WOODY, CISCO, & ME

WOODY, CISCO, & ME

WITH WOODY GUTHRIE IN THE MERCHANT MARINE

JIM LONGHI

ibooks
new york
www.ibooks.net

DISTRIBUTED BY SIMON & SCHUSTER, INC.

ibooks, inc.
24 West 25th Street
New York, NY 10010

The ibooks World Wide Web Site Address is:
http://www.ibooks.net

ISBN 0-7434-8004-X
First ibooks, inc. printing April 2004
10 9 8 7 6 5 4 3 2 1

Printed in the U.S.A.

FOR WOODY *&* CISCO

CONTENTS

ACKNOWLEDGMENTS

Gabrielle, my wife, is part of

this book — her editorial art and

her constant encouragement

made it possible. I am grateful to

her as well as to our son, Jaime,

for his inspired coediting.

WOODY, CISCO, & ME

PROLOGUE

It's the spring of 1943, the middle of World War II. Woody Guthrie and Cisco Houston ask me to ship out with them in the Merchant Marine. *The Merchant Marine?* Me, a certified unadulterated coward, volunteer for the *most dangerous job of the war?*

The Merchant Marine had more dead, proportionately, than all the war services put together. Hundreds of our hastily welded ships were fighting their way across the North Atlantic through wolf packs of Nazi submarines, carrying bombs, tanks, food, and gasoline to England and far on up to Murmansk, Russia's only open port. Russia had twenty million dead, and England was barely hanging on. They were desperate for our supplies. If Hitler could cut that lifeline, the world might be his. By the spring of 1943 he was about to succeed. His submarines had already sunk nearly seven hundred of our ships, and more than six thousand of our seamen were dead. Our government was begging for volunteers. All honor to the brave men who volunteered, but I'm not a brave man—why should I volunteer? *Woody and Cisco, that's why! It's their fault!*

Woody Guthrie, thirty-one, only four years older than I, was a legend. The little bantam-rooster Dust Bowl Okie was hailed as the greatest folk balladeer America had ever known. He had written nearly a thousand songs, mostly about plain people during the Great Depression. He sang them to the migratory workers in their California camps, to the jobless in the hobo camps, to the hungry on soup lines, and to the unorganized workers across the country—getting his head busted a few times along the way. It wasn't their fault, he sang; it was the system that wasn't working right. He belonged to no political party: "Right wing, left wing, chicken wing, makes no difference so long as the common people unite with love and without greed." His songs were in the Library of Congress;

RCA released his album *Dust Bowl Ballads;* he had a national radio show that he quit rather than accept the sponsor's censorship; his autobiography, *Bound for Glory,* was hailed by the critics; and Woody himself was called a "national possession like Yellowstone and Yosemite."

Woody's long-time partner and best friend, Cisco Houston, was a Californian, tall, rangy, quiet, blond, blue-eyed, extremely handsome, guitar-playing, golden-voiced Pasadena Playhouse student—perfect Hollywood cowboy star material. But he began to listen to Woody Guthrie's radio show, and he soon quit the Hollywood world to join Woody. Together they had fought for the underdog; now they would fight the big fight against fascism.

Neither Woody nor Cisco had to go to war. Woody had four children and could have stayed out of it or gotten a soft job in the army. Cisco was legally blind; he couldn't see three feet ahead of him. But they volunteered for the Merchant Marine.

When they asked me to ship out with them, I was honored, thrilled, and terrified. I was trapped between two heroes. I felt like a slice of salami in a hero sandwich. I said, "Great! Let's go!"

Millions know Woody Guthrie the "national possession," but very few know Woody Guthrie the war hero. He and Cisco, besides performing other deeds under fire, risked their lives to save mine. Their story must not die with me.

Each detail is etched on my brain—trauma and stress are master etchers—the story writes itself.

The WILLY B.

1

"... and there's a blonde in every lifeboat! A blonde in every lifeboat!" The dispatcher's voice squawking over the loudspeaker was nearly drowned out by the din of the more than five hundred seamen who filled the union hiring hall. "She's a beauty of a ship! A regular luxury liner with beds instead of bunks and silk sheets on every bed! And . . ."

I watched the seamen mill about, talking, laughing, calling to each other. It was like a giant cocktail party. The only quiet ones were those who lay on folding chairs, asleep or drunk.

"She's a fine-feedin' ship! A fine-feedin' ship!" the dispatcher shouted into his microphone. "They tell me her chief steward was the mater dee at the Ritz before the war! Now there's only a few jobs left on this beauty, just a few, and she won't be on no long cold trip like Murmansk, because her captain was seen buyin' a pair of Bermuda shorts, so it's probably a short, safe sugar run to Cuba and back to little old New York! But if she does make the Atlantic run, there ain't a submarine can touch her, 'cause she's the fastest thing afloat, and she can zigzag her pretty ass across that ocean faster than any Nazi submarine in . . ."

Submarines! I looked toward the exit.

You cowardly bastard, I cursed myself. Just the mention of submarines, and you're ready to run, after all that bullshit about fighting fascism. You should have shipped out or joined the army the day war was declared. Instead it's eighteen months later, and you're still here. You've got overcooked spaghetti for a backbone and tomato sauce instead of blood in your veins. The government's begging for seamen. If you weren't a coward, you'd look around for Cisco and sign up instead of hiding in a corner behind this wall of brave men. Look at them — more than seven hundred ships sunk and six thousand dead, and still they're shipping out. Look at them!

I was especially ashamed to see that the men were older than I'd expected, mostly between thirty-five and forty-five. I was also surprised to see that a third of them were Filipinos, Cubans, Puerto Ricans, Jamaicans, and Chinese. They reminded me of the crews in Conrad's novels. Most of them wore wild Hawaiian shirts. The June sunlight streaming through the high windows penetrated the swirling clouds of tobacco smoke and spotlighted the colorful crowd. There were plenty of younger men too, but the flavor of the crowd was definitely old sea dog misted over by the smell of whiskey. They were the professional seamen, the backbone of the Merchant Marine from before the war.

"Awright now, who's gonna fill these last few jobs? Who's the lucky stiffs?"

Although the men seemed to ignore the dispatcher's voice, they kept an eye on the ten-foot blackboard on which his assistant constantly chalked and erased entries, with the names of the ships in the left column and their open jobs across the board.

"Awright, you guys!" The loudspeaker fought the noise of the crowd. "Let's go! We gotta fill these goddamned jobs right now! Let's go!"

"What's the dispatcher pushin', Hank?" a middle-aged man asked loudly of another middle-aged man standing in front of me.

"Number three!"

"Number what?"

"Number three!" The second man pointed to the blackboard. "The *Susan Jones*, a real dog! Her last two times out she went to the Mediterranean. The way they're knockin' them off there, the odds on her stink! I got a good tip on number six!"

"The *Blue Star*? Are you kiddin'? I heard she's loadin' crates with Russian markings, which has gotta mean Murmansk, right? I wouldn't give you even money on her! I like — uh — number seven." The first man pulled out a red handkerchief and wiped the back of his neck. "I hear they just put mosquito netting over the bunks, so at least she ain't goin' to Murmansk, right?"

"Right. And she's named for Paddy Whelan — he's the guy who went down shaking his fist, yelling 'I'll get you yet, you Nazi bastards!' So what the hell. Even if she's going to the Mediterranean, somebody's gotta ride her."

"Okay. Let's go."

I watched the two men push their way toward the dispatcher's cage. Murmansk! The Mediterranean! The Battle of the Atlantic! It's the war!

Right here in this hall on 17th Street! It seemed incredible that outside, people were living their lives as though the war were thousands of miles away, when in fact the front began just beyond the dimmed-out lights of Coney Island, where German submarine U-boats lay waiting in wolf packs.

"Believe me, Pedro, no man can live more than three minute!" a small Chinese seaman said to a man standing near me. His voice was shrill, not from fear or anger, but just to make himself heard. "No fucking man can live more than three minute in the water on Murmansk run — no fucking man!"

"I glad I no make that run! How many ship your convoy lose?" Pedro asked loudly as he fanned himself with a copy of the *Daily News*.

"No can tell — maybe lose fucking half!"

"Mediterranean pretty bad too." Pedro fanned himself faster. "Last trip two tankers blow up, boom, right in front of me!"

The Chinese man smiled and said, "Me think frying to death can be no worse than freezing to death, Pedro, so why we not take the job dispatcher he hollering about?"

"Okay, Lee — shake hands for good luck!"

I watched them as they made their way through the crowd. Why are they going? For two hundred dollars a month? They could earn more working in a shipyard. Then why? Is their understanding of the war better than mine? Wasn't I raised on antifascism? Did Pop ever allow me to drink a glass of wine without toasting "Morte" — death — to Mussolini and his blackshirts? Was I ever allowed to pass any man dressed in black without touching my balls and muttering "Fongul a fascismo?" And with a heritage like that, I'm dragging ass while these guys ship out? But Jesus, to die fried in oil or drowned in freezing water! Okay, and what if the army sends me to the front? Is it any better to die in God-forbid hand-to-hand combat? Yes, but with two years of law school, maybe they'll give me a desk job. All right then, its decision time; I can't go on standing here like a mope. If I can't ship out, I can't ship out. The draft letter is in my pocket; why don't I go down to the army office and be done with it? Why? Because that goddamned Cisco asked me to ship out with him, in front of Gabrielle, that's why! So what, she'll be just as proud of me in the army, and as for Cisco, my commitment to ship out with him wasn't an irrevocable one. I told him I'd meet him *if* I could work things out in time. Right, right; nothing wrong with going into the army, nothing at all. Settled! So what if I wasted half a day getting my seaman's papers; what's a half-day in a lifetime?

I looked at my watch and saw that it was noon. Unbelievable! I'd been arguing with myself for over an hour. I wanted to tell Cisco my decision, but I couldn't see him in the crowd. He had probably gotten tired of waiting. Anyway, it certainly wasn't an irrevocable commitment I had given him; irrevocable is when a ship's gangway is pulled up. I headed for the exit.

"Come on now, there's three jobs left on this lousy tub," the loudspeaker blared as I pushed open the swinging doors leading to the lobby. "Ain't there three red-blooded men left in this friggin' hall? There's still three jobs . . ."

The doors shut behind me, and I headed for the street, but when I came to a glass case in the center of the lobby, I stopped. Inside the case there was an open book that looked like a big Bible. I sensed what it was before I read the brass plaque: "We take this solemn oath — we will continue your struggle. We will never rest until the cause for which you died has triumphed. We will keep 'em sailing in your hallowed spirit — the spirit of free men who never have and never will surrender to fascist slavery."

It was the book of the dead, the list of the National Maritime Union members who had died in the war. A sign explained that each day a new page would be turned. I read: Sanders, Santiago, Schwartz, Smithson, Suarez. Phil Katz's name was in one of those pages, and Ted's name and Tony's. My eyes started to cloud. I thought I'd better get the hell out of there. As I turned to go, I became aware of the music coming from inside the hiring hall — it sounded like Woody Guthrie singing "The Sinking of the *Reuben James*": "Tell me, what were their names? Tell me, what where their names? Did you have a friend on the good *Reuben James*?"

I opened the door to see what was going on. The music was coming from the loudspeaker; evidently they played records during the dispatcher's breaks. Then, suddenly, I spotted Cisco in the center of the crowd, his tall blondness towering above the men around him. He must have been sitting down when I had looked for him.

"Cisco!" I shouted. He waved to me. I pushed my way to him, and we embraced. I was proud of him for not allowing his Anglo-Saxon inhibitions to stand in the way of my Italian-American exuberance.

"I'm sure glad to see you." He patted my back.

"Why?" I held him at arm's length. "Did you have any doubts about my coming?"

"No — not really." His deep-blue eyes searched my face. "Did you?"

"No — not really."

"Good."

Cisco didn't talk much, but when he did, you listened to every word of his gentle western drawl. He was twenty-five — two years younger than I — yet he seemed older and wiser. He had stopped his schooling after high school, but like his hero, Jack London, he educated himself while he crisscrossed the country as a cowboy, fruit picker, union organizer, Hollywood extra, and guitar-playing singer in bars and union halls. He had the richest, sweetest, lonesomest voice I'd ever heard. With his talent and his rangy matinee-idol looks, he might have gone far if he had stayed in Hollywood. And he could have stayed; the army had rejected him because of his eyes. When I met him, he had already made a couple of trips in the Merchant Marine. Although Cisco's patriotic example made me uneasy — especially in front of my girl, Gabrielle — I liked to be with him. We had met the week before at a party given by his girl, Bina Rosenbaum, and I was pleased when, after knowing me for so short a time, he had asked me to ship out with him.

"Tell me, what were their names, tell me, what were their names," the loudspeaker continued playing.

"It's going to be a good trip." Cisco pointed to the loudspeaker. "Woody Guthrie's coming too."

"Woody Guthrie?"

"We're buddies. He's meeting us here."

"Why didn't you tell me you knew him?"

"You never asked me."

What interesting coincidences — the book of the dead, the lyrics of "The *Reuben James*" and now Woody Guthrie himself about to join us.

Everybody in my world knew Woody Guthrie. He was a folk hero, part of the Great Depression — the Dust Bowl, Steinbeck's *Grapes of Wrath*, Woody's songs. I saw him once at a Madison Square Garden rally for the unemployed. He sang his song "This Land Is Your Land," and twenty thousand people stood up to sing it with him as though it were the national anthem.

"Geez, I hope he likes me." I said to Cisco.

"Don't worry, he will. Otherwise I wouldn't have asked you to come. Shipping out is a little like getting married!"

"I'm beginning to feel like I'm on a blind date."

"Awright," the loudspeaker blared, "I've got three more jobs on another beauty, only this ship's got *two* blondes in every lifeboat. Now who's gonna . . ."

"Two blondies in every danged lifeboat? Godawmighty, what are we waiting for?" It was Woody Guthrie, looking up at us, head cocked, one eyebrow raised. He was short, wiry, with dark curly hair and a guitar slung across his back, looking just like his publicity pictures, except that he wasn't wearing his usual rough clothes — he was wearing a brand new khaki shirt with neatly rolled-up sleeves and a sharply creased, brand-new pair of khaki trousers, at least three inches too long, bunched around his shiny new shoes. He was freshly shaved and altogether as spic and span as a kid on his first day at school. "Well, come on!" He uncocked his head. "Let's go get a piece of that there blondie boat the man's hollerin' about!"

Cisco put a hand on Woody's shoulder. "Got some things to do first. To begin with" — he put a hand on my shoulder — "this is Jim."

"Hell, I know this here's Jimmy." Woody stuck out his hand and gave mine one sharp shake. "But let's go get those jobs! I know a good job when I see one. Ain't I sold papers, polished spittoons, picked cotton, bootlegged whiskey, practiced divine healing, painted signs . . . ?"

"Slow down pardner, don't be nervous. No fear of the dispatcher running out of jobs."

Woody looked up at us. "T'aint losin' the jobs I'm worried about. Truth is I'm afraid of losin' my dee-ter-my-nation, unless we get it over with right away."

"Don't tell me you're scared, Woody." I tried to laugh.

"Well, I don't exactly feel like a condemned man, but I ate me a hearty breakfast just in case."

This time I burst out laughing.

"Don't worry; we'll be all right," Cisco said. "Now let's go get your union cards." He picked up a guitar that was leaning against a chair and slung it over his shoulder.

"Woody, they just played your record of '*Reuben James,*'" I pointed to the loudspeaker. "Isn't that something?"

"Sure is. Every time somebody buys a record of mine, I get two cents. I've sold so many records, I'm only ten dollars short of buyin' me a new guitar. Do you play?"

"No, I've got no musical talent."

"Mmmmmm." Woody looked up at Cisco. "Okay, let's go get them union cards." Cisco led the way to the lobby and up the stairs to the union offices.

"Woody." I stopped climbing and waited for him to turn around. "I want you to know that it's an honor to ship out with you."

"Don't worry. Everybody's got some musical talent." He started climbing again.

His non sequitur silenced me for a moment, but then I continued, "I love your songs."

"Even if you just learn to play the kazoo." He kept climbing.

I followed him, wondering whether he'd heard what I said or whether he just couldn't take a compliment. I tried again: "Your songs are wonderful."

"But I'm sure we'll have you playing the guitar before too long," he said, without looking at me.

"Here we are." Cisco stopped in front of the door that said "Ferdinand Smith, General Secretary." Smith's office was a big one, with three girls typing away. His private office was behind a closed door. Cisco explained to one of the girls that Woody and I needed union cards, and she started to take down the information.

"Woodrow Wilson Guthrie?" She looked up at Woody. "Hey, you're Woody Guthrie! I bought one of your records!"

"Thank you, ma'am — that's another two cents toward my new guitar." The girl laughed and told us to wait. She went to call Ferdinand Smith.

"Well I'll be damned — Woody Guthrie!" Smith's Jamaican accent sang. "Every time we get on a picket line, somebody's sure to sing your song." He boomed out, "No you can't scare me, I'm sticking to the union, I'm sticking to the union, till the day I die!" He put out his hand. "I'm sure glad to know you!"

"Likewise." Woody shook the black man's hand. "If you and your buddies hadn't got your heads busted so often, we wouldn't have a seaman's union to join."

"Is the Dust Bowl refugee problem still as bad?" Smith asked Woody.

"Oh, it's a little better, but the solution of the worker's problem has to wait. The war has to have top priority." Woody's Oklahoma accent was still there, but the country-boy comic effect was gone.

"I agree with you, Brother Woody." Smith handed us our union cards. "And I hope you all have a safe trip."

I was proud to hold the card, but it felt like a living thing in my hand — a dangerous living thing. I slipped it into my pocket and tried to put out of my mind the picture of a gangway being pulled up.

We shook hands all around and headed back to the hiring hall. On the second floor we were stopped by the sound of conga music coming from behind double doors. Without any hesitation Woody pushed open the doors — it was the union social room. The music was coming from a phonograph; a buxom woman, six feet tall, was teaching ten rough-looking seamen how to dance the conga. She led the line of dancers; the man behind her held her hips, the second man held the first man's hips, and so on down the line, all of them wagging their behinds to the rhythm of the lady shouting, "One, two, three," and then violently thrusting out their right legs when she shouted, "kick!"

The seamen followed their tall Lorelei as she snaked the line around the floor. "One, two, three, kick! One, two, three, kick! You got it! Come on," she waved to us. "Join the line!"

Woody grabbed the last man's hips and followed him as though he'd been doing the conga all his life. "Come on," he called to us, "help the little lady! One, two, three, kick! It's all part of the war effort!"

Cisco and I joined in, and when the record finished we introduced ourselves to the lady. She was Helen, the social-director volunteer from the Ladies Auxiliary of the National Maritime Union. She was thrilled when she realized that Woody was Woody Guthrie, and when he agreed to sing a song, she clapped her hands and jumped two feet off the floor.

"Wrote a little song about gals like Helen here." Woody tuned his guitar. "Or in other words where we would be without the Ladies Aux-ill-eye-ree!" He tickled his guitar strings and started to sing, sounding just as he did on his records, dry, twangy, tough-as-leather, all his concentration on his words. Cisco joined him. On the second chorus, Woody nodded to me. "Just hum along." I did, and on the third chorus I tried harmonizing, which I hadn't done since I was twelve, when my brother and I sang "Carolina Moon."

By the end of our second song, my harmony got better. Our last song was "Midnight Special," and although I'd never heard it, I worked out a third-part harmony. In the middle of the song Woody turned to me and muttered, "Louder!" I did as he said, and while I sang I thought, hey, I'm singing with Woody Guthrie! We've got a trio — a Merchant Marine trio, with Woody, Cisco, and me.

■

When we got back to the hiring hall, the dispatcher was still blaring out jobs.

"Well, what's our strategy for winning this war?" Woody looked up at Cisco.

"Take the first three open jobs!"

"Since this is the first trip for Woody and me, instead of going to Murmansk or the Mediterranean, couldn't we try to get a short sugar run to Cuba and back to little old New York?" I asked as nonchalantly as I could.

Cisco studied me for a moment before answering. "Useless, buddy — nobody knows where they're going."

"I've got three jobs open," the dispatcher called, "three jobs in the steward department on this darling ship! Now who's the lucky stiffs gonna . . ."

"Might as well take those three." Cisco nodded toward the loudspeaker.

"In the steward department? Waiting on tables?"

"Yes." Cisco smiled. "Or washing dishes, or making up officer's beds, or scrubbing pots."

"Couldn't we be — uh — regular seamen, like working on deck?"

"Regular seamen?" Cisco's voice was patient. "No department's more important than the steward department. Ask any one of these guys. They don't much care how well the deck gang can steer a ship or how well the black gang can make the engine run. All they care about is the steward department. If she's a lousy feeder, it's a lousy trip. If she's a good feeder, it's a good trip. Anyway, I can't work on deck — my eyes aren't good enough — but you can take a deck job if you want to." His eyes searched my face; when Cisco's eyes focused on something, they shifted slightly from side to side while his head shook with a noticeable tremor. The moving eyes, the tremor, made him all the more compelling.

"No, I want to work with you," I said quickly.

Cisco looked at Woody. "How about you, Woody?"

"Hell, somebody's gotta wash the dishes."

"Okay then, you guys wait here." Cisco went toward the dispatcher's cage.

"I don't mind working in the steward department," I said, offering Woody a cigarette. "It just sounds a little more glamorous to work on deck or in the engine room." Even as I said "engine room" I wanted to bite off my tongue. Imagine being trapped in an engine room while under attack. You might as well join the submarine service!

"Cisco can't work in the engine room, no more than he can work on deck. He and his young brother Slim inherited the same bad eyes."

"He didn't tell me he has a brother."

"Had a brother." Woody pressed his lips, looked down at the floor, and then suddenly snapped his head up. "Slim's ship was hit off the coast of Maine. Went down in three minutes. They say he probably couldn't find his way out of the engine room."

Cisco was coming toward us. "Two messmen and a dishwasher." He waved three slips. "On a ship called the *William B. Travis.*"

"Yep!" Woody looked like he was tasting something. "I like the sound of her name — the seamen three on the *Willy B.*"

From the union hall we walked into the ship company's office, where we were told to sit in the waiting room. After a few minutes a beautiful girl stood in the doorway.

"Someone will be with you in just a minute." She grinned and disappeared before Cisco could turn around to see her.

Cisco jumped up, hands frozen in midair, eyebrows nearly up to his hair line, nostrils quivering. "Mmmmmmmmmmm!" he groaned as he pointed toward the door, "Mmm! Mmm! *Mmm!*"

"Down boy!" Woody commanded.

"Geez, he didn't even see her. How could he . . . ?" I looked at Cisco with new appreciation.

"Folks with bad eyes can hear and smell better." Woody sniffed the air.

"You mean he probably smelled her perfume?"

"Or something." Woody continued sniffing.

Cisco shook his head, went back to his seat, picked up a magazine, held it about three inches away from his eyes, and proceeded to read. Woody stopped sniffing. "No doubt about it, he can hear and smell better'n anybody I know. One time the two of us were singing union organizing songs at a migratory workers' camp. Everybody was a'whoopin' an' a'hollerin' along with us when all of a sudden Cisco stops playing, hangs his guitar on the branch of a tree, picks up a length of two by four, and announces to the crowd that he can hear the deputy sheriffs' cars coming down the lane, which gave us just enough time to prepare a decent welcome for our uninvited guests."

"Do you know each other a long time?"

"Three years don't sound much, but three days together in a freezin' freight car is a long time, and standin' back to back fightin' off a pack of company goons for three minutes is even longer."

An officious-looking man in a blue uniform came in. "You'll have to wait for the doctor," he said brusquely and left.

"Doctor?" Cisco was on his feet. "Goddamn it — this line never asked for a physical before! I wouldn't have taken the jobs. I can't pass the eye test!"

"Then let's go back and get three other jobs," I said.

"Not allowed to; once you accept a job, you're stuck with it."

"Does that mean I've got to ship out alone — with Jim?" Woody's face was absolutely expressionless.

"No. If a man refuses to ship out after he's been assigned, the army grabs him, but they can't touch you or me. My eyes are no good, and you've got kids. We two can go back to the hall and get another ship, but Jim's stuck. He's got to take this job, or —"

"No, sir! I'm not shipping out without you guys. I'd rather go in the army."

My, my, I thought, how nicely problems solve themselves sometimes. I won't have to ship out after all! And my honor intact too! If the Merchant Marine wouldn't allow me to ship out with my buddies, to hell with the Merchant Marine!

"Too bad," Woody said. "I kinda liked your third-part harmony."

Cisco put his hand on my shoulder. "You know I wanted you to ship out with us."

"Wait a minute. You guys are not rid of me that easily. For one thing, what have you got to lose if you take the physical? Maybe you'll pass the eye test."

"Impossible; I can't see beyond three feet. Anything beyond three feet is distorted, and glasses don't help."

"Vincenzo Long-eye," the uniformed man called out.

"Here, sir." I stood up. "But it's pronounced Longhi — rhymes with 'shorty.'"

"Gilbert Houston?" he called, without a smile.

"Here."

"Woodrow Wilson Guthrie?"

"Yup!"

The man looked up sharply and stared at Woody, obviously feeling that the two stripes on his sleeve entitled him to more than that "Yup!"

"All right, come with me." He led us down a corridor.

"Go on." I prodded Cisco. "Maybe they'll skip the eye tests."

"In here!" The officer opened a door and gave Woody a dirty look. "Strip down — everything!" He pulled the door behind him and left us standing alone in a doctor's office.

"Goddamn it, Woody," Cisco muttered as he started to unbutton his shirt, "you got more ways for starting trouble than you got hair on that wooden head!"

"Cain't help it — somethin' about a officer's uniform makes me nauseous. If I'd of opened my mouth to say more'n 'yup,' I mighta throwed up."

"Come on, Woody." I took off my trousers a little self-consciously. "If you want to do your part in this war, you can't be allergic to officers' uniforms."

"You're right, but my allergy's been with me ever since I was a kid and used to see our town sheriff's uniform all sweated and stained with the blood of some poor Indian that got persuaded into signing away his land. However, I ain't gonna let that keep me from carryin' out orders and doin' my dang bustinest best to beat them Nazis!" And in a flash of dazzling speed he pulled off his shirt, kicked off his shoes, stripped off his trousers, whipped off his socks, jumped out of his underwear, and snapped to rigid attention.

Cisco and I started at his shiny, bony body.

"The man said strip!" Woody continued standing at rigid attention. "What are you guys waitin' for? Dontcha know there's a war on?"

"Congratulations!" A pot-bellied doctor, smelling of whiskey, had come in unnoticed. His remark was for Woody. Woody stayed at rigid attention as the doctor came up to him. "For a little guy," the doctor continued, "I'd say you were pretty well endowed."

"Why thank you." Woody looked down at himself, though still standing at rigid attention. "For a long time I had an inferiority complex about that. You see my cousins used to call me Shorty, which, according to theirs, mine certainly was, until one day my grandma said, 'Pay no attention to them idiots, little Woodpecker, t'aint the size that counts, it's what you do with it.' So I'd be much more obliged to you, Doctor, if you paid a compliment to the size of my brain instead." He bent his head. "Here, feel it."

"Never mind the jokes, wise guy." The doctor poked Woody's groin. "Just cough." Woody coughed as though his lungs were bursting. "All right, wise guy, that's enough!" The doctor scribbled something onto a card. "What's your height?"

"Five-feet six and one-eighth."

"Read the eye chart on the wall, wise guy." Woody read each letter very slowly, to give Cisco a chance to memorize the letters. "That's enough. Next man. Height?"

"Six feet one." I stepped ahead of Cisco; I too was going to call out the letters as slowly as I could.

"Read the fourth line backwards." The doctor started to examine my groin. I read as slowly as I could. "Did you say the last letter was M?" the doctor asked without looking at the chart.

"No, N."

"Okay, next man. Height?"

"Six feet two." Cisco looked at me, nodded toward the eye chart, and shook his head hopelessly.

The doctor finished poking Cisco and went to the sink. "Read the fifth line down, if you can," the doctor called to Cisco as he started to wash his hands.

"F-X-T-L-E-M." I read quickly, trying to sound like Cisco.

Without turning around, the doctor said, "Okay — you guys can go."

2

"How do you get Jim from Vincenzo?" Woody asked as the three of us walked to our ship, which was tied up at Hudson River's 20th Street pier.

"It's an old Irish custom that the Italian Americans took over — the Vincents become Jim. But as a matter of fact I have more names than anybody I know." I went on to explain that my birth certificate says Vincenzo, my family calls me Enzo, my teachers called me Vincent, my high school girlfriends called me Vinny, and my neighborhood friends called me a variety of names having to do with my eyes. Because I read a lot as a kid, my eyes were like slits, so they called me Chink, Banjo-eyes, or mostly Popeye. But when I went to Columbia I called myself Jim, for two reasons: first, to avoid being called Vinny, since Vinny made my flesh creep; second, all the rich guys in my class had middle initials, so I gave me a middle initial — J. I picked J because it gave me a better title to the name "Jim." When my father called me a phony for taking a middle initial, I told him the J was to honor his name, Joseph. That shut him up.

"And that's how I get Jim from Vincenzo. Now you clear up something for me. Back in the ship's office Cisco said you were exempt from the army because you had kids. I thought you just had one — Cathy."

"No, Miss Stackabones is not my only one. I've got three kids by my first wife." Woody looked straight ahead as we walked. "Let's say we were casualties of the depression, Oklahoma, Dust Bowl — things like that." He turned to look at me. "We're all right now, though, their mother and me — we write — they're taken care of. Goin' out to see them as soon as this war's over."

Although we were still two blocks from the waterfront, we could hear its hum. The waterfront's noise had always fascinated me: the banging and clanging of freighters spilling the riches of the world onto the sidewalks of New York; winches shrieking; seagulls shrieking; truck horns blasting; longshoremen crazily driving forklifts, shouting at pedestrian longshoremen, nearly colliding with other machines; everybody yelling; tugboats whistling; ships' horns blowing; and the awesome call of the big passenger ships — all augmented by the noise of the West Side Highway overhead.

Just to drive down that highway, from 57th Street to Canal Street, was a magic-carpet ride, especially when the *Queen Mary* and the *Normandie* were in port at the same time, their bows almost touching you as you drove by. Pier after pier of exotically named freighters, together with the smell of spices and the smell of the sea, transported me to places I dreamed of, and the signs above the docks added to the poetry: Bombay, Valparaiso, Capetown, Mombassa, Algiers, Durban, Port Said, Ceylon, and on and on and on.

The war changed the cargo, but the scene was the same — except for the sabotaged *Normandie*. She lay on her side at her pier, fire-gutted. But the *Queen Mary* still carried passengers — fifteen thousand soldiers at a time.

Cisco, Woody, and I dodged our way past the overloaded forklifts, showed our passes, and entered the dark wharf, which was filled with the noise of men and machines. The sudden change from the bright sunlight outside nearly blinded me, and I was almost knocked down by a fast-moving forklift, which would have been the end of a trip not even begun.

Our ship was tied up at the pier. "That must be the biggest damned ship in the merchant marine!" Woody said as we looked up at the SS *William B. Travis*. The black freighter was more than two city blocks long, and because she was empty, her midship loomed over us at least five stories high — six, seven stories counting her smokestack. She was immense — frighteningly immense.

Jesus, Joseph, Saint Anne, and Saint Mary — I silently invoked my mother's gods — so this is the monster that's going to swallow me and take me to Christ knows where. I had never seen a more evil-looking ship. In all the world there couldn't be another ship like this. "She's no different from any other Liberty ship, you landlubber," I said to Woody, who was still staring up at her with his mouth open. "They're all ten thousand tons with three holds up front and two in the back."

"And do they all have machine-gun turrets and cannon up front and back?" Woody's neck stretched like a rooster's as his head turned from bow to stern, stern to bow.

"Cannons? Machine guns? Where?" I croaked.

"Nothing to worry about." Cisco nudged us to lead the way up the gangway ladder. "All aboard."

Woody waited for a man who was already halfway down the ladder. He had red hair and he looked mean. By way of greeting, Woody said to him, "I still think this is the biggest damned ship in the Merchant Marine."

The man looked back at the ship. "You mean the biggest steel coffin you ever seen." He stepped off the gangway.

"Uhhh, why do you happen to say that?" I tilted my head back, my eyelids blinking nervously, as though I had been personally insulted.

"I happened to say that, buddy, because it happens to be true. Look at that pile of junk! Mass production my ass! A thousand Liberty ships a year — what good are they? Every time there's a rough sea, you're wonderin' whether she's gonna split in two!"

"Stop exaggerating, old-timer," Cisco said.

"Exaggeratin'? Look at her! Not a rivet in her; everything's welded together with spit! With rivets there's give to a ship, but with that fuckin' welding she's all of one piece, stiff, no give, so wham! They break in two. We just heard about one that broke her back in a storm and went down in two minutes." He turned and spit at the ship, "*Ptui!* You can't trust these rat bastards! They're all —"

"If you don't cut it out," Cisco interrupted him, "you'll scare these guys to death before their first trip. There's two thousand Liberty's; they don't all split."

"You're right, mate, you're right, but at least it's our duty to warn these new men about the rolling." He turned to Woody and me. "If the sea just ripples, a Liberty'll roll worse than the rolling barrel in Coney Island. On this last trip the captain was seasick for a week, which serves the lousy dictator right, 'cause the sonofabitch is worse than Hitler."

"Well, thanks for the encouragement." Cisco looked up at the ship. "But we have no choice — we've been assigned."

"Dispatcher buggered you, eh?" The seaman grinned.

"Yeah," I added, "and you know the old saying, buggers can't be choosers." The seaman laughed. Cisco and Woody didn't.

"Well, at least is she a good feeder?" Cisco called out as the seaman walked away.

"Oh, sure, that's why I'm signing on again. My name's Red — see you later." He waved as he walked toward the wharf.

Woody charged up the gangway ladder and stopped on the top landing. He turned around to the admire the view. "Now ain't that something?" It *was* beautiful: the Empire State Building, the midtown skyline, the Jersey Palisades, and the Washington Bridge way up the river. I took a good look before stepping onto the ship.

The feel of the steel deck under my feet was shocking — it was the first time I'd ever been on a ship. This was the main deck, Cisco explained. The crew's cabins and the navy gun crew's cabins were on the main deck, midship. The officer's cabins were above, on the boat deck.

"The walls are welded too," I said to Woody.

"Stop worrying." Cisco jabbed me in the ribs. "And they're not walls, they're bulkheads. These are not floors; they're decks. Those are portholes, not windows. The ceiling is called the overhead, and the toilet is the head." He led the way inside.

Before my eyes could adjust to the change of light, I caught the smell of fresh-baked bread. A five-foot wide corridor, called an alleyway, ran the length of the midship, and just in front of us, fronting on the alleyway, was the galley. It was caged in by wire mesh with holes as big as halfdollars, and it was spotless. The big black stove was immaculate; the hanging pots and pans gleamed. A short, dark man in a clean white jacket grinned and said with a Puerto Rican accent, "Allo boys. You look for chief steward?" He introduced himself as Roberto, the chief cook. "I make a little overtime — take care of skeleton crew. I think steward in his cabin, but maybe he's in messroom, I think."

As he spoke, I looked carefully at every detail: the square red tiles on the galley floor, the steel deck of the alleyway, and the steel handrail along its side.

We stepped over a threshold into an empty messroom. "Crew's mess," Cisco said. "We feed about thirty men here. The navy kids have their own messroom — they're about twenty — and the ship's officers, about twelve of them, eat in what's called the saloon."

The crew's messroom was rectangular; it had two rectangular tables fixed to the deck, each table seating twelve. The seats were fixed revolving stools with wooden backs. There were two portholes — the room looked small and cramped.

We followed Cisco through a steel archway into a small pantry. It had a porthole, two big sinks, and a big coffee urn. The pantry connected with the gun crew's messroom. It was the same size as the crew's mess. We stepped into the alleyway and followed Cisco.

"What's in there?" I pointed to an oak door.

"A crew cabin." Cisco opened the door and switched on the light. Prison cells had more room. In a space six feet by ten there were four bunks (two uppers and two lowers), four steel lockers, and a sink.

"I know the dispatcher was kidding when he said luxury liner," I said, "but this is worse than a submarine."

"Submarines don't have portholes." Cisco opened the steel cover of the single porthole, but that made the place look even more like a prison cell.

"Are they all like this?" I asked.

"Yep, but don't worry. It'll soon feel like home." Cisco led the way up the corridor to a much larger messroom that ran across the width of the midship. It had four square tables, each seating four, and four portholes looking out toward the ship's bow. It was the officers' saloon mess.

We followed Cisco through the room, out the other side, down the parallel alleyway, and up to the boat deck. My heart beat faster when I saw the lifeboats, two on each side of the ship. I looked up at the big, black smokestack, at the bridge, and at the gun turrets forward and aft.

We found the chief steward in his cabin, seated at his desk. He took our slips without rising. He was about thirty-five, dark, lean, and as neat looking as his cabin, with its drum-tight bunk and spotless deck.

"You've shipped out before, right?" He looked up at Cisco, but without waiting for an answer, he continued, "You can be the crew's messman." He looked up at me. "First trip, right? What do you do ashore?"

"Law student."

"Okay. You can be the officer's messman. I'll show you what to do. And you?" He looked at Woody. "What do you do ashore?"

"Guitar picker, fruit picker, potato packer, poker player, piano —"

"Dishwasher," the steward interrupted, "you're the new dishwasher."

"Yes, sir!" Woody saluted him sharply, but the steward turned away as though he hadn't seen.

"We're leaving in an hour," he said.

"An hour?" I was stunned. "I don't have any clothes — my books — I've got to say goodbye to my girl, my parents, my —"

"We're going to Jersey City, across the river. Report tomorrow morning at nine — pier three, Caven Point." He turned back to his desk.

Outside I made sure we were far enough away from his open porthole before I said, "What a lovely fellow."

"Don't judge him too hard; he runs a good-feeding ship." Cisco sniffed the air. "And maybe he's a worried man."

"He could have told us in the first place that we're only going to Caven Point!"

"That's what he's probably worried about."

"What's so terrible about Caven Point?"

"That's where ships load dynamite — you know, bombs, ammunition, things like that. But don't worry" — Cisco saw the look on my face — "they may not all be big blockbusters. Might get a lot of little ones," he chuckled.

"What the hell's the difference between a few big ones or a lot of little ones? If we get hit, we won't even know it!" I looked to Woody.

"Count your blessings." Woody pulled his guitar in front of him. "We might get hit in the middle of a song. Trick is to keep singing or keep thinking of sex; that way you're bound to die a happy man."

3

The day already seemed ages old, but it was only three o'clock. "What are you guys doing the rest of the day?" I asked.

Woody wet his forefinger and held it in the air. "Wind's blowin' in the direction of McSorley's saloon. Let's make for that — do a little singin' and wet our whistles."

"Okay," I said, "but first let's stop at Broadway and Eleventh Street — *L'Unita del Popolo*. It's a little Italian antifascist weekly where I've been working. I want to say goodbye to some guys you'll be proud to meet."

On the way to the *L'Unita* office, I told Cisco and Woody something about the newspaper. It was run by two Italian history professors, Giuseppe Berti and Ambrogio Donini; both had escaped to New York after serving more than ten years in Mussolini's prisons, but even in New York, their lives were in constant danger. Carlo Tresca, one of Mussolini's enemies in the Italian-American community, had recently been shot dead near *L'Unita*'s office.

We climbed the old stairs to the newspaper's musty little two-room office. I introduced Woody and Cisco to the professors; to Mary Testa, a good-looking Italian-American girl who was my boss on the English page; and to Mike Sala, the business manager, a forty-year-old ferocious-looking Sicilian ex-barber who could barely read or write but without whose wild passion and reckless courage, the little weekly would long since have died.

Woody promptly took some dollar bills from his pocket and pushed them into Mike's hands. "I'd like a year's subscription, but don't send it yet. I'll be doing a lot of moving around for a while."

Mike counted out five dollars, grabbed Woody's hand, and forced the rest of the money into it. "You take back! Five dollars is enough!"

"The rest is a contribution." Woody tried to hand it back.

"*No!*" Mike's loud cry shocked us. "You gonna make a more big contribution!"

We stared at him as he fixed his eyes on Woody with hypnotic intensity. "*You gonna go and kiss my mother for me!*" His voice trembled. "I don't see her for twenty-five years."

There was a moment of silence.

"Mike," I said, "your mother's in Sicily."

"Yes!" He turned his stare on me. "And you gonna go and kiss her for me!"

"But Mike," I said, "we haven't invaded *Sicily*; we're only in *North Africa*."

"You gonna go and kiss her for me!" He shut his eyes, and in the silence that followed, we could see him willing the invasion of Sicily — willing the Allied commanders to act — willing our convoys and our armies straight to his native land. "The village of Altofonte." He opened his eyes. "Near Palermo — and tell her I'm coming."

"You crazy bastard." I opened my arms to him.

"For my mother." Tears rolled down his face as he hugged me tightly and kissed me on both cheeks. There were tears on everybody's cheeks, except for Cisco and Woody — they blew their noses. Mike grabbed Woody and kissed him, then he did the same to Cisco. Mary and the professors embraced us and urged us to be careful.

"Don't forget," Mike called after us as we left, "Altofonte, near Palermo!"

"Crazy Wops!" Cisco muttered as we headed for McSorley's saloon.

■

After three songs and four beers, it was time for me to meet Gabrielle at her job in the Empire State Building.

"There's a party at Leadbelly's tonight." Woody wrote out the address. "Why don't you bring her?"

Gabrielle Gold's love of life lit up her young beauty and sparkled over everything around her. Example: when her friends played "Botticelli," a twenty-questions kind of group game, Gabrielle's participation changed the game from a pleasant time killer into a happy romp. She would toss her long, mahogany-red hair, throw back her tawny, freckled face, open her wide, gorgeous mouth, and dazzle her fellow players with a lusty laugh that challenged, complimented, questioned, and seduced you, all at once.

In political arguments her passionate optimism more than made up for her lapses in logic. "Of course the Red Army will destroy the Nazis! Otherwise, what's the use of getting married?" And she usually won against the most reasoned kind of pessimism.

I adored Gabrielle. She could persuade a friend to go with her at six o'clock of a stormy winter morning to stand in front of a subway entrance, cajoling signatures against the House Un-American Activities Committee or badgering sleepy subway riders into pledging blood donations, until nine o'clock, when she would go to her own job. She worked as a legal secretary for five lawyers until six o'clock, when she would go to university classes, and then, more often than not, she would meet me, untired, full of life, her voice singing, "Hi, Jim!" And she was always immaculate and always sensuously perfumed. She usually wore a white blouse, opened over her glowing bronze skin to the cleft of her firm breasts. In the summertime her pure white shorts, almost too brief, accentuated the long line of the sexiest pair of legs I'd ever seen — especially from the back. When she danced with somebody else, I gritted my teeth — she was *my* girl since the first day I met her several months before, and on that very first day I had asked her to marry me, even though I was afraid I wasn't good enough for her.

I had never told her about my fear of fighting. All she knew was that I was waiting for my army draft call. We never talked about why I had not volunteered at the start of the war, but in her presence I was always aware of my weakness, and my guilt increased as the world learned more and more about the German death camps. Gabrielle was Jewish. Marrying Gabrielle would wash away some of my guilt because I would become one with her, Jewish with her, my kids would be Jews — and shipping out would help earn me the right to marry her.

"Baloney, Jim! You're only shipping out because Cisco asked you!" she said when I told her about my decision.

"Sure, Cisco asked me, but what's that got to do with it? I'm shipping out! In two days I'll be smack in the middle of the war!"

"What's it's got to do with is that Cisco is a very romantic guy."

"Sure he is, and what's more, he's a buddy of Woody Guthrie's, and Woody's shipping out with us."

"Now I understand — how could you resist? What's getting killed compared to shipping out with Cisco Houston *and* Woody Guthrie?"

"Gaby, will you cut it out? I'm shipping out because I want to be in the middle of the fight as soon as I can — because I want to make up for the eighteen months I've wasted!"

"I said baloney, Jim! You don't have to feel guilty about the eighteen months. Your parents needed you; you could go into the army without feeling guilty. You're shipping out because you see Cisco and Woody Guthrie as romantic heroes, and you're so goddamned impressionable, you'd follow them on a suicide mission if they asked you."

"Jesus — you're jealous!"

"No — you're stupid!" Tears filled her eyes.

I kissed her and held her, but I couldn't find the words to explain my decision, and as for what she said about my being led by two guys like Cisco and Woody, well, maybe the truth lay somewhere between us.

"All right." She smiled. "No use carrying on — it's done. Next?"

I kissed her and said, "Let's celebrate!"

Instead of going to the 14th Street Cafeteria for our usual thirty-five-cent special, we went to Joe's Villa Splendor and blew a dollar apiece on a three-course spaghetti dinner plus a half-bottle of wine.

Leadbelly's tenement apartment was near 10th Street and 1st Avenue. The downstairs bell said "H. Ledbetter," and from the hallway we could hear Leadbelly singing on the fourth floor. We were greeted by his wife, Martha, a handsome middle-aged woman. She led us down the corridor of the little three-room apartment. Leadbelly's voice carried loud and clear above the noise of the guests who were arguing politics in the kitchen and in the bedroom. Clouds of cigarette smoke and the smell of whiskey filled the air. In the living room thirty or more guests sat on the floor listening to Leadbelly. He sat on a chair, singing and shaking his great, bald, black head in mock annoyance at the arrogance of his big twelve-string guitar — as though the guitar played itself. He talked to it imperiously, and it answered him just as imperiously. Seated at Leadbelly's feet were Woody, Cisco, Brownie McGhee, Sonny Terry, Laura Duncan, and Josh White, and they were there not to sing but to listen to this king of black music, who had been sixteen years on a chain gang. John Lomax had rescued him so that he might record his work songs, his blues, and his hope songs before he died.

I squeezed Gabrielle's waist. "Are you enjoying?" We had been there for more than an hour.

"Yes, but I can't understand Leadbelly — it's another language."

"It doesn't matter; you've got to feel it."

"I'm feeling, I'm feeling — look how I'm feeling!" She kissed me hard on the mouth.

"Woody," I called to him, "we've got to go."

"It's early."

"Yes, but we've got to be at Caven Point at nine."

"Of course, of course, you lucky Wop. Goodbye, Gaby." He kissed her on the cheek.

"I know why he's a lucky Wop," she said, squeezing my arm, "but what's Caven Point?"

"That," said Woody, "is an explosive subject best left alone tonight. Sweet dreams to both of you."

■

The Caven Point pier stretched out toward the middle of New York Bay, far enough away from the surrounding residential areas and the skyscrapers of downtown New York for them to be safe — or so the public hoped. How many thousands of tons of explosives were stored at the point was a military secret. In fact everything at the point was hushed — almost silent. There was no sound of trucks, no banging of cargo, and no yelling. The longshoremen were paid triple time. They spoke softly and handled the bombs very gently. Before we were allowed to board our ship, we were made to cover our shoes with cloths, for a steel-cleated heel could cause a spark that might set off the whole shebang. The three of us watched silently as the longshoremen quietly and quickly laid crate after crate of two-ton blockbusters into our ship's holds. They had been loading her all night.

"Are you guys hypnotized by dynamite or something?" the chief steward yelled to us. "Let's go; we've got a job to do!"

He put us to work down below, stacking supplies into the wooden bins of the storeroom, which was about thirty feet by fifteen. We broke open tons of boxes and neatly packed away hundreds of cans, bottled condiments, paper products, and piles of fifty-pound flour sacks. It was hard work, what with the heat and the flour dust in our mouths and on our sweating skins. Then the chill-box — a room as big as the storeroom — had to be filled with crates of vegetables, fruits, cartons of milk, butter, and cases of eggs. The chill-box was clean, with no moldy smell. Cisco said it was a sure sign of a good-feeding ship.

The freeze-box had to be filled too, with sides of beef, frozen poultry, and meats of all kinds. Although the job was hard and required a lot of concentration, my mind was never totally on my work; I was constantly aware that I was surrounded by thousands of tons of high explosives. The danger of instant catastrophe electrified the air — I could feel it crackling on my skin — and my eyebrows ached from being constantly arched. The other men in the skeleton crew must have felt it too; I'm sure that Cisco and Woody did, because, like the longshoremen, they worked with a minimum of talk. The presence of dynamite was not conducive to conversation.

At lunchtime Roberto fed us sandwiches and coffee, but we didn't eat much. Without discussing it, we went back to work before the hour was up. I think we felt that the harder we worked, the sooner the ship would leave Caven Point. The longshoremen also worked faster. But they worked there day after day, ship after ship — working faster wouldn't free them from the danger. Maybe dynamite dampened logic as well as conversation. It did speed up work, though, because by 4:30 the *Travis* was ready to sail with her quota of Caven Point cargo tightly packed in the bottom of her holds. By 4:45 we were pulling away from that pier and starting on my first sea voyage — to Red Hook, Brooklyn, across the bay.

The pounding of the ship's engine, the letting go of her ropes, the sound of her horn, the smell of salt water, and the longshoremen calling good luck to us were thrilling; I was a real seaman — no more need to pretend, as I always did when I rode the ferries. Now I leaned against the rail like an old hand, flicked my cigarette over the side, and waved condescendingly to the crowded passengers on the Staten Island ferry. Nobody waved back.

"God bless that ferryboat!" Woody blew her a kiss. "Many's the time Cisco and I rode her back and forth, until we'd sung enough to earn us a meal and a bottle of rum."

Cisco, sitting on the hatch cover, struck his guitar and sang, "In the mighty crystal glitter of that wild and windward spray, I fought the pounding waters and met a watery grave." It was one of my favorite Guthrie songs, "Grand Coulee Dam."

Woody pulled his guitar around and joined him. "Well she tore our boat to splinters, but she gave men dreams to dream, on the day the Coulee Dam crossed that wild and wasted stream." I joined them on the next verse, my third-part harmony blending well with Cisco's beautiful top tenor, and our singing calmed the air. It neutralized the dynamite's electric charge and it soothed us.

The light of the five o'clock sun turned the bay's brown water to crimson and made the skyscrapers even more fantastic. Our ship steamed slowly through the maze of crisscrossing harbor traffic, past dozens of anchored ships, past Governor's Island, and into Buttermilk Channel, where a tugboat eased her alongside the Red Hook dock, successfully ending my first sea voyage.

The sun, much lower now over the far Jersey hills, backlighted the Statue of Liberty in an astounding way. "Look!" Woody pointed to her. "Miss Liberty's got a halo!"

"I wonder if that's an omen." I muttered.

"Of course it is." Cisco slung his guitar over his back. "It means that I'm going to have a great Guinea dinner tonight — right?"

"Right!" I had almost forgotten that my parents had invited Cisco and Gabrielle to my farewell dinner. Woody was going home to say goodbye to Marjorie and Miss Stackabones.

While we waited for the ship to tie up, I told my mates the story of the first time I brought a friend home to dinner. It was my way of telling Cisco what to expect and also a way to tell both of them something about me.

I told them how in the depth of the Great Depression, 1932, my parents worked twelve hours a day to send me to college. They were very proud of me because I had finished high school at fifteen and Columbia had accepted me. They worked at bottling acrid-smelling laundry bleach in an unheated four-car garage in the Bronx. My fourteen-year-old brother, Fred, helped after school.

I worked too: I faked my age and got a truck-driver's license so that I could deliver the bleach to stores around the city. I would load the truck each morning, drive to Columbia, and park on 124th Street — eight blocks away from the campus — to avoid being seen by my classmates, most of whom came from rich families. Some were so rich that, even though their families lived in the city, they boarded at school. Of the few who didn't board, half of them were delivered to school in limousines. I must have been the only Ivy League student ever to go to campus in a 1928 two-ton Ford truck. After classes I would walk to the truck, change into work clothes, and begin my deliveries, never getting home before eight.

Most of my rich fellow students were sons of chairmen of the boards of important companies, and they would often brag about it. I dreaded the question "and what does your father do?" Fortunately, after a while I had an answer. I talked to my father about the benefits of incorporating our little business. Our neighborhood lawyer would do it for only five dollars, and my father agreed. I chose the name. From then on, when my rich friends asked, "and what does your father do?" I would answer, "Oh. He's the chairman of the board of the Bronx Chemical works."

Everything at Columbia was a deception. Lunch was another deception. My friends ate in the campus restaurant, served by white-coated waiters. I had to sneak my lunch in the street, usually a bar of the biggest and cheapest peanut candy in the world: Mr. Goodbar, which cost five cents. Sometimes I'd use my nickel to buy an apple from the unemployed. When I finished my lunch, I'd go into the campus restaurant, and after sitting at a dirty table for a while, I would fake a yawn as though I'd had a big meal, get up, and mix with my classmates.

A worse deception was my age. I could pass for eighteen because I was six feet tall, but I was sure that my classmates, most of whom were eighteen or nineteen, wouldn't talk to me if they knew the truth. The Barnard girls I occasionally dated would have died.

But my biggest deception was provoked by the social order that prevailed on the campus. The order was based on more than just money; everybody had friends who had lost all their money in the depression. Columbia's social order was based on family history: the longer a family had lived in America and the older its wealth, the more superior it was. Columbia was a New York school, and because New York was founded by the Dutch, the sons of the rich, old New York Dutch families considered themselves the most superior of the superiors. My father and mother were poor Italian immigrants. I was provoked into using the big lie when one of the most superior (let's call him Van Cortlandt) befriended me.

Despite Van Cortlandt's general smugness and his patronizing attitude toward me, I was thrilled to be seen with him — although ever aware of the risk of falling off the tightrope of deception that I had strung. I took every precaution to cover up any evidence of my poverty. He took for granted that the handful of Italians and Jews allowed to attend Columbia were from well-off families. For instance, I spent the weekend with Hannibal Zumbo, the only other poor Italian American in our class. Hannibal lived in Little Italy bordering Chinatown, in a cold-water flat with a hall toilet.

"Have a good weekend?" Van Cortlandt asked me on the next Monday morning.

"Great."

"Where?"

"Zumbo's."

"His country place or his town house?"

"His town house," I said without lying. But my act became increasingly more difficult to perform, and our relationship reached a danger point when Van Cortlandt invited me to his parents' town house for dinner.

Their mansion, just off Fifth Avenue, was a revelation to me. Nothing, not even Hollywood, had prepared me for such a world — the giant entrance doors; the marble-columned foyer; the library stacked with precious books up to its twenty-foot ceiling; the smell of flowers; the dining room, with its Renaissance fireplace; and the uniformed couple serving just the four of us.

I carefully imitated every move the Van Cortlandt's made at table, and my performance was going quite well until Van Cortlandt senior uttered the dreaded words, "Tell me about your parents."

After a moment's silence, I looked up and said, "They're poor — they're poor, but they're both of the nobility." I let the words sink in, pleased with my coup — with one sentence I had ennobled my parents. "Not the newly created nobility of the king; they're of the papal aristocracy, from the eleven hundreds." Might as well be hung for two lies as one.

"How interesting." Mr. Van Cortlandt's dry smile indicated that although he appreciated aristocracy, he did not appreciate Roman Catholics.

"Yes, they are of the papal aristocracy, but my father rebelled against the decadence of the Church." That would go well with these Dutch Protestants. "And he also fought against the monarch." That clinched it — I had transformed my atheist-socialist father into a Protestant Republican, just like the Van Cortlandts. "And so my parents were forced to leave everything behind and come to America, the land of democracy." That was the capper — religious-political aristocratic refugees, and from the eleven hundreds! So much for the Van Cortlandts' three-hundred-year-old bourgeois ancestors. Van Cortlandt also invited me to his parent's country home on Long Island. The visits were fascinating, but with each visit my social debt increased, and I had no way of repaying it. I was trapped. If I invited my friend to my parents' home, I was faced with the terror of being exposed as a fraud. If I didn't invite him, I faced the shame of being labeled a sponger, a freeloader, a schnurrer.

For a while I succeeded in fending off my friend's hints that I reciprocate, but his hints soon became insistent requests. "Come on Longhi, when am I going to get a real Italian dinner?" Or "Come on Longhi, what difference does it make if your family lives in a three-room flat? I'd love to meet them after all the things you told me about them!"

When I couldn't put him off any longer, I confessed my lie to my mother. "Lie? That's no lie! We *do* come from high, high society!" She immediately switched from Neapolitan dialect to the purest Italian, pushed back a loose strand of her jet-black hair from her handsome face, removed her apron, and straightened herself to her full height. "Did you forget that your father's mother's sister married a Ventrella? The Ventrella's were high — high! They never did a day's work in a thousand years! Of course our family is high!" And as she continued to illuminate the history of her husband's mother's sister's husband's family, her Italian became more and more majestic.

Although my mother had to leave school after the fourth grade, she was brilliant, and she had a prodigious memory that enabled her to memorize the greatest Italian poetry. She never forgot a line, just as she never forgot a rebuff — real or imagined. She regarded my ignorance of our nobility as a slur on the honor of our house.

With offended regal dignity, she began to pace our small living room, and with each line that she declaimed about the nobility of our family, she became more and more convinced of the truth of her lines — just as any great actress would. At a certain point in her recital it became clear, without either of us referring to it, that she was in fact auditioning for the role I would need her to play to save my honor. And by God, right there in front of my eyes, she transformed herself into a great lady, taller and more handsome than I'd ever seen her. Cousin Minny always said that when it came to acting, my mother made Leonora Duse look like an amateur. When Mom ended her audition, she sat down as though her chair were a throne and ordered me to issue an invitation to my aristocratic friend immediately.

The dinner was set for the following Sunday. During the next three days Mom cooked heavenly fragrant dishes, and while she cooked and cleaned, she never stopped rehearsing her role, nor did she once raise her voice, not even to my father. She moved around the house in a stately manner, as though our top-floor, three-room apartment was the Pitti palace, and she didn't allow a single word of dialect to pass her lips. She was going to be a letter-perfect aristocrat.

As for my father, I hadn't the slightest anxiety: he was a quasi intellectual whose normal behavior was so bizarre that he could easily pass for a highly inbred aristocrat. His looks helped too — tall, lean, and good-looking, despite his bald head, beaklike nose, and eagle eyes.

Sunday, at precisely one o'clock, the bell rang, and I opened the door to welcome my friend. My mother stood in the doorway of the steaming kitchen just off the tiny entrance area. In all her rehearsals, she had never looked more regal. When I presented my friend to her, he half-bowed and told her that he had heard many wonderful things about her. She made no reply except to smile modestly and bow her head slightly — she was not going to ridicule herself by trying to use her broken English. The little English she learned from my brother and me was used only when there was no other way to express herself. From the way Van Cortlandt reacted to her, however, it was obvious that her pantomime was far more expressive than any words.

As Mom gracefully retreated into the clouds of aromatic steam, I led my friend into the combination living room–bedroom, where my father and my brother were seated at a beautifully set table. Pop heartily slapped Van Cortlandt on the shoulder, pushed him into the best chair, poured a huge glass of wine for him, and began joking about the three days' work his vain wife had put into this dinner for her son's honored friend. Van Cortlandt made amazed and grateful comments, loud enough for my mother to hear. He seemed overwhelmed by the heroic effort of a lady who might once have had a dozen servants to wait on her.

After twenty minutes of more wine and more paternal jokes about maternal cooking, the noise from the kitchen reached a crescendo of pot banging and hissing steam, until my mother appeared, worn-looking but still regal, carrying an enormous platter of pasta. Van Cortlandt promptly stood up for her, embarrassing the rest of us into standing too. As she put the heavy platter on the table, she gave my father a contemptuous, devastating glance. Then she tried to ease herself into the chair Van Cortlandt held for her, but at the last moment she flopped into it, exhausted. She looked up at the appreciative, well-mannered aristocrat, and with the most dignified and grateful smile, she shook her head slowly and said to him, "Ah'm so fuck-na tired!"

As long as I live, the scars of those four words will never disappear from my psyche. As for Van Cortlandt, he had not understood her heavily accented English; he thought she had said something in Italian.

"Well, that's the end of my story." I waited for Cisco to stop laughing. Woody kept shaking his head. When Cisco stopped laughing, he said, "Did your fancy friend ever learn the truth about your 'noble' mother?"

"Never."

"Somebody ought to write a song about her." Woody scribbled something in his pocket notebook.

"Can't wait to meet her," Cisco said.

"Then let's go." I grabbed Woody and Cisco by the arm and led them toward the lowering gangway. "She'll kill me if we're late."

"Take it easy!" Cisco panted as he tried to keep up with me. "There's got to be a phone booth on the next block."

"We probably have to go all the way to Court Street." I kept walking at the same fast pace I had started when we left the Red Hook dock.

"What time is she expecting your call?"

"At 6:30."

"Hell, it's only a quarter to seven!"

"You don't know my mother — fifteen minutes is her deadline. If I'm sixteen minutes late, she calls the Missing Persons Bureau."

"That's very funny."

"It's not funny for me. She's a first-class anxiety nut. When she answers the phone, she never says hello; she always says 'Watsa matter!'" I increased my pace — there was a candy store on the corner. I dialed hurriedly, but her line was busy. "And she's a mass of contradictions; she can behave with such majestic dignity and then cut you with the foulest collection of curses you ever heard. If we're with people who don't understand Italian, and she's angry with me for some reason, she'll act like a queen-mother and smile benevolently, while under her breath she's saying to me, 'Your sister's a whore and she's going to die in the electric chair!' — and I don't even have a sister!"

I dialed again. Her phone was immediately picked up. I held my receiver so that Cisco could hear her. "Watsa matter!" It wasn't a question; it was a definite assertion that some terrible tragedy had struck, and she was demanding to be told about it.

"Nothing's the matter. I told you I'd call you, and I'm calling you." I spoke English for Cisco's benefit. "Now wait a minute, wait a minute — Ma, come on, will you? Your phone was busy! What? You called Minny?" Cousin Minny was our family's Missing Persons Bureau. "But Ma, I've only been missing for seventeen minutes, not seventeen years!"

"You promise to call 6:30. You don't call 6:30." She spoke English to establish the full gravity of her accusation, her tone controlled and as formal as a prosecutor's. "You are not a man of your word and you not nice. You know I worry — if you can't telephone on time, don't tell me you gonna telephone. I don't know, I don't wait, I don't worry. You say you call, I wait, I worry, and you are a skunk. Goodbye!"

"Ma, Ma, wait a minute! Don't be mad! Come on, tell me, what did you cook for us tonight?"

"Cazz, cuccuzill, e uova!"

"What did she say?" Cisco had his ear close to the receiver.

"She said she cooked a prick, with baby squash and eggs."

Cisco pushed his way out of the phone booth so that he might better hold his sides. I shut the door to block out his laughter.

"Come on, Ma, don't be mad! No, we won't be late! Where are we? We're in Brooklyn, but I swear we'll be there in an hour!"

"Sure, sure," she said, "te mitt a cavalla nu strunzo e arriva a ora de pranzo."

"What did she say?" Cisco pushed the door open.

"She said, 'Sure, you'll mount a turd and get here in time for dinner.' But Ma, I told you we're going to be on time."

"You'll be on time," she continued in Italian, "when Minny's ass grows teeth!" and she hung up.

The subway trip to the Bronx took longer than expected. I rang the downstairs bell to let Mom know we'd arrived, and we hurriedly climbed the five flights of stairs. She greeted us at the door in her best regal manner, wearing her most saccharine smile.

"Ma, I'm sorry we're late!"

"Gentleman" — she ignored me and addressed Cisco — "I hear so much about you. You are the good friend who will take care of my Enzo! May God keep you both in good health for a hundred years!"

"I'm honored to meet you." Cisco almost bowed.

"You forgot the pastry?" She turned her saccharine smile on me.

"Oh, damn! I'm sorry Ma."

"With all that gorgeous food, who needs pastry?" Cisco sniffed the air.

"You need! I wanted to make a feast for the friend of my dear son! Come!" She led the way, past me, into the living room, where Pop, Gabrielle, and my brother, Fred, stood waiting for us.

"What did she just mutter to you?" Cisco whispered.

"Nothing. She just called me a cretin and wished me a touch of cholera."

"With that angelic smile?"

"I tell you, she's a mass of contradictions."

"Mass?" Mom looked up at Cisco, hopefully. "You go to mass?"

Cisco hesitated.

"Mass, my ass!" Pop gave Cisco's shoulder a hard slap. "A strong, beautiful, intelligent young man, what the hell he needs with mass? Shake hands, my dear Cisco!" He nearly wrenched Cisco's shoulder with one powerful shake.

Mom muttered something and disappeared into the steaming kitchen.

"Is your mother angry?" Cisco asked.

"Not really." Fred pulled some cotton from a package. "She just asked God to bust my father's atheistic belly wide open." He handed Cisco two wads of cotton. "Here, put these in your ears if you want to survive this meal."

"Hey, you shit!" Pop tore the cotton from Fred's hands in mock anger. "Why you always make fun of me?"

Fred was Cisco's height; he pulled the three of us in a ring around Pop, who was only five feet ten. Fred kissed the top of Pop's bald head. "Pop, if you don't behave today, we three are gonna pick you up and sit you on top of that closet." Although Fred had already drunk a couple of glasses of wine, it was not enough to dim the twinkle in his eyes or dull the intelligence of his kind, open face.

Despite the theological tensions, the dinner was a great success. "I'm so glad you come to my house, Cisco." Mom poured him another demitasse of coffee. "I'm gonna pray for God to watch out for you and my boy. You believe in God, no?"

Again Pop came to Cisco's rescue. "No religious discussion in this house!" He banged a wine bottle onto the table. "Eat! Drink! Be happy!"

"Mussolini!" Mom pointed angrily at Pop. "He look just like Mussolini!"

"Hey! Hey! Hey!" Pop rubbed his bald head. "Mussolini is bald, short, and ugly. I'm bald, tall, and beautiful!"

"Same thing — dictator is dictator! Cisco, you think that's nice? You and my son gonna fight dictators, and we have dictator in this house?" Cisco stammered; he was getting a taste of what it was to be caught in the crossfire of a religious war.

"*Cisco, don't believe her!*" Pop fired his salvo all in one breath. "In this house there is *democracy!* The law is the same for everybody: no religious discussion allowed!"

"Hitler." Mom pointed at Pop. "He look just like Hitler! I can't have a picture of Jesus in my house, I can't have my babies baptize . . ."

"Don't remind me of that day of infamy!" Pop shouted. "Traitors! Fifth Columnists! Jesuits!" Cisco stared at my father.

"Don't worry." Fred calmly poured anisette into Cisco's coffee. "He gets like that every time he remembers our baptisms."

"Double-crosser!" Pop yelled to my mother.

"Dictator!" she yelled back.

"My cousin Louise," I quickly explained to Cisco, "she kidnapped Fred and me when I was twelve, and she had us baptized."

"This woman!" Pop's accusing finger shot toward my mother and shook in front of Cisco's eyes. "This woman was the traitor!"

"He's a lousy dictator!" Her accusing finger shot toward my father and shook in front of Cisco's eyes.

Cisco took the two opposing fingers in his hands, "Well, Mrs. Longhi, at least your children *were* baptized."

"Too late!" She withdrew her finger. "Some injection only work for some people — the baptism work for my Freddie — he's a good Catholic, but" — she pointed her finger at me — "for that sonofabitch it no work!"

Gabrielle nearly fell off her chair with laughter.

"And whatta you laugh, Jew?" Mom tried to keep back her own laughter.

"That's enough!" Pop stood up. "Everybody on the roof! Come on Cisco, play the guitar! Su fratelli —" he began singing the Italian socialist anthem as he led the way. Mom chanted a Latin litany in counterpoint to Pop's anthem as she followed him up the stairs.

"What's she chanting?" Cisco asked me as we joined the procession.

"Her own Latin words for 'Fuck all of his ancestors — the dead and the extradead.'"

We sat on the roof, talking, singing, and slowly recovering from Mom's gargantuan dinner. Pop and Mom told stories of Italy. Cisco told us about California and about his mother and his sister. He said nothing about Slim. We talked of everything except the war, until it was time to go.

Pop said, "Stay until the moon comes up."

We stayed, but the mood changed. Cisco sang some lonesome songs like a sad troubadour from olden times, and Mom sang some ancient lullabies.

Fred took me aside. "You take care — right?" His eyes were shiny. "And don't forget to look up and down before you cross the ocean." Fred was making a private joke; when we were kids, my mother had warned me to look up and down before crossing the street. I carried out my mother's orders to the letter. I wouldn't cross until I had looked up and down — up to the sky and down to the sidewalk. Fred handed me ten dollars. "Here — for your maiden voyage. I thought of buying a bottle of champagne to break over your head, but I figured you'd rather have the money." I tried giving it back. "Keep it," he said. "We army rejects are gonna make a fortune out of this war." He embraced me hard, and I felt his wet cheek against mine.

Pop's good-bye was like a top sergeant's drill order. "Strength and courage! — Write every week! — Be a man!" It wasn't until we embraced that his voice broke. "Remember — we love you."

My mother's good-bye was amazingly unemotional, the same three bursts of Neapolitan she always gave me whenever I was about to leave her house for more than a day. They were like bursts of machine-gun fire catching me across the back, and I would always go through the charade of stumbling as though mortally wounded. This time though, she let me have it as I went to embrace her. First burst: "Mit-tit-too-ka-putt!" (Wear your coat!). It got me in the gut, and I doubled over. Second burst: "Mas-teek-a-bone!" (Chew your food well!). I stumbled toward her. Third burst: "Stah-tah-kort!" (Be careful!). I fell into her arms. As we kissed, she slipped a small medallion into my hand. "Wear this for me," she whispered into my ear. "Saint Michael will protect you."

Gabrielle and I said our good-byes alone until early morning, when she went to the Empire State Building and I went back to the floating arsenal waiting for me in Red Hook.

■

Cisco was on board when I got to the ship; Woody was a little late, but it was no wonder, considering what he was carrying. We could barely see him under the load: a seabag over his shoulder, a guitar strapped to his back, a violin case, a mandolin case, a stack of at least ten books, and a portable typewriter, all tied together by a length of clothesline and somehow wrapped around him.

"Hey!" a longshoreman called out, "looka the walkin' pawnshop!"

Cisco picked out a cabin for us, on the portside forward — less noise, he said. He and Woody chose the two lower bunks; I was glad to get an upper — more romantic for me. The other upper bunk served as a temporary storing place for some of Woody's stuff.

"Momma mia!" I looked at Woody's books — Darwin, Gibbon, Rabelais, Emerson. "These are heavy enough to sink a ship."

"Hell, that's just a little light reading. Here, this one's for you!" He threw me a copy of his autobiography, *Bound for Glory*.

Cisco brought Jack London's *Martin Eden*, *A History of the U.S. Labor Movement*, and an anthology of James Thurber.

My library consisted of some law books and a Bible I stole from a hotel room.

Woody riffled the pages of a law book. "Well, if we read all of these carefully, we'll come back with a pretty good education."

"Right." Cisco pulled two life jackets from under the bunks. "But now we start a different kind of education — the art of getting back to New York in one piece. Here, try these on."

Woody was delighted with his life jacket and insisted on wearing it when we went out on deck for a smoke before starting to load stores down below.

"Put those cigarettes out!" an officer on the boat deck screamed at us. "What's the matter with you guys? Don't you know you can't smoke on deck here!"

We looked around; all five cargo holds were being loaded with fifty-gallon black drums — on top of the bombs.

"What are we loading?" I asked an Italian longshoreman who was signaling to the winchman.

"Gas-u-leen."

"Gasoline?" I looked at Cisco and Woody.

"Yes, but no just any kinda gas-u-leen." The longshoreman slapped his chest. "Angelo's gang give you the best — high test!"

"What's the difference?" Cisco said in answer to the look on my face. "If we get hit, the thing to remember is collect your wits and pull yourself together. Don't go to pieces, don't lose your head, don't fall apart, don't —"

"Yeah, very funny," I cut him short, "very funny."

"Sir!" Woody called up to the officer on the boat deck, "Oh, sir! Ain't no use you issuing us these life jackets. What I believe we urgently need is parachutes!"

Cisco grabbed Woody by the arm and led us down below to the storeroom.

We had been working a couple of hours when DRRRINNNGGG! The deafening ring of an alarm bell struck my ears with paralyzing force. I had never heard anything so loud and so frightening as that brain-shocking, relentless ring. I turned to Cisco, but he disappeared through the doorway, shouting "Run!"

Woody and I raced after him up to the main deck. Hundreds of long-shoremen were pouring out of our ship's holds, scrambling, pushing, racing each other down to the dock, where hundreds of other longshore-men from the ships alongside us were already racing wildly toward the dock gate, out into the street, all of us running as fast as we could up the four-block slope to Court Street, speeded by a continuously shrieking siren.

"What is it?" I yelled as I caught up with Cisco.

"Time bomb." He looked back to see if Woody was with us.

"Joey-y-y-y-y!" a woman screamed, but other than that there was no sound from anybody, just panicked, silent running.

My lungs were near bursting when I collapsed onto a brownstone stoop three blocks up the slope. Woody and Cisco flopped next to me. It turned out to be a false alarm.

The crowd walked slowly and silently back to the dock, relieved and, I think, humiliated — as I felt humiliated for having been made to show my frantic fear of death. As I climbed the gangway back onto the ship, it occurred to me that I could still get out of shipping out — my commitment wasn't irrevocable until my ship's gangway was pulled up.

5

We worked until five and didn't have to be back until ten that night. We decided not to phone our girls — we had said our good-byes.

"Let's find us a nice gin mill that appreciates some good music." Woody strapped his guitar onto his back. Cisco did the same.

"What's the matter?" I asked Woody, who was looking at me with his head cocked and one eyebrow raised.

"You look naked without a *gee*-tar." He pulled his guitar around. "While we were running up that hill this morning, I promised me, if I survived, I'd treat me to a new guitar — one with a little wider neck, like the one I've seen on 6th Avenue. I'll give you this one — you can pay me fifty dollars at the end of the trip. He started playing softly. "She's got a sweet tone — plucks nice an' easy — been everywhere with me — seen me through many a bad time and some pretty good ones. It would grieve me to part with her, but seein's how she's goin' to you, and since I'm sure you'll keep her in the style she's been accustomed to, then I don't feel like I'm losin' a guitar; I feel like I'm gaining a son." He took off the guitar and hung it around my neck.

I was so moved I tried to embrace him, but the guitar kept getting in the way.

When we got to the 6th Avenue store, Woody greeted his new guitar like a lover: he caressed it and tickled its strings; he showed off its rich tone, its beautiful shape, and its high color. He even made us smell its varnish.

Sam, the guitar dealer, looked worried. "Remember, Woody, she's not waterproof, so you watch out for them submarines, you hear?"

"Don't worry, Sam." Woody cut off a piece of wrapping paper on which he quickly crayoned something in big block letters, then he taped the paper onto the guitar. "Ain't no need to worry about them Hitler submarines." He held up the guitar, across whose shiny face the big letters proclaimed, "THIS MACHINE KILLS FASCISTS."

■

On the subway back to Brooklyn Woody played his new guitar, to Cisco's accompaniment, and I got my first guitar lesson. By the time we got to Red Hook, my fingers were raw with deep string grooves, but I was proud of the guitar, which I too strapped to my back, and I was very aware of the interesting picture the three of us made as we walked back to our ship.

A black man walking toward us stopped short and in Neapolitan dialect said, "What the prick are you doing here, Jimmy? I heard you went in the army."

The man was Whitey, one of the few black longshoremen on the "Italian" docks. We had become friends when I was doing missionary work for *L'Unita* among the Italian longshoremen. Whitey spoke Neapolitan fluently, and he knew that I loved to hear him use it.

"Are you coming to the meeting?"

"What meeting?"

"For Pete — a memorial meeting for Pete at Saint Stephen's."

I translated for Woody and Cisco and started to explain about Pete Panto, but they knew the story of the young rank-and-file leader who was murdered by the underworld dock bosses for saying no.

■

It was just ten when we got back to the *Travis*. There wasn't a sign of life from the darkened ship; blackout curtains covered her open portholes, but as we climbed the gangway ladder, we heard the noisy chatter of her full crew.

The crew's messroom was crowded and filled with the noise of old friends meeting, new friendships in the making, beer cans clanking, and sandwiches and coffee being passed around. The only quiet came from the table where a seven-man poker game was going strong.

The gun-crew messroom was much quieter — there was no happy chatter of reunion or of new friendships in the making. Unlike civilian merchant seamen, who could change ships after every trip, the U.S. Navy gun-crew kids were permanently assigned to the *Travis*. Most of them sat around writing letters. One of them had a bright-looking little monkey that kept interfering with his letter writing.

"I'm your new dishwasher," Woody called out to the gunners, "and these are my buddies." He stuck his hand out to the nearest letterwriter.

The young gunner stood up, slightly flustered, and said, "Hi!" He smiled as Woody pumped his hand. One by one the gunners stood up to have their hands pumped by their new dishwasher. Woody also shook hands with the monkey.

"New dishwasher!" one of the gunners called out, "How's about a tune!"

In no time Woody had a singing, stomping, and hollering party going, what he called a hootenanny. The regular crew quickly joined us, all except the poker players, and the room was jammed — standing room only for our first performance on the *Willy B.*

We were a hit with everybody except the monkey, who kept his hands over his ears. I banged my guitar like a drum, Roberto the cook banged a pot, and nearly everybody played something — harmonicas, kazoos, spoons, or just a banged-on table — Woody leading the ensemble through his war songs, work songs, hillbilly songs, blues, talking blues, and several kinds of hoedowns. It didn't matter that there was no room for square dancing; they danced in their chairs or where they stood. Bottles of whiskey came out of hiding, bottles that were meant to be saved for the high seas.

Things were going so well that two poker players joined us, and after a while the gunner's lieutenant commander came in with his ensign, followed by two of the ship's officers and finally by the captain himself, a stocky, red-faced middle-aged man with a heavy Norwegian accent. The whiskey bottles disappeared as the men made way for him.

"We leave at midnight." He looked sternly at the officers, clearly communicating his displeasure for their fraternizing with the crew. "If any man turns out drunk, he'll be put in irons for a week." He looked around the packed room, stared at Woody for a moment, and then exited, followed by the officers.

"I told you — worse than Hitler!" Red took a swig from the bottle he had hidden behind his back.

"Time to make up our bunks anyway." Cisco put down his guitar, and the party broke up.

■

"Where do we get the sheets?" Woody put his guitar under his bunk.

"Well," said Cisco as he put his guitar away, "if the wheel is in the wheelhouse, the sheets got to be in the sheethouse, which is where I think we all are going to be with that captain."

The linen room was down below. Its bins were stacked with fresh bed linens, blankets, and towels, which were handed out by one of the steward department men. The dirty linen went into big bags and was laundered ashore.

Cisco showed us how to make our bunks drum-tight. I was about to climb into mine just to test it when I felt the tremor of the ship's engine. "It's five minutes to midnight. Let's go out on deck." My heart beat faster.

"You guys go." Cisco stretched out on his bunk. "I'm tired."

Woody and I reached the deck just as the ship's horn gave its first deafening blast; the sound waves beating against my skin both thrilled me and frightened me. I looked over the side and saw the gangway ladder being pulled up slowly.

"Woody, do you spell *irrevocable* with one *r* or two?"

"Two."

The horn's second blast shuddered through me as the mooring lines were cast off. I watched the ship inching away from the pier. I turned to Woody. "Bon voyage, old buddy."

"Amen," he replied.

A tugboat eased the *Travis* through Buttermilk Channel and into the bay, picking its way slowly past the anchored ships in the darkened harbor. The city was browned out, not because of fear of air attacks, but to cut down the sky glow against which our ships were silhouetted — sitting-duck targets for the U-boats waiting offshore.

Woody went to the bow; we would be passing by his house just as soon as we rounded Coney Island. I went to the stern, to look back at Manhattan, where Gabrielle was now probably sleeping, and beyond her to everything I'd been in my twenty-seven years. The dimmed lights of Manhattan receded and then disappeared as we passed through the narrows and began our turn around Coney Island. I took one last puff on the cigarette I held carefully cupped in my hand — one last look astern, and then I joined Woody up in the bow.

"Just there — right there." He pointed ashore. "3580 Mermaid Avenue."

Past Coney Island, out off the Rockaways, the ship began to roll slightly, and I got my first squeamish feeling, but I forgot about seasickness when I realized that we were coming abreast of Fire Island, where several ships were supposed to have been torpedoed. The city's sky glow had dimmed, but the three ships behind us were still clearly silhouetted against the ghostly light.

"You know somethin'?" Woody said as we made our way back to the crew's messroom. "Considering the cargo we're carrying, if the Nazis did blow us up, we wouldn't even feel it — so the last laugh would be on them."

The brightly lit messroom looked reassuring: the poker game was still going strong; several men on watch were taking night lunch from the refrigerator filled with cold cuts, cheese, bread, and milk; and the steady beat of the ship's engine had a far more comforting sound than it had outside.

"You guys better get some sleep — we get called at six." Cisco put down Woody's copy of Darwin and turned out his bunk light.

Woody undressed quickly, slipped into his bunk, turned out his light, and immediately began snoring.

"That's one of his great talents." Cisco looked at Woody, who was lying flat on his back, mouth open, dead to the world. "I've seen him trapped between two freight cars doing sixty miles an hour in the freezing cold, sleeping peacefully."

I put out my light, but I couldn't sleep. "Could we open the porthole curtain? It's stuffy in here."

"Can't. We might accidentally turn on a light or somebody might open the door — one ray of light is all a U-boat needs. But count your blessings; we're only three in this cabin."

In the pitch black I became more aware of the pounding of the ship's engine — whoom pah-boom, whoom pah-boom, whoom pah-boom — pushing us closer and closer to where the wolf packs were waiting. I shut my eyes tightly as though that might shut out the engine's noise, but instead I saw the ship from a submarine's-eye view — her gigantic keel moving through the dark silent water, everything dark except for the white of her churning propeller and the white wake of a torpedo speeding straight toward our dynamite-laden holds.

I shut my eyes tighter, but my mind saw every detail of the torpedo tearing through the hull, the explosion catching me trapped in my cabin, everything bursting in a chaos of jagged steel and torn legs and arms and blown-off heads, and the water rushing in to drown those of us still breathing.

I rubbed my feet together; warm as it was, my feet were ice cold. I tried to ignore the pounding of the engine — there were other sounds. The ship creaked as she rose and fell with the sea. I was amazed to feel her flexibility. Red had warned us that Liberty ships had no flexibility, yet I could actually feel her decks bending and straightening, breathing in time with the sea — so much for Red's estimate of Liberty ships.

I listened for other comforting sounds. There was a faint high-pitched creaking, an intermittent creaking that seemed to come from several places inside the cabin. I soon realized that the sound came from our heaving bunk springs. It was not the ship's deck that was flexible; it was my bunk spring that bent and straightened and breathed with the sea. What Red said was probably right: a welded ship is a goddamned stiff — a steel coffin.

I stopped listening for new sounds. There was a new insistent one, a gnawing sound, a steadily gnawing sound. I turned on my bunk light, and the noise stopped. I could see nothing. Soon after I put out the light, the noise started again. Rats? The ship's sounds were giving me no help in getting through my first night at sea. My only comfort was the thought that as long as there were rats on a ship, the ship was not about to sink.

■

"Six o'clock!" somebody shouted and then banged the door behind him.

The ship was rolling noticeably. I was pleased that I had fallen asleep without getting seasick, and I turned on my bunk light. Cisco and Woody gave no sign of being awake. I climbed down from my bunk and opened the porthole. Bright sunlight struck my eyes. Although the ship was rolling, the sea was blue and smooth as glass. Red was right again: the *Travis* was a Coney Island rolling barrel. I stuck my head halfway out the porthole to get a better view, and I blinked twice before I realized that the forest of masts I was staring at was not a mirage.

"Cisco! There must be a hundred ships out there!"

"Maybe more. Go up to the boat deck and count them, then come back in ten minutes to wake us up," he said without opening his eyes.

The sight of the convoy was staggering — more than a hundred ships. There were at least ten lines stretching out toward the horizon and at least ten ships in each line. They were spaced about five hundred yards apart. I was awed by the seamanship. How could so many ships find each other in the dark — blacked out, in strict radio silence — and still organize themselves into such a perfect pattern?

The forest of masts and booms looked vaster and denser from the boat deck. How much cargo were they carrying? Most of the gray and black ships were Liberties, but many of them were bigger than ten thousand tons. We must have been carrying a million and a half tons of supplies. There were troopships too — I could see three. If there were six troopships in the convoy, at five thousand men per ship, this convoy alone was carrying thirty thousand men. I wondered if we were part of an invasion fleet.

Naval escorts double-ringed the convoy. Our ship was on the left outside line, second from the end, and I could see two destroyer escorts patrolling our exposed flank, their decks laden with antisubmarine dynamite "ashcans" ready to be catapulted for underwater explosion. Two other destroyers on the horizon patrolled the outer ring, and toward the center of the convoy, up forward, there was a big-gunned cruiser. I was grateful for the sight of the escorts, but they seemed such flimsy protection for so many ships. If a U-boat succeeded in launching a torpedo in the general direction of the convoy, it *had* to hit something.

I woke Cisco.

"What's our position?"

"Outside line, second from the end."

"Shit! But don't worry; you'll live to be a fat bald-headed Wop with a lot of grandchildren."

"What's wrong?" Woody opened one eye.

"Nothing much." Cisco started dressing. "It's just that for the rest of the trip our address is Torpedo Junction, also known as Coffin Corner."

Cisco showed Woody how to clean the big coffee urn in the dishwashing pantry and how to make good coffee, which was part of the dishwasher's job. He showed him how to use the two sinks and the drying racks, shortcuts on drying cutlery, what to do with the garbage, and how to mop the deck. While he taught Woody, he sent me to the storeroom for bread, milk, butter, jams, jellies, ketchup, mustard, salt, pepper, paper napkins, oranges, grapefruit, cans of assorted fruit juices, and pitchers of water.

I set up the tables in the officer's messroom, and at seven I was ready for my first customer. Everybody complimented me on my table decorations — I had commandeered some celery leaves, one branch for each table, and it made for pleasant conversation until the captain came in. He made no comment on my floral display, and the conversations died down.

The captain just wanted tea and toast; everybody else wanted eggs. Breakfast would be a simple meal to handle.

"I said three and a half minutes. These are not even three minutes!" The second engineer, my first egg customer, looked disgustedly at the soft-boiled eggs.

I took the eggs back to the second cook and tried to explain my problem while he shouted to himself, repeating the precise egg orders being shouted at him by the other messmen. While he shouted, he ran up and down in front of the long stove, flipping fried eggs with one hand, juggling boiled eggs with the other, scrambling others in between, shouting constantly, "Two over soft! Two three-minutes! Two over hard! Two scrambled soft! Two scrambled hard! Two on a raft soft! Two bull's-eyes hard! Two, three and a half! Two, four!"

I tried to get the cook's attention. "Cookie, the second engineer insists on —"

"Two bull's-eyes soft! Adam and Eve on a raft hard, and fuck the second engineer!" he shouted without turning round.

"Don't argue with him," Cisco whispered. "Feed 'em to the fishes." I did, and when I reordered the engineer's eggs, I timed them myself and cajoled the cook into taking them out promptly.

The very least I expected from the engineer was a nod of gratitude. Instead he ate his eggs with obvious annoyance at the delay, as though getting perfectly cooked eggs without delay was a right guaranteed to him by the United States Constitution. His behavior was reasonable, however, compared with that of some of my other customers.

It was made very clear to me that an egg is not just an egg; a two-minute egg can be repulsive to a three-minute man; a bull's-eyes up-soft man will not tolerate bull's-eyes up hard; and the same for hard-over and soft-over and poached eggs and scrambled. A man who might eat the worst food with only a grumble will become indignant, obstreperous, or insulting — or, even worse, might silently refuse to eat — if his eggs are not made to his exact specifications.

That first morning I learned that there was no ship's job tougher than messman. A deckhand had to learn to splice five-inch hawsers, rig up tackle, sling scaffolds, toss lines, overhaul gear, take soundings, lower lifeboats, batten down hatches, stand watch at the wheel, operate a steam capstan and a winch, take blocks apart and grease them, make cargo slings, lower booms, secure deck cargo, take a rolling hitch in a rope, and swab and chip and paint a ship. And a black-gang man had to learn how to load the fuel oil, fire the boilers, keep the proper pressures, oil the moving parts, wipe every part of the engine room, tear down a piece of machinery, put it back again, and blow the ship's smokestack. The deck gang and the black gang had tough jobs, but they weren't subject to insults and threats of bodily assault. If a messman served eggs not made to exact specifications, he ran the risk of getting the offending eggs smack in his face. We messmen just managed to keep everybody satisfied by swapping eggs with each other, by cajoling the cook, and by a good deal of fish feeding.

Breakfast over with, I cleared the tables and stored the perishables, and after sweeping and mopping the deck, Cisco and I went to see how Woody was doing with his dishwashing.

The pantry was a shambles — dirty dishes piled three feet high, spilled garbage on the deck, and the big coffee urn hissing dangerously. From the gun-crew messroom came the sound of music — Woody's music. Twenty gun-crew kids were gathered around, listening to him singing "The Ballad of Tom Joad," his version of Steinbeck's *Grapes of Wrath*. They listened in fascination, their breakfasts half-eaten.

"Jesus Christ, Woody!" Cisco broke the spell. "This is no fucking cabaret! This is a gunners' messroom, and that's a dishwashing pantry, which is where you're supposed to fucking be!"

Woody's audience let out an uproar. "Finish the song, Woody! Finish the song!"

Woody looked up at Cisco. "Those dishes ain't going anywhere, and neither am I. They'll all be washed in good time."

"Get your ass in that pantry, you crazy bastard! If the captain comes by, he'll log you a week's pay!"

"Oh, well." Woody put down his guitar. "I guess we're just gonna have to postpone the political, socio, and economical education of these poor little children who've been lied to all their innocent lives by the bourgeois press and phony Hollywood movies."

The gunners hollered louder and started to chant. "The dishes can wait, our economical education cain't! The dishes can wait, our economical education cain't!"

"Okay, okay!" Cisco hollered back. "Finish the goddamned song and then get the hell in here!"

Cisco and I withdrew to the pantry and began washing dishes as quietly as we could — we too wanted to hear the story of Tom Joad once more.

"Now the deputies come and Preacher Casey run," Woody continued singing.

> And then he got away
> And then he met Tom Joad on the old river bridge,
> And these few words he did say, poor boy,
> These few words, he did say:
>
> I preached for the Lord a mighty long time,
> Preached about the rich and the poor,
> Us workin' folks is got to get together
> 'Cause we ain't got a chance anymore,
> We ain't got a chance anymore.

Woody sang the long ballad to its very end, when Tom Joad says:

> Wherever little children are hungry and cry,
> Wherever people ain't free,
> Wherever men are fightin' for their rights,
> That's where I'm gonna be, Ma,
> That's where I'm gonna be.

When Woody finished, there wasn't a sound. The gunners just sat there as he put his guitar away; then they quietly thanked him and offered to help wash the dishes.

"Hell, no, I don't need anybody to clean up my mess! Out!" He shooed Cisco and me out of his pantry.

"When he's finished," Cisco said to me, "give him a hand with the slop pail. We'll take turns helping him." The slop pail was a big garbage can. Woody and I carried it out to the deck and flung its contents over the rail. The wind promptly flung the garbage back in our faces. Right there and then we learned the meaning of two more nautical terms — windward and leeward.

Despite our little misunderstanding with the wind, Cisco congratulated us on our first day's work.

"What about my floral display? You didn't think I was being a fink?"

"Not at all. I would do the same thing in the crew's mess, but if I did, the guys would think I was a queer."

∎

Ordinarily we'd have had time off, nine to eleven thirty, but on our first morning we had to report to our assigned gun stations. There were three gun turrets on the stern — one for the big five-inch cannon and two twenty-millimeter machine-gun turrets on each side — at the bow there was a three-inch cannon with two machine-gun turrets, and there were four more machine-gun turrets on the boat deck.

Cisco explained that the machine guns were obviously of little use against submarines; they were supposed to defend us from dive-bombers. Dive-bombers, he explained, would attack us when we were near enemy land bases. However, he said, our machine guns weren't very effective against planes, because they weren't proper antiaircraft guns; furthermore, he assured us, the Nazi dive-bombers would swoop down on us with terrific speed, usually with the sun behind them to prevent us from seeing them. But, he went on, our guns *did* fire very pretty red tracer bullets. The only trouble with the tracer bullets, he said, was that they showed you how badly you missed your target. He did say that the machine guns might come in handy if pirates tried to board our ship. He was less encouraging about the cannons. Cannons might be effective as antisubmarine weapons, Cisco said, if a submarine surfaced, turned belly-up, and said, "Fire."

Despite the guns' limited efficacy, twenty-four U.S. Navy gunners with their lieutenant commander and an ensign were being paid to man those guns, and we civilian merchant seamen had to help. Because of Cisco's eye problem, we maneuvered so that he and I were put on the five-inch cannon as loaders. I would pick up a heavy shell, slam it into Cisco's arms, and he would pass it to a gunner, who would shove it into the cannon. There was no actual firing practice that morning, but that didn't stop Woody; he was made a machine gunner's assistant in the turret next to us. In no time he talked the gunner off the firing seat, happy as a kid with a new bicycle. He aimed his machine gun all over the sky, making bullet sounds with his mouth.

"Need a lot more practice," he said to the navy kid. "I missed at least three of them Nazi dive-bombers."

In the hour left before lunch, Cisco showed us around the ship. From

the bridge we saw the huge convoy beginning to change direction —
ninety degrees to starboard — wheeling around with the precision of a
military parade. The mate let us watch while he studied something
through his binoculars and issued orders to the helmsman. Another man
on the bridge, the radio man, was working the blinker semaphore, re-
ceiving and sending messages to the commodore's ship leading the convoy. There would be radio silence for the entire trip.

"Sir?" I addressed the mate. (I used the "sir" not because I was required
to — only with the captain and the chief engineer was it mandatory —
but because it might help me get an answer.) "Sir, do we know our general destination?"

"Southeast."

"The Mediterranean?"

"Probably."

"How long will it take to cross the ocean?" I asked Cisco.

"As long as the slowest ship in the convoy — about ten knots — fourteen, fifteen days to Gibraltar."

"Jesus — but once we get to Gibraltar, the worst is over — right?"

"Wrong. The Mediterranean is much smaller than the Atlantic, but
like a lot of small guys, it can be a helluva lot tougher than the big ones.
But don't worry about it. Come on, I'll show you the engine room." He
led the way for Woody and me.

A blast of noise shook us as we opened the door leading to the engine
room. We were on a landing, looking three stories down on a confusion
of boilers, tubes, and machinery; giant pistons pounding, turning the
block-long drive shaft that powered the great propeller that drove us
across the Atlantic.

Cisco motioned us to follow him down into the roaring maze. The
smell of fuel oil was so strong I could taste it. I held tightly to the ladder's rail and started my descent, happier and happier with each step —
happy that I had chosen the steward department.

An engineer officer, a fireman, an oiler, and a wiper were on duty. I
couldn't understand the answers they shouted to our questions, not only
because of the noise, but because I kept thinking that we were deep below the waterline, separated from the sea by steel plate only two inches
thick. I looked up at the landing, two stories above us — what would it
be like if a torpedo hit the engine room? I pictured us trying to find our
way out as the sea poured in on us. "Let's go!" I shouted. "My ears hurt."

Lunch was a simpler meal to serve, although the menu was much richer. There were cold cuts for hors d'oeuvres, a good soup, two kinds of meat, well-prepared vegetables, and good pie. The officers' conversations were livelier, the captain ate without frowning, my service was smoother, and there was no mistaking windward for leeward.

In fact there was little wind, the weather being summer-perfect and the sea getting bluer as the convoy steamed toward the south. Most of the crew sunbathed on the canvas hatch covers aft and listened to Frank Sinatra on the gun crew's portable phonograph. "I'll Never Smile Again" never sounded more bittersweet. The destroyers moved slowly across the blue horizon; the seagulls, their wings motionless, hitchhiked on the ship's airwake; Cisco lay on his back with his eyes closed; and Woody sat cross-legged, now and then scribbling something in his pocket notebook.

I sat near Woody as I read his book, fascinated by the story of his life, the struggles of his family, his mother's tragedy, Oklahoma poverty, the Great Depression, the fruit-picking camps, riding the rails — I kept looking from the book to Woody. The printed word gave him another dimension. There was my Woody, sitting there cross-legged on the hatch cover, and there was the Woody Guthrie of the printed page — another person, ten miles high. Woody's words lit up images of a suffering America I'd never seen, but his words were filled with hope for "a better world a'comin'" and charged with the certainty that the freight train he rode was "bound for glory." I wondered if Woody would someday write of our ship that it too was bound for glory.

Dinner went well too, and as soon as it was over, we crowded into the crew's messroom for our first union meeting. The bosun called for order. The main thing on the agenda was the election of the ship's chairman. The ship's chairman would be our representative regarding working conditions, and he would also be our delegate to our union's national convention.

The union's national officers were divided into two groups, left and right. Both sides, about equal in strength, were already maneuvering for a decisive battle to be fought at the next national convention. The same division was evident in the packed messroom.

Pete Harmon and Manny Gordon were good friends of Cisco. Manny was tall, dark, and as aristocratic-looking as a Hebrew prince. Pete was of medium height, blond, and as aristocratic-looking as a Boston Brahmin. Both were two of the toughest union men on the waterfront.

"I nominate Brother Cisco Houston!" Manny stood up. "I've shipped with him before. He's got guts, he's smart, and —"

"He's a Red!" somebody called out from the rear of the room.

"Fuck you, Newington!" Manny shouted at the interrupter.

"Order! Order!" The bosun banged the table with the handle of his Bowie knife. "Brother Newington, if you want the floor while another brother's talking, you ask the chair for a point of order. And you, Brother Gordon, you got any requests to make about any illegal interruptions, you make the request to the chair — you understand?"

"Brother Chairman!" Manny held up his hand. "I have a request to make about Brother Newington's illegal interruption."

"What is your request, Brother Gordon?"

"I request that you tell Brother Newington to go fuck himself."

"Point of order! Point of order!" Newington was on his feet.

"What's your point of order, Brother Newington?"

"My point of order is that I request you tell Brother Gordon that he can do the same in spades!"

"Both requests denied!" The bosun banged the table. "Any seconds to Brother Houston's nomination?"

"I second the motion!" Pete Harmon called out. "I shipped with Cisco too. He's a good man and he's fair, and Brother Newington is a red-baiting fascist!"

The right-wingers nominated Newington, "to knock out the Reds!"

"Point of order!" Woody got the floor. "Just want to clear up this business of color. I've worked side by side with Cisco, organizing the Dust Bowl refugees against the fruit growers and their deputy sheriffs. He taught me what it is to be a good union man. That we're not members of the Communist party is beside the point — I'm not a communist, but I've been in the red all my life. It don't matter what color a man's politics is as long as we're fighting for the same thing — like the Red Army and us fighting together to beat Hitler. If a man's a good union man, it don't matter one damn if he's left wing, right wing, or chicken wing." Woody sat down. The right-wingers booed.

The bosun banged for silence. "Brother Woody's right. The union is the thing. Before the union, we had to live in small cabins with twelve men piled three high, on bare mattresses. Once I had a top bunk under a dripping steam pipe, and I had to learn to curl up like a pretzel so the scalding water wouldn't drip on me while I slept. Now let's vote for the best union man."

Cisco won by twenty to twelve. We celebrated and healed some of the wounded feelings by holding a hootenanny. It was a good one, but it didn't last long because we were tired — our first day at sea had been a long one.

I lay in my bunk, unable to sleep. I read Woody's book, but although it was fascinating, the underwater image of the ship's keel and the Nazi-marked torpedo kept intruding — and the gnawing sound continued until near morning, when I finally fell asleep.

That morning, after breakfast, the chief steward told Woody to switch jobs with the gun-crew messman — the messman had twisted his ankle badly and couldn't do the running around required for the job. Woody was delighted with what he considered to be a promotion and couldn't wait to prove that he should have been given the job in the first place.

Woody listened impatiently to Cisco's detailed instructions about the job. "Hell, I know how to be a waiter!"

"There's more to it than that. You've got to set up properly and bring up all the supplies in time for —"

"Godawmighty, don't you think I know that?"

We each went to our messrooms. Cisco and I finished setting up with a couple of minutes to spare, and together we went to the gun-crew mess to see how Woody was doing. Not a table was set up — two minutes before chow time, and not a plate nor a fork was in sight. Woody was standing before the menu blackboard, chalk in hand, putting the finishing touches on the most ornately decorated menu imaginable. The dishes, written in a beautiful flowing script, were framed by birds, flowers, mermaids, and black and white children playing together. The dishes themselves were given new names. Beef stew became "Aunt Jenny's Prize-winning Saturday-night Special, made of choice chunks of prime Texas beef braised in golden butter, cooked with fourteen carat carrots, plump tomatoes, California celery, and sweet Spanish onions, seasoned and stirred every ten minutes by a beautiful virgin if available or by the youngest gunner on the crew." The meatloaf was renamed and described just as poetically. Before Cisco could open his mouth to yell at Woody, the chow bell rang, and the first rush of diners took their seats.

Woody, still decorating the menu, called over his shoulder, "I'm your new messman. I'll be right with you." The gunners watched dumbfounded as Woody put a last delicate touch on a lovely mermaid's breast. There wasn't a sound of complaint about the unreadiness of the messroom.

Woody stepped back to examine his handiwork, head cocked to one side, and then turned to the men and said, "All right, men, what'll it be?"

The gunners stared at the menu until one of them said, "I think I'll try Aunt Jenny's Special."

"Me too!" called another gunner.

"Three Aunt Jenny's Specials here!" came from another table.

"Lickety split!" Woody scooted out of the messroom, leaving his bewildered customers to ooh and aah over his artwork while they set up their own tables.

Speechless, Cisco and I followed Woody to the galley, where we heard him call to the cook, in a voice not loud enough for the gunners to hear, "Five beef stews."

At dinner Woody covered the blackboard with new decorations, which again transformed the prosaic menu into irresistible gastronomic poetry. The gunners set the tables.

After dinner Cisco threw a blanket over a crew's mess table. "Five card stud poker game is open." He riffled a fresh deck of cards. Woody and I rushed to grab two of the seven places. The other players were Manny, Pete Harmon, Bosun, and Newington.

Since most of us had no cash, the betting had to be on credit — traditionally the bets are settled at the end of the trip, on payoff day. Everybody, including Newington, agreed that Cisco should be trusted to keep the record.

"Look, you two," Cisco said to Woody and me, "why don't you play chess or something? These guys are rough players, and we play fifty cents and a dollar — a man could lose all his wages in no —"

"Lookee here, Mother Houston, will you stop worrying about me for a while?" Woody said.

"Just deal 'em." I drew a long pull on my cigarette.

Cisco snapped a card at each of us, and thus began our first lesson in sea-going poker. Thirty minutes later the lesson was over. Woody and I had been at sea two days, and we'd already lost two weeks' wages.

"How's about a game of chess?" Woody moved over to the empty table.

"Can't." I sat down next to him, still stunned from the poker lesson. "There's no chess set on board."

"Plenty of mops, though." Woody unscrewed a mop stick from its mop. "And we can use the checker board."

I watched him as he began to whittle the mop stick. By the time the poker game broke up at one in the morning, Woody had carved out a creditable-looking chess set. But we were both too tired to play.

The next morning, our third day at sea, we saw golden weeds and green grasses in the blue-green sea; the bright sun shimmered on the water like a million golden fish. "That's the Gulf Stream," Cisco said. The vegetation and the blue-green color clearly demarcated the Gulf Stream from the rest of the colder and less colorful waters surrounding it. "What a plumbing job," Cisco said as he shook his head. "A steady flow of hot water, a hundred and fifty miles wide, streaming right across the cold Atlantic, heating up London, making it warmer than New York in the winter, although London is a thousand miles further north."

"Well I'll be damned!" Woody looked up at Cisco, dumbfounded.

"I don't blame you for looking so astounded," I said to Woody. "It sure is some plumbing job."

"Oh, I know about the Gulf Stream." Woody kept looking at Cisco in amazement. "But that was the longest speech I ever heard him make."

We worked well that day, and after dinner we went to the ship's fantail to watch the Gulf Stream. The convoy was now steaming straight east, all out for the long haul across the Atlantic. The seagulls that had accompanied us since we left port were now gone, but the flying fish took their place. They shot out of the water in a long, low, silver-streaked trajectory, smashing into the sea, a hundred, two hundred, even three hundred feet ahead. They looked two feet long, with a two-foot wingspread. We watched them until the dolphins came, a whole troop of them, splashing, whirling, and waving to us, practically shouting, "You ain't seen nuthin' yet!" They leaped, rolled over, and nudged each other and the ship as well, acknowledging the crew's applause with what certainly looked like big grins.

The bosun said it wasn't true that the dolphins were accompanying us for our garbage — there was plenty of food for them in the sea. They were accompanying us just for the pleasure of our company and would probably stay with us all the way across the ocean. He swore that he once saw a dolphin push an exhausted seaman to a lifeboat.

After the dolphins, the next attraction was the sunset. The latitude I've lived in all my life never showed me a sunset so stunningly beautiful — it was enough to make an atheist doubt his faith.

The next attraction was the sky itself — it was enormous. I'd never before seen it from horizon to horizon. You could actually see and understand that the earth is a globe. As it turned away from the sun, the stars began to take their places. They were so dazzling that they lit up the blacked-out convoy — even the destroyers on the horizon were silhouetted against the stars that reached clear down to the sea behind them, and the Milky Way curved over us like a triumphal arch.

Most of the crew joined us to watch the sky and listen to Woody sing the song he'd been writing since we left home. He called it "Talking Merchant Marine." He sang it as a talking blues:

> In bed with my woman just a'singin' the blues,
> When I heard the radio tellin' the news,
> Said the big Red Army took a hundred towns,
> And the Allies dropped them two-ton bombs;
> I started hollerin', yellin' — dancin' up and down like a bull
> frog.
>
> Doorbell rang, in come a man,
> I signed my name, I got a telegram,
> Says, "If you want to take a vacation trip,
> Get a dish-washin' job on a Liberty ship,"
> Woman cryin', me a-flyin',
> Out of the door and down the line.
>
> 'Bout two minutes, I run ten blocks,
> I come to the ship there on the docks,
> I walked up the plank and signed my name,
> They blowed the whistle and I was gone again,
> Right on out into the stream,
> Ships as far as the eye could see,
> My old lady just a-waitin'.
>
> Ships loaded down with TNT,
> All stretched out across the rollin' sea,
> I stood on the deck and watched those fishes swim,
> Prayed them fishes wasn't made of tin:
> Sharks and porpoises, jelly beans, rainbow trouts, mud-cats,
> jugars,
> All over the water.
>
> This convoy is the biggest I ever seen,
> It stretches out across the sea,

An' the ships blow their whistles and ring their bells,
Gonna blow them fascists clean to Hell:
Win some freedom, liberty,
Stuff like that.

Well, I walked to the tail, I stood on the stern,
And I looked at the big brass screw-blade turn,
Listened to the sound of the engines pound,
Sixteen feet every time it goes around,
Look out, you Fascists!

I'm just one of the merchant crew,
Belong to a union called N.M.U.
I'm a union man from head to toe,
I'm U.S.A. and C.I.O.
Fightin' out here on the water,
Gonna win us some freedom,
On good dry land.

"Hot damn, Woody, that's pretty good!" one of the gun-crew kids sang out. "Did you really write that?"

"Yup."

"Did you write any others?"

"Yup."

"How many?"

"Oh, not countin' the ones I lost or threw away, 'bout a thousand."

"A thousand? Godawmighty, Woody how can you even get the ideas for a thousand songs?"

"Easy. There are two kinds of songs — living songs and dying songs. The dying songs — the ones about champagne for two and putting on your top hat — they tell you that there's nothing to be proud of in being a worker, but that someday if you're good and work hard, you'll get to be boss. Then you can wear white tie and tails and have songs made up about you. I like living songs that make you take pride in yourself and your work, songs that try to make things better for us, songs that protest all the things that need protesting against, and God knows there's thousands of them, and if you think of them you'll think of a title, which is half the battle in writing a song. There's the 'Single Girl Blues,' the 'Starving Family Blues,' 'Leaky Roof Blues,' 'Hock Shop Rag,' 'Pawn Shop Rag,' 'Pawn Shop Polka,' 'Down Payment Scream,' 'High Price

Gallop,' 'The Dying Landlord,' 'The Dead Landlord' . . ." and Woody went on calling off song titles — the men laughing at every one of them — winding up with "Gone Woman Blues, Gone Man Blues," "Scabs in My Factory, Scabs in My Hair, Scabs in My Bed," "Shoo, Scab, Shoo," "Union Mattress, Union Baby," and "My World Union."

"Godamighty, Woody you must have made a million dollars!"

"No, but he could have," Cisco said.

"Maybe," Woody continued. "I once had my own radio program, but the sponsor — a big tobacco company — wanted me to sing dying songs, so I quit."

"Tell them about your resignation letter." Cisco nudged Woody.

"Oh, I just wrote 'Dear sirs, I've smoked your tobacco, I've chewed your tobacco, and I've even snuffed your tobacco, but I'll be goddamned if I'll have your tobacco shoved up my ass.'"

That night I read more about Woody's life. His pages almost made me forget the image of the keel and the torpedo.

7

Abandon-ship drill was held next morning. My gray life jacket, tightly tied around my middle and holding my head like a neck brace, had a moldy smell. The jackets made us look grotesque. A navy kid giggled nervously when the deckhands uncovered our lifeboat. He giggled again when the boat was swung out over the sea.

The ship had four lifeboats and four rafts, each capable of holding twenty men. There was room enough for one hundred and sixty men, though our crew was only sixty, but the older hands said that if we were hit, we'd be lucky if we could launch two out of the eight lifecraft, because of panic, listing, or lack of time.

"If we get hit, try for the rafts." Cisco read my mind. "All you have to do is knock out the pin, watch the raft slide into the sea, and jump after it."

Later that afternoon, DRRRINNNGGG! — the ear-shattering, mind-paralyzing general-quarters bell summoned us for live firing practice. It was impossible to understand how a bell only twelve inches in diameter could make such a terrifying noise. All the twenty-millimeter guns firing together were not enough to drown out the alarm bell I could still feel ringing in my ears.

Lunch and dinner went smoothly. After dinner there was a not so smooth political discussion. Woody said that true freedom consisted in the right of every person to have a decent job, as well as the freedom to say his piece, and that socialism might be the way to guarantee that.

"They're *all* motherfakkers! Marx, Engels, Lenin, Stalin!" Davey Bananas yelled to Woody across the crowded messroom. "They're all motherfakkers." Bananas's New York Jewish working-class intonation, plus his broken nose, made him sound like Slapsie Maxie Rosenbloom, the prizefighter, whose speech was filled with adenoidal "aahs." His face got redder as he laced into Woody. "Aaah, as Brutus said, aah, power corrupts and turns all idealists into motherfakkers! Stalin's knocked off millions of his opponents, and some day, aah, his own people are going to shout it to you naive fucking idiots!" Bananas banged the table. "Socialism means law. Aah, law means politicians, and *all* politicians are motherfakkers!"

He got a lot of applause.

"You're just a goddamned anarchist!" I jumped into the argument. "It's possible to have socialism with democracy."

"Aah, you can shove your idealism up your ass!" Bananas interrupted. "Read Engels, aah, *State, Society and the Family*, read Lenin's *Imperialism*, aah, read Marx's *Das Kapital!* They're *all* motherfakkers! *All* a bunch of —"

DRRRINNNGGG! The terrifying general-quarters alarm bell interrupted Bananas like a bomb exploding in our mist.

"Submarines!" somebody shouted.

"Take it easy!" Cisco yelled as we all tried to get through the door at the same time.

I raced down the alleyway, thinking, "What a shmucky way to die — almost knocked out by an anarchist — saved only by the bell." But what the hell was I saying, saved by the bell? That fucking bell blasting in my ears was the bell of death.

A bright-red rocket exploded somewhere up ahead in the convoy, just as I got to my gun station. "A ship's hit!!" a gunner shouted.

"The rocket's her SOS." Cisco anticipated my question.

It was still light enough to see the destroyer escorts catapulting their depth charges as they raced up and down our side of the convoy. Whoom! Whoom! Whoom! The explosions threw up columns of water and reverberated against the side of our ship with heavy thuds. I clutched the rail. "My heart stood still"; "My heart was in my mouth" — now I knew the truth of those expressions. All my senses stretched to the extreme. If we were to be hit, I wanted to hear the explosion before I died. To not hear it, to die without knowing it, like being clubbed on the back of the head, would be a disgusting insult. Whoom! Whoom! Whoom! Each depth charge made the air around me more electric. I looked at my shipmates. Nobody moved; they seemed as electrified as I was. The entire convoy seemed electrified. The hundred ships were like one living thing tensed to the breaking point. Suddenly the ship behind us, in coffin corner, began firing all of her machine guns at the sea. Without waiting for the ensign's order, our machine guns opened fire too, and in an instant half the ships in the convoy were blazing away wildly at any dark spot in the sea. Red tracer bullets flew in all directions. After a few seconds the shooting stopped, and we began laughing at our hysterical idiocy. It was a miracle that we hadn't killed each other.

We tried to spot the torpedoed ship, but it was too dark. Anyway, nobody could stop to pick up her survivors. They would have to wait until the destroyers were done with the U-boats; only then could the destroyers go back for them.

The general-quarters ended at midnight. "We gonna hear from the sonabitches again." Roberto the cook spat into the sea. "This convoy is the biggest one I ever see. We gonna hear from the sonabitches all right."

Most of us went to the messroom for coffee and to hear the radio. Although static usually prevented us from understanding what the British news reader was saying, the tone of his dignified voice was enough to make us feel better about our chances of surviving the Nazis, and when Vera Lynn sang "There'll be bluebirds over the white cliffs of Dover," it was the guarantee that we couldn't lose. That voice with the teardrop was a beacon to us, a beacon leading us straight to victory. A fireman put it a little differently: "As long as Vera Lynn keeps singing, Hitler might as well shove his armies up his ass."

And when she sang, "We'll meet again, don't know where, don't know when," there was a long silence. Nobody mentioned the stricken ship, and there was no speculation about the fate of her crew.

The three of us turned in, but it was difficult to fall asleep — the air was still charged. Many of the men stayed in the messroom, and their voices carried; the card players sounded angry, some of the men were arguing over trivial things, and even the monkey's chatter seemed shriller.

Our door flew open. "They're *all* motherfakkers!" Davey Bananas shouted into our dark cabin and then slammed the door.

"Crazy, anarchist bastard." Cisco turned on his bunklight and lit a cigarette. "And the next time that fucking alarm rings, you guys *walk*, don't run to your stations. Alleyway collisions kill more guys than U-boats." He put out the light.

After a couple of minutes of silence, Woody said, "No, I wasn't scared," as though somebody had asked him the question; then he went on talking in the dark about the only thing he was afraid of — fire. He spoke quietly, steadily, unashamedly. Perhaps the fact that we couldn't see his face made it easier for him to talk.

He started by telling us of his earliest recollection: his beautiful mother, Nora, singing strange, sad songs to him, old ballads handed down from her Appalachian ancestors. Even as a child he was aware of her sadness, and he always tried to make her laugh. As he got older he became more aware of the tension between her and his father, Charlie. Charlie Guthrie was a two-fisted real-estate trader who cheated and frightened Indians out of their land. Nora hated his work, couldn't bear to see his guns, and lived in a constant state of anxiety. Charlie, though, had a soft side — he loved his wife and tried to help her, but her illness really had little to do with him. She became more and more depressed until she became afflicted with "spells" that made her say wild things and do wild things, like throwing over furniture or flinging away whatever she had in her hands. During one of those spells, an overturned oil lamp burned down the new house they just moved into. Shortly after that Woody's twelve-year-old sister was horribly burned when her dress caught fire. Nora and Charlie wept by her bedside as she lay dying, but Woody didn't cry, because his sister begged him not to.

Neither Cisco nor I broke the silence Woody had fallen into at this point. When he resumed the story, he told us that his mother became progressively worse. She began to stagger and move jerkily, like a drunk. One night Woody's father suffered terrible burns. He told everybody it was an accident, but the next day he committed Nora to an insane asylum where, eventually, she died.

Woody paused to pull out a cigarette. "But I'm sure that she was not insane. I'm sure she had a physical illness of some kind. The talk in our family is that she inherited it." He struck a match. "And the fact is that I'm beginning to suspect that I have it too." I couldn't see Woody's face, but I could see that the light of the match trembled slightly. "The doctors don't know much about it — maybe only Jesus can help me." Woody fell silent.

After I recovered from my surprise, I said, "Woody, I didn't know you were religious." Cisco said nothing.

Quietly, Woody said, "Hell yes, I'm a religious man, but I don't have a favorite. I sorta like 'em all."

"You mentioned Jesus."

"Yes — the ones I admire most in the world are Jesus and Will Rogers." He blew out the light.

After a while I said, "I finished your book — it's great."

"Thanks." Woody continued smoking in silence.

Long after he and Cisco were asleep, I lay awake thinking about Woody's strange contradictions. From the first day I met him, he gave the impression of being a closed man. Despite his camaraderie, kindness, and humor, he would never allow his feelings to show. For one thing, he never laughed. He made everybody else laugh, but he never laughed; he would smile or give a quick sardonic grin to express defiance, but I had not yet seen him laugh. If somebody said or did something funny, Woody would say — with a deadpan face — "That was very funny." Nor did he ever use foul language, as we all did, or show anger or fear. His emotions seemed to be tightly locked within him — except for his writing. His writing held back nothing; it was filled with innermost feelings, passion, and uninhibited self-analysis of the deepest kind. Therefore, I wasn't surprised at the openness with which he had just revealed what he did. What was strange was the cold, flat way he had told us of his family's tragedy and of his fear of finishing like his mother — never for a moment allowing his emotion to show. I wondered whether this mask had been imposed on him by his dying sister when she begged him to stifle his tears.

I tried to fall asleep by listening to the ship's engine, but the image of the keel and the torpedo kept intruding, and then the gnawing started. I turned on my light, climbed down from my bunk, and began to trace the sound. It was near Cisco's bunk. It was in Cisco's bunk. It was Cisco — he was grinding his teeth. Cool, brave Cisco, what kind of dream could cause him to clamp his teeth with such pressure as to make such a hideous sound?

■

Breakfast went badly that next morning. The tension was still in the air, and the egg-eaters were more finicky than ever. Halfway through the meal, DRRRINNNGGG! the general-quarters alarm sounded. I grabbed my life jacket and tried not to run to my gun station — I trotted.

My stationmates were already at their gun positions. They were pointing at the empty space behind us. We were in dead coffin corner! The ship that had been there yesterday was gone. One of the men on the bridge said that she had developed engine trouble and was forced to drop out of the convoy during the night. The destroyers on our flank and rear dropped their depth charges in an ever-widening ring until they drove the U-boats beyond the horizon. As my eyes swept the sea for signs of the enemy, I realized what a hateful thing the horizon could be.

The horizon was a circular prison only twenty-two miles wide. No matter how fast we traveled, we were always in its bull's-eye center — a sitting-duck target for the U-boats waiting just beyond its circumference. At the end of a day's steaming, there you were, in the dead center of that ever-present twenty-two-mile-wide circular lake, and the next morning you were still there. You had to take the captain's word that we'd made any progress, and though it would take two weeks to cross the ocean, the boredom of seeing the same circle of sky and the same circle of water could stretch the two weeks into an eternity — if you let it. But I devised a method for calculating time that made the days fly.

To begin with, I figured that since the earth is round, you could, with a little effort, imagine that we were steaming downhill, which right away is easier and a lot faster. Second point in my method: the average trip from New York to wherever and back took three months — a monstrously long time to be a sitting target — but I broke up the three months into magic segments. The first segment was getting to Gibraltar. Once there, we would probably have to wait no more than a week for a new convoy escort to take us to our destination, which would probably be no more than a week's sail away. As soon as we arrived at our destination, we would already be on our way back. So getting to Gibraltar was the only long haul, and since getting there took only two weeks, we would be practically within sight of the rock after only one week. And since we'd already been at sea for four days, the first week was almost over, and if you really thought about it, we were already on our way back home.

The general-quarters order remained in force throughout that morning, but we were allowed to return to our duties, with our life jackets on.

Lunch was awkward. The men ate little and hurried back to the open deck. It seemed safer to be out in the open.

"I'm going to take a shower." Cisco said.

"Are you nuts? What if we get hit?" I tightened my life jacket.

"It'll make the gun-crew kids feel safer, and anyway, with what we're carrying, what difference does it make? Furthermore, if we do get hit, it'll be the last time I'll be caught with my pants down." Cisco's example had a quieting effect, but not for long.

"How many times you been torpedoed, Bosun?" a gunner asked.

"Twice."

"Where?"

"On the Murmansk run, last winter. Then, on the *Walter Gresham* three months ago, not far from here. But don't worry; we'll be all right." He started to walk away.

"Come on, Bose, we can take it," one of the black-gang guys said. "How many ships did your convoy lose on the Atlantic run?"

Bosun hesitated. "About fifteen out of forty-five." After a dead silence, Bosun said, "One of the ships was carrying ten thousand tons of powdered milk. She went down in a mountain of white foam."

"How many men did your ship lose."

"Twenty-seven." Bosun walked away.

"Is it really going to take us ten more days to cross the ocean?" I asked Bosun.

"That's it." He looked around at the convoy. "You just can't go faster than the slowest ship."

"Why the fuck did that ship have to drop out?" The black-gang guy stared at the emptiness behind us.

"Is better we in this position." Roberto the cook grinned. "If we get hit, we don't blow up the whole goddamned convoy."

"Anyway," Pete Harmon added as he turned to look at the destroyers, "somebody's got to be in coffin corner."

"I realize that!" the black-gang man snapped back. "I just wish this fucking convoy would move a little faster!"

Nobody said anything. After a while Woody left. In a few minutes he came back carrying two empty wooden crates. He sat down and began to break the crates into different pieces of assorted sizes. At first nobody paid much attention to him, then more and more then men turned away from the destroyers to watch Woody.

"What are you making?" Chips, the ship's carpenter, asked as Woody whittled away at a piece of wood.

"A wind machine," he said without looking up.

"A wind machine? What's that?"

"Somethin' to make this convoy go a little bit faster." He looked up at the carpenter for a moment and then resumed his whittling.

Everybody heard what Woody said. There was a moment of silence, followed by an explosion of hysterical laughter. Some of the men fell to the hatch covers and rolled over, legs pumping the air; some doubled up and groaned with laugh pains; others just sobbed, pressing handkerchiefs to their eyes and stamping their feet. Nobody was able to speak. They tried to repeat Woody's words, "Somethin' to make this convoy go a little bit faster," but all they could do was point to the destroyers, then point down at the hatches and the cargo we were carrying, and then point at the empty space behind us. One of the men staggered across the deck, knees bent, choking with laughter, imitating a slow ship. He pulled on an imaginary ship's whistle and cried, "Woo-woo!" as he pointed to Woody and the empty wooden boxes beside him.

Woody looked at the laughing men calmly, forgivingly, with a they-know-not-what-they-laugh-at look that threw the men into new paroxysms of rolling, doubling up, side holding, and sobbing, while Woody steadily whittled away.

"What happened?" Cisco, back from his shower, surveyed the bizarre scene.

"Woody's making a wind machine!" I managed to get out.

"Oh, that." Cisco went to sit next to Woody.

"You know about it?" Chips tried to catch his breath.

"Oh, sure," Cisco said.

Cisco's remark helped the men to control their spasms. They wanted to hear what Cisco had to say.

"The machine — the machine," Chips gasped as he tried to control himself, "the machine is going to make the ship go faster?"

"Yup." Cisco turned to watch Woody's whittling.

When the new gale of laughter died down, Chips said, "How?"

"Explain your theory to the good brothers." Cisco nudged Woody.

The silence was instantaneous as Woody stopped whittling and looked up at the men around him. "Well, the thing involves certain advanced principles of aerodynamics which, put simply, goes something like this: the machine is only about two feet long and one foot wide, and its propeller is only about a foot long, but small as it is, it generates a flow of thermo-propulsion airwaves which pass over the ship's topography, creating an aerovacuum force behind the stern, which squeezes the ship forward, thus increasing its velocity in an infinitesimal but measurable way, and since we are in the rear, or the asshole of the convoy, the wind caused by the machine will propel the entire convoy, however imperceptibly, just a little bit faster, and since torpedoes are delicately balanced so that the slightest variation causes them to miss their targets, the slight variation this machine will cause may be just enough to save you nonbelievers."

There was some chuckling, but no laughter.

"Have you ever built one before, Woody?" a gun-crew kid asked.

Cisco nudged Woody. "Tell them about the cyclone."

"Well there was this cyclone warning in East Texas." Woody went on whittling as everybody hung on his every word. "Wind about to bear down on us at more'n a hundred miles an hour, so I built a wind machine with the help of my wife and my two little kiddies and waited for the big wind on the porch of our rickety old house, which would have blown away with one weak puff from a sickly wolf, when sure enough, here come that big wind blowing a mile-high wall of Oklahoma dust straight at us, at more'n a hundred miles an hour. So I turned my little machine to face that mean old cyclone, and as sure as I'm sittin' here, that big wind got no further than the town limits when it turned plumb around and pushed clear out towards the Pacific Ocean, and the last we heard of it was three weeks later, when it flattened a town called Yokahama, in Japan."

After a moment's silence, one of the men said, with a straight face, "Godawmighty, Woody, aintcha afraid somebody'll steal your idea?"

"Cain't." Woody kept on whittling. "There's a patent pending on it, number three seven four six eight eight two nine six on the Woody Guthrie Anticyclone and Ship Speeder-Upper Aerodynamic Wind Machine."

"Hell, we got nothin' to lose in tryin' it," the gun-crew kid with the monkey said as a particularly loud depth charge reverberated against our ship's side. "The damned thing just might work." He clutched his monkey to him.

Everybody looked at the kid.

"Of course it will." Chips put his arm around the young gunner's shoulders. "Woody, is there anything I can do to help?"

Woody looked up at Chips. "Sure — cut these boxes into eighteen-inch planks."

"What about me?" asked the young gunner.

"And me?" asked another.

"Get me as many rubber bands as you can find," Woody said, and in a few moments he had issued orders to twelve very willing volunteers.

Woody and his helpers worked all that afternoon. When a man had to go on watch, another man took his place. The master builder never had less than a dozen men around him, cutting, whittling, notching, and nailing, building a pile of finished wood, rubber bands, lengths of string, nails, and carved-out little wheels. Only Woody knew what form the wind machine would take. He diplomatically put off all questions, and the crew's curiosity grew in proportion to the growing pile of parts.

Production was suspended pending Woody's completion of his dinner chores, but two of the crew helped him with the chores so that not a second was wasted in building the mysterious machine. The pile of parts was placed on one of the cleared mess tables, and Woody proceeded to assemble them. His helpers handed him various parts or tools as he called for them.

First Woody constructed a solid base about two feet long. On that base he built a strong track along which a sturdy shaft would slide back and forth; attached to each side of the shaft were two powerful, smaller shafts that also pounded back and forth and turned a series of wheels. The foot-long propeller was attached last. We were all dying to ask questions, but there was no talk, just Woody calling for knife, wood, pliers, and rubber bands as we watched in fascinated silence.

"What a crock of mystic shit!" Davey Bananas broke the silence like a clap of thunder.

"Brother Bananas" — Pete Harmon always spoke with the tone of an Anglican minister — "why don't you mind your own fucking business?"

"It is my fucking business! I'm supposed to be shipping out with an N.M.U. crew, aah, not with a bunch of aborigines sucking around a witch doctor!" Bananas picked up one of the wooden parts and waved it under Pete's aristocratic nose.

"We're not aborigines." Pete spoke calmly. "Woody's not a witch doctor. You're a prick, and put that fucking part down if you know what's good for you."

"Mystics are motherfakkers, you goddamned idiots! Medicine men, priests, wind-machine makers — they're *all* motherfakkers!" He flung the wooden part onto the table, and before anybody could get at Bananas, DRRRINNNGGG! The general-quarters alarm bell blasted our ears.

Cisco Houston, Woody Guthrie, and Jim Longhi
singing at the National Maritime Union Hall, New York City, 1943.

Woody and Marjorie Guthrie, New York City, 1944.

Cisco Houston and Bina Tannenbaum, New York City, 1944.

Jim's favorite picture of Woody, 1943.

Cisco and Woody at Moe Asch's recording studio, New York City, 1944.

Left: Jim and his mother, Rose, when she slipped him her St. Michael's medal, the Bronx, N.Y., 1943. Right: Jim, Cisco, and Woody with Mike Sala's mother, whom they found — miraculously — in Sicily, September 1943.

Left: Jim and Cisco, trying to look like Arabs to avoid MPs during a port stop in Oran, Algeria, 1944. Right: Woody and black GIs.

Jim and Gabrielle Longhi, New York City, 1944.

8

There was another red rocket that night, in the rear coffin corner on the other side of the convoy. When the general-quarters order ended, Woody and his helpers returned to the assembly table and worked faster, so that by midnight Woody was able to affix the sturdy one-foot-long propeller to the rubber-band mechanism of the double shafts. When he finished, he covered the machine with a towel and pronounced it ready for installation. He said it would be done in the morning, after breakfast.

I woke up early the next morning, but Woody was already out, and when I went on deck for my usual look around, I saw some men gathered around him on the rear deck. He had, without anyone seeing him do it, fixed the wind machine to the starboard rail, about twenty feet from the stern. The towel still covered his mysterious creation. "It's not to be unveiled until after breakfast," Woody said and walked away.

The crew ate breakfast hurriedly, and some of the younger officers who had heard about the wind machine also ate a little faster. At ten o'clock precisely, fifteen men, three junior officers, and the naval ensign gathered around the messman inventor on the afterdeck.

"Okay, Woody?" Chips asked, ready to assist Woody in untying the towel.

"Let her rip!" Woody flipped away the towel, and there, in all its insane complicated glory, stood the Woody Guthrie Anticyclone and Ship Speeder-Upper Aerodynamic Wind Machine, its propeller whirling madly in the strong breeze, its powerful little shafts pushing and pulling away furiously, and its wooden wheels spinning stunningly as the audience cheered and slapped Woody's back.

"Hot damn!" the monkey gunner shouted as he held his hand over the stern. "I can feel the aerodynamic vacuum, and I'll be a monkey's uncle if this ship ain't movin' faster!"

"Of course it is," Woody said as the cheering continued.

"You crazy fuckin' fetish worshipers!" Bananas could not contain himself any longer. "It's nothin' but wood and rubber bands. It can no more make this ship go faster than if I farted off the stern. Use your logic, you fuckin' idiots. Religion is the opium of the people!"

"Religion," said Klotski the Polak, an able-bodied seaman, "is what my mother believes in. She says not everything can be explained by logic. Some things you gotta have faith in, and they'll happen — like I have faith that if you put one finger on that machine, you gonna find your fuckin' ass full of seawater!"

"You dumb motherfakkers! Your barbaric superstition is gonna put a fuckin' jinx on this ship!" Bananas stormed away, leaving us to contemplate Woody's machine, on which in bold letters was written "Patent pending, number three seven four six eight eight two nine six."

Bananas came back a while later with three converts to his idea that Woody's machine was a jinx. They stood about making obscene remarks about the moving shafts, the revolving propeller, the whole thing, but they dared not come closer than arm's length. At least fifteen of Woody's followers guarded the wind machine as though it were the Holy Grail, and it was made perfectly clear to Bananas and his scoffers that touching the machine would be the height of imprudence.

Manny Gordon looked steadily at Bananas. "Like Polak told you before, put a pinky on that machine and your asshole'll be full of seawater."

However strong Manny's threat might have been as a deterrent, we worked out a system of guarding the machine without really discussing it; it was just understood that at least one man should be near it at all times. Even at night the men on watch would find an excuse to visit the stern to make sure that the aerodynamic vacuum was still there.

One of the oilers asked Woody for permission to lubricate the machine's dozens of moving parts. Woody thought about it with a deep frown, lips tight, head down, and then he took out his pocket notebook and pencil, made a few calculations, and finally told the oiler to proceed, but with many admonitions against overlubrication. "No more than three drops on the torque-tension resistor, two drops on the piston-thrust dynamo injector, and none at all, absolutely none at all, on the negative compressor!"

The propeller whirled away furiously, throwing its steady flow of thermopropulsion air waves over the ship's topography, toward the stern, where it created the aerodynamic vacuum that would increase the speed of the ship and the entire convoy.

The believers sat on the hatch covers, just watching the machine without talking, ignoring the patrolling destroyers, just watching the machine with beatific smiles on their faces. The men on duty who couldn't sit and watch would smile as they went past the machine and then nod happily to the off-duty watchers on the hatch covers.

"Superstitious motherfakkers!" Bananas went around mumbling for the rest of the day. After dinner, instead of sitting down at the blanket-covered poker table, where he was a consistent winner, Bananas opened his wallet and brought out several twenty-dollar bills. He flung them onto the blanket. "All right — a hundred says you're all a bunch of superstitious motherfakkers. Let's see how many miles we logged yesterday and how many we're gonna log today with your mighty machine."

An immediate silence fell over the men. No church was ever quieter than that messroom. A distant depth charge rumbled against the ship's side. Klotski slowly pulled a ten-dollar bill from a little pouch that hung around his neck, next to a religious medallion. He kissed the bill, kissed the medallion, and carefully laid the money on the blanket. His act of devotion was quickly followed by the other believers, and in no time Bananas's hundred was covered.

Our singing for the men that night sounded like a revival meeting. The crew kept calling for songs like "Precious Lord, Take My Hand," "A Jewel on Earth," and "Keep Your Hand on That Plow." They kept us singing until after midnight.

Just as we turned out our bunk lights, two distant depth charges drummed against the side of our ship. Doom-doom. Some fucking lullaby! I lay on my back for a long time, eyes open, too scared to smoke. Faith. If only I had some. Then maybe I might get some sleep instead of staring at the same silent torpedo speeding toward the same dynamite-laden keel. Would it really all be over in a flash? The end? Finished forever? Could it really be like that — an instant of life and then nothing, for all eternity? Such a stupid ludicrous joke could destroy your mind. Blessed are they who believe — like Klotski and my mother. I looked down at Cisco and Woody. Their cigarettes glowed in the dark. I was glad that they weren't sleeping either. I lay back on my pillow without saying anything. Another depth charge rumbled, and the image of the speeding torpedo lit up sharper than ever. I was breathing much too fast. I touched my wrist to feel my pulse, but I couldn't find it and I was beginning to sweat. Then, just as my haunting torpedo was about to smash into our keel, I blurted out, "Faith is the substance of things unseen and the proof of their existence!" I looked down at my startled mates. "Dante said that, but I think Klotski said it better when he was talking about the wind machine, 'Some things you gotta have faith in, and they'll happen.'"

"It wasn't Dante, it was Saint Paul," Cisco said matter-of-factly. "But if Dante also said it, then he's full of shit too. And you needn't worry; those depth charges are far enough away."

"It's not the depth charges that's bothering me; it's Klotski." I waited for Woody to say something in support of the wind machine's chief devotee, but the wind machine's creator just went on smoking in the dark. "Klotski's faith," I continued, "may be a lot closer to the Ultimate Truth than our scientific logic can ever bring us. To get closer to —"

"If the subs get any closer, the general alarm'll go off. Then you can worry." Cisco put out his cigarette. "Now go to sleep and —"

The rumbling of another depth charge interrupted him, and before he could continue, I shot out, "What good is our scientific logic when it comes to the Ultimate Truth?" My head hung down over Cisco's bunk. "Scientific logic can't even answer a child's simplest questions, like where does space end, or when did time begin? It can't even —"

"Will you stop worrying and goddamn go to sleep?"

"Okay, okay, you needn't get so hot. I just wanted to make the point that man can only think and experience in three dimensions. Einstein discovered the fourth dimension, but he says he cannot *experience* it — he only knows that it exists — and he says that life has endless dimensions and that our three-dimensional logic can never answer —"

"For Christ's sake!" Cisco snapped on his bunk light. "I can understand your being scared shitless, but why can't you have ordinary diarrhea, instead of diarrhea of the mouth? It's keeping me from sleeping!"

"Never mind the vituperation; just answer one question, and I'll stop. What good is your logic if you can't even *conceive* of infinity?"

"It doesn't matter one fuck whether I can conceive of it; I just accept it! Now will you go to sleep?"

"You just accept it?" Another depth charge beat against us. "Then you're exactly like Klotski and Dante! You're just accepting it on *faith!*"

After a long pause Cisco turned out his light and grumbled, "Dante and Klotski are still full of shit."

"Then so are you," I said. I heard Woody give a short chuckle as he put out his cigarette. Despite the continuing depth charges, I soon fell asleep and dreamed about the wind machine.

There were no red rockets in the sky that night, and in the morning the log book showed that the ship had traveled thirteen miles more than the day before.

The crew beamed with joy; men punched each other's shoulders; those on duty, passing each other, would grin and say, "Ain't that somethin'?"; the messrooms rang with laughter; and the second mate broke the captain's rule against fraternizing with the crew just long enough to stick his head in Woody's messroom to announce that he too had bet on the wind machine and won five dollars from the captain himself. Bananas doubled his obscenities and his bet. The believers covered his bet and doubled the guard on the wind machine.

Woody said very little, and when the men, in awed voices, asked him many questions about his machine, he managed to deflect their questions by saying that he had already explained the general principles and that the machine's specific technology was too complicated to discuss unless the questioner had some advanced knowledge of aerodynamic thermo-vacuum propulsion.

After breakfast the gun-crew kids followed Woody onto the windy deck. There, under his strict supervision, he allowed the oiler to add a few more drops of lubricant to the machine's whirling propeller, to the pushing-pulling shafts, and to the spinning wheels — again, with the strictest admonition to "never ever put a single drop of oil on the negative compressor!"

Although the day was gray and chilly, most of the gun crew and some of the regular crew sat on a hatchcover watching the sturdy little machine holding its own against the steadily increasing wind. The wind presaged rough weather, but that was good — heavy seas would make it difficult for the submarines to hit us. On the other hand, as the wind increased, so would the Germans increase their attacks, hoping to sink as many of us as they could before we reached the protection of the rough seas ahead.

A young gunner pointed to the machine. "You notice, the more the wind blows, the faster the propeller turns — that's to help us make up for the speed we're losing on account of the head wind. Isn't that right, Woody?"

"Uh-huh." Woody gave Cisco and me an embarrassed look.

Most of the gun crew and some of the regular crew sat on the number-five hatch cover, one eye on the wind machine and one eye on the destroyer escorts racing up and down our flank. A column of water shot up in the wake of the destroyer nearest us, and a few seconds later the force of the depth charge hit us. Nobody spoke, except me; quietly I said to Cisco, "If we get hit, what makes you so sure that it'll be all over for us? Maybe in some mysterious way life does go on. We can't possibly know. The universe, life, it has endless dimensions, while our minds have only three, so how can —"

"Duck, Woody!" Cisco trumpeted. "The shit's starting to fly again! Longhi's got another attack of diarrhea!"

"Go ahead, make fun." My voice rose to the level of Cisco's. "But just remember that if religion is the lowest depth of ignorance, atheism is the height of presumption!"

"Stop squabbling, you two!" Woody rose and glanced anxiously at the men. "Tension upsets the wind machine — cuts down its efficiency. If you guys want to argue go to the —"

DRRRINNNGGG! The general-quarters alarm interrupted Woody and sent everybody flying to his station. "I told you," Woody panted as he caught up with me, "too much tension!"

The destroyers dropped their depth charges in an ever-narrowing circle. The U-boats were closer to us than ever before. I shoved a cannon ball into Cisco's gut. "Take this, you presumptuous bastard!" Cisco grinned, passed the heavy shell to the loader, and kept his silence during the rest of the attack.

After a while the depth charges began to recede. "Hey, Woody," a gunner called, "your machine is workin' just fine! Lookie how we're outrunnin' them Nazis!"

"You see?" Woody called to Cisco and me. "When you two cool down, the machine works better."

When the general quarters ended, each man from the afterdeck stations stopped to say something grateful to the cocky wind machine whirling and pounding away against the snapping wind.

"Hey Woody, looks like the wind is getting mad at your baby," a gunner called as a shower of spray hit the machine, causing its propeller to stop dead for just an instant before it furiously resumed whirling away.

The next night there was another general-quarters alarm. The wind was strong, and the sky was so black we could barely make out the ship in front of us, let alone the destroyers ringing the convoy. But we *could* hear the sturdy wind machine clanking and pounding as we watched for red rockets.

For the next two days a steadily increasing head wind tried to slow us down, but the tough little wind machine beat against its enemy with increasing speed. The convoy didn't lose a single ship, and Bananas lost all his money.

On the wind's third day the sea was bad enough for the submarines to quit. After dinner we celebrated in the crew's mess with the holleringest, drinkingest, smashingest hootenanny yet. Woody, flanked by Cisco and me, was surrounded by an adoring gun crew and most of the regular crew — even those on watch popped in, drenched and cold, not to warm up, but to join in singing praise to Woody and his machine. And this time the monkey didn't cover his ears — he jumped from one man's shoulders to another's, grinning and screeching as he pointed to Woody.

The audience shouted for Woody's own songs, one after another — "Hard Travelin'," "Pastures of Plenty," "Bound to Lose" (you fascists bound to lose) — and even Bananas got carried away long enough to ask for "Hard, Ain't It Hard."

But the rolling of the ship got worse with each song, until we couldn't stand up anymore. We sang sitting down, and even then it was difficult to keep our seats. At one point Cisco wanted to quit, but I was afraid to and urged Woody to sing on; as long as I kept singing, I would forget about capsizing. The singing was also good for my stomach. It was only when I stopped singing that I felt the first panic signs of seasickness. "Sing it, Woody boy!" I shouted as I tried to concentrate on the F chord.

Then the pitching started, up one wave and down the next, which added to the rolling created an unbeatable combination, and the singing had to stop.

The three of us lurched down the alleyway, past the smell of seasickness coming from the head. We clutched the handrail with one hand while protecting our guitars from being smashed against the bulkheads. We secured them as best we could when we reached the cabin, and then we tried to undress. Instead of unbuttoning my shirt, I pulled it over my head, but before I could complete the operation, a roll sent me flying blindly against the sink. On the next roll Woody was caught with one leg out of his trousers and sent hopping and then flying against the door. "Yippee!" he shouted as another roll threw him into his bunk.

"Sonofabitch!" I shouted as the roll flung me into Cisco's arms.

"Nightie night." Cisco helped me into my bunk.

I lay flat on my back. The ship pitched and threw me hard against the bulkhead, then back, hard against my bunkrail, back and forth, back and forth. Next it rolled so hard I was almost standing upright. Then the ship snapped back, and my feet went over my head. I was too terrified to be seasick.

"Nightie-night your fucking ass!" I hurled down at Cisco.

A heavy pitch flung me harder than ever against the bunkrail as the ship's bow rose higher and higher. The backbreaking crash of the falling ship hitting the sea was accompanied by the even more frightening sound of pots, pans, and kettles breaking loose from the galley wall. A sickening shudder went through the ship, from her keel, through her rigid, welded steel plates, right up our bunk posts, and into my body.

"And furthermore!" I shouted down to Cisco, "Einstein himself says man can never know the whole truth about life and death!"

"Go to sleep." Cisco turned off his light. "Chances are we're not going to capsize."

"You don't understand! If we knew everything, we'd die of boredom!" I called out as a roll lifted my feet above my head and my heart fell into my mouth. When I recovered I continued, "The fact that we don't know what's coming next is just the thing that makes life such a fantastic scenario!"

"And the next thing you're going to say is that God wrote it! For Christ's sake, will you turn off your diarrhea and go to —" Another great roll, accompanied by crashing pots, interrupted Cisco.

"Don't laugh, wise guy!" I yelled down, "Einstein says the order he finds in the universe is the product of a supreme intelligence which he calls God!"

Cisco snapped on his bunk light and looked up at me. "Are you seriously saying that Einstein believes in God?"

Even Woody turned to look up at me.

"Of course!" The roll nearly threw me onto the deck, but I managed to grab a bunk post. "And he says that as we discover new dimensions, we'll be dazzled by what'll be revealed to us about life, about death, about everything! We'll be dazzled and ecstatic even though the ultimate truth is forever beyond us."

The door burst open. "Hey, Woody!" A seaman in oilskins stood in the doorway. "The storm is raisin' hell with your machine! We'd better take it down!"

Woody was silent for a moment, then he said, "Can't — it wouldn't like that. But thanks for telling me."

The seaman hesitated. "Okay, Woody — you know what you're doin'." The ship's heavy roll banged the door behind him.

"Goodnight." I turned out my light even though I knew that sleep was impossible. "And the least we should do is try to understand what Einstein was talking about." Cisco put out his light without saying anything.

The dark made the rolling and the pitching even more frightening. I remembered how, when I was eight, I stopped crossing myself. Despite my father's assurances, it took great courage to defy my mother's God. I remembered the bouts of doubt I had until I was twelve, how I would then cross myself endlessly to make up for all the nights I'd missed. As the rolling and pitching became worse, I thought: "If there is a God, please Sir, don't let this Liberty ship break her back. I want to see Gabrielle once more."

■

"Six o'clock!" The waker-upper opened and slammed our cabin door just as I was falling asleep.

The storm had worsened during the night — I could barely climb down from my bunk. Cisco and Woody were rolling from side to side, fast asleep. I woke them and made my way up to the boat deck. The shrieking wind pinned me against the bulkhead, pushed my breath down my throat, and hit my face with a driving rain. For a moment I stood there breathless, watching the ugly, black clouds colliding with each other at frightening speeds. I was so angry with myself for once again coming out onto the windward side instead of the leeward side that I decided to fight the wind as punishment for my landlubbing stupidity. As I opened my mouth to suck in some air, I was hit in the side of the face by a jet of spray coming from abeam. I couldn't help but grin at the thought of being outboxed by the sea — a left cross to the jaw after falling for a sucker's head-on feint — and for a split second the salty water in my mouth tasted good, until I realized that the frenzied wind hurling itself at the ship was actually stopping the ship dead in her tracks, lifting her, sea spray whipping wildly about her, and holding her as she trembled, teetering on the brink of a trough four stories deep.

I gripped the rail as I looked down at the incredible incline. Jesus Christ! The ship tilted forward, her rear end sticking out of the water, her propeller screaming at the indignity as it frantically beat the air, then down the slope she went — ten thousand tons of steel smashing against the unbreakable sea. Boom! Boom! Boom! Her bow was pushed under and held there until she sprang up, tossing off tons of swirling water. The shudder that passed through the ship passed through me as I hugged the rail, wondering how the ship did not break in two. A wall of gray water rushed toward us. I tried to steer the ship with the force of my mind, willing her to take the wave at an angle instead of hitting it head on. Turn! Turn! But before I knew it, we were being lifted and left teetering on the brink of another trough. A destroyer appeared off our starboard beam, four stories below me, and in the next instant I was staring at it four stories above me.

The bosun staggered toward me. "Tell Woody, half the propeller's gone!" he shouted. "The whole machine'll blow away if he doesn't take it down!"

In the lull before the next wave, I heard moaning coming from the gun turret. I climbed the turret and saw a gunner kneeling beside another gunner who lay on a water-soaked mattress. The prostrate gunner was dead white. He looked unconscious.

"He's so seasick he can't stay inside!" The kneeling gunner rubbed the sick man's wrist.

"Anything I can do?" I shouted.

"Yeah! Tell me if the wind machine's still there!"

"It's still there all right! It's crippled, but it's still there."

"You hear that, Eddie boy?! The wind machine's gonna blow this old storm away yet!" the gunner shouted to his sick mate.

I found Woody in his messroom, trying to set up. I gave him Bosun's warning about taking down the wind machine.

"Can't take it down." Woody continued setting up. "It would die of shame."

A gunner said, "Woody, will you let me give it some more oil then?"

"No, it's too dangerous out there!"

"I'll be all right, and don't worry, I won't put a drop on the negative conductor."

"Okay," Woody said reluctantly, "but about the negative conductor, I think this time we'd better give it just a drop."

The gunner grabbed his oilskin coat, and as he went out he bumped into the chief steward. "No feeding!" the steward announced as he stuck his head in the doorway. "It's too rough! No breakfast, no lunch — just serve sandwiches and coffee!"

"You can't believe what the ocean looks like," I told Woody. "You can't believe it!"

"Then I'd better take a look." Woody borrowed a gunner's oilskin and went outside.

After breakfast I saw Eddie, the near-dead seasick gunner, coming out of Woody's messroom. He looked alive and fit as any of us, despite the ship's rolling and pitching.

"My God, what happened to you? A little while ago you were lying up there . . ."

"Woody cured me!" He grinned as he walked down the pitching alleyway.

"How the hell did he do *that?*"

"Ask him! I gotta get back to my station!"

Woody was mopping the messroom deck. "How in God's name did you cure that kid?"

"Talked to him." Woody continued mopping.

"Talked to him? What the hell did you say to him?"

"Well, for one thing, I told him I'd have to charge him my regular faith-healing fee — fifty cents."

"Come on, stop joking."

"Hell, faith healing's no joke. Practiced it during the depression. Was pretty good at it. I'm especially —" A giant wave threw me against Woody, and we both hit the bulkhead as the ship rolled near to the point of capsizing.

"Oh, my God!" I groaned.

Woody steadied himself. "As I was saying, I'm especially good at curing diarrhea, in case you —"

Another giant wave pitched me across the messroom. "Fuck you, Guthrie!" I shouted as I went hurling through the doorway.

By nighttime the storm had reached hurricane force. It was sandwiches again for dinner.

"What the hell's goin' on up there?" the second engineer asked the grim-faced first mate, who ate his sandwich standing up, his oilskins dripping water.

"Don't ask." The mate gulped his coffee and rushed out.

"The old man's been on the bridge for twenty-four hours," the third mate said to no one in particular.

I watched the starboard portholes rise. I clutched a table, sure that the ship would never right itself, but she did, with a backlash that flung me downhill toward the starboard portholes, which were now thirty degrees below me. I might as well be topside — if we were to capsize, I did not want to be below.

I hurriedly made two sandwiches for the captain and filled a mug of coffee for him, but by the time I got to the wheelhouse, half the coffee was gone, and when I looked out at the storm, there seemed to be nothing left of the whole world except the helmsman, the mate, and me.

The helmsman gripped the wheel and ignored my question about the captain's whereabouts. The mate, without taking his eyes off the big wave bearing down on us shouted, "He's on the flying bridge! Wants a better feel of the storm! He's never seen anything like it!"

Just then the door slid open and the captain came in, his face streaming with water as though he had been weeping. "Put that tray down and get the hell below at once!" he shouted at me in his rough Norwegian accent. But I couldn't move; dark as it was, I saw or felt the giant wave coming at us.

"Hard right!" the captain shouted as he grabbed the wheel and tried to take the wave at an angle, but the wave picked up the ship and shook her before casting her down. The deafening, backbreaking crash of ten thousand rigid-steel tons was immediately followed by a great moan from deep down in the ship itself — her decks groaned, her beams creaked loudly, and every welded plate of her strained in agony. In that instant I understood that our ship was a living thing. Captain Sandburg was her brain, the engine room her heart, and all sixty-four of us different cells, each with a duty to perform. The *Willy B.* was a living thing, and she was capable of feeling pain.

"Get the hell down below!" the captain shouted without taking his eyes from the next giant wave coming toward us. I ran out the wheelhouse and fought my way back to my cabin. I managed to climb into my bunk.

"You may well ask," I shouted to Cisco and Woody as I slammed the cabin door behind me, "if our logic can't lead us to the truth, then how can we say that Hitler's wrong? In which case what the hell am I doing on this stinking ship?"

"Now don't start that again." Cisco swayed with the roll and lay down on his bunk. "Stop worrying and lie down — you're liable to tip the ship over."

I grabbed a bed post to steady myself. "Well if you *must* know, I'm on this ship because everything in my blood, in my bones, tells me that Hitler is *wrong!* That's why I'm on this stinking ship!"

"Good for you, but I'm trying to go to sleep on this stinking ship, which I'm on because of logical conviction and not because of your mystical bullshit!" Cisco snapped off his light.

"Bullshit! Bullshit!" I managed to climb into my bunk. "I try to open your mind to new ideas and all you can say is —"

Boom! A tremendous wave hit us broadside. The ship staggered. For an instant she lay perfectly still. Then she began to go over. My lowering feet told me the degree of incline — thirty — thirty-five — forty! At forty-two degrees a Liberty ship would capsize. My feet said forty-five degrees. The ship stopped rolling, but she didn't roll back; she hung there, trembling. The slightest wave would tip her over. Her trembling changed to violent shaking. Then boom! She flung herself backward, almost capsizing the other way, and then thrashed from side to side.

"You close-minded fuck!" I shouted down at Cisco. "If we do capsize and somehow find ourselves in a glorious hereafter, you'll probably still go on arguing that my ideas are bullshit!"

"Which they are."

"Woody!" I shouted, more from fear than from exasperation, "you heard both sides of the argument. Who's right?"

"You're both right."

"Come on now, this is no time for comedy! How can opposite parties to an argument both be right?"

"Well, as the wise old rabbi said to the neutral party who asked the same question — 'You're right too.'"

The door burst open. "Woody, Godawmighty!" a drenched seaman shouted, "the propeller's gone and the negative conductor's half torn away! Why don't you let us take the wind machine down?"

"I know how you feel, Andy, but there's some things we just can't interfere with."

Andy shook his head and closed the door behind him. Woody put out his light without saying good night.

I left my light on, because the dark exaggerated the degree of the ship's rolling. With the light on, I could see my feet. My feet told me the true degree of the ship's rolls.

Sleep was impossible. I tried to think of Gabrielle, but I couldn't stop thinking about what I would do if we turned over. How would I get out? The deck would be the overhead and the overhead would be the deck. The end would be long and agonizing. I prayed for the storm to end. Let the submarines come; at least the end would be just a flash.

By dawn the sea was stilled, and the convoy was perfectly reformed.

There was nothing left of the wind machine except for its splintered base still gripping the rail. The gun crew and some of the regular crew gathered around Woody as he tenderly removed the base from the rail. He placed the base and the grips that held it into an empty flour sack. The ship's carpenter solemnly handed Woody a piece of steel chain and some rusty bolts. Woody carefully placed them in the sack. He closed the sack with three safety pins. No one uttered a sound, not even the monkey. Woody held the sack over the rail for a long moment.

"She did stop the storm," a gunner cried out, "even though it broke her poor little heart."

Woody released the sack. Everybody strained to watch it sink into the sea, then, one by one, as they left, they patted Woody's shoulder — even Bananas.

9

After breakfast most of the crew sat on the afterdeck hatch covers enjoying the warm sun and the sky-blue sea. The gun-crew phonograph played Tommy Dorsey's "Getting Sentimental over You." Some of the men wrote letters, some played gin rummy, two played chess with Woody's chess set, and some were even in a mood to do their laundry.

The dirty clothes were put into an empty orange bag. The net bag was tied to a line and thrown over the after-rail. The force of the seawater rushing through the clothes washed them cleaner than any washing machine could — but if the bag were pulled up a minute too late, the clothes would be torn to shreds.

When Charlie from Ohio finished his laundry, he brought out his guitar — he was a professional jazz guitarist — and played "Bye-bye Blues." Woody listened, fascinated by the complexity of Charlie's chords. After a couple of more jazz classics, Charlie passed the guitar to Woody and induced him to sing "Philadelphia Lawyer," one of Woody's great ballads. I watched the whole happy scene with mitigated pleasure — it was perfect submarine weather.

Three strange warships appeared on the horizon. As they steamed toward us, we realized that they were British destroyers come to help us across the last dangerous stretch to Gibraltar. The Nazis had U-boat bases along the coast of Spain, their "neutral" ally.

One of the destroyers came within fifty yards of us. She looked as though she hadn't been in port since the war had begun for England, three years before. Part of her smokestack was shot away, and large patches of rust ate away at her gray sides and superstructure. Even her crew, lining the rail, looked worn and rusty, with their dirty patched khaki shorts and their scraggly reddish beards, and they all looked underfed.

"What a fucking mess!" a gun-crew first-tripper snorted and was about to laugh when Bosun grabbed him by the neck and doubled him over.

"Bow to her, you dumb bastard! That's the British navy, the bravest seamen in the world. Without them the Nazis would have beaten us long ago."

The destroyer was now only twenty-five yards away. "Hi, Yanks! Welcome to the tea party!" one of the Britishers called out as he held up his fingers in a V for victory sign.

"Good to see you, Limey!" Bosun returned the victory sign. "How's it going?"

"Just beautiful matey! Just one big, beautiful, bloody tea party!"

"God bless Vera Lynn!" Woody shouted.

"And the same to Frank Sinatra!" the Britisher shouted back.

Their captain's bullhorn interrupted the exchanges. "I say," it called out in a most upper-class English accent, "have you a doctor on board?"

Our captain's bullhorn answered, "Sorry, we have no doctor on board. There's one on the commodore's ship up ahead!"

"Thank you!" the British captain called back as he accelerated his ship. "Cheerio and good luck!"

"There now, aren't you glad they're with us?" The Bosun put his arm around the first-tripper. "God knows how long it'll be before we reach Gibraltar."

"It won't be long Bosun!" Cisco called as we wiped something from his arm. "I've just been hit by bird shit."

"Look! Seagulls!" somebody shouted happily. Three or four gulls were lazily riding in our ship's airwake, their wings motionless.

"That means we can't be more'n two days away from land!" A gunner slapped another gunner on the shoulder.

"Yeah, and it looks like we'll make it." Cisco continued wiping himself. "With the British as sea escorts and the seagulls for sky cover, we ought to make Gibraltar without any trouble at all."

Cisco was wrong. For the next two nights we were threatened by brightly lit ships steaming straight toward our blacked-out convoy. They were Spanish ships. Spain was supposed to be a neutral country, yet they were lighting the way for the U-boats, guiding them straight to us. But thanks to our escorts, we lost no ships that we could see, and on the morning of the fifteenth day, the rock loomed before us — the fortress rock — Gibraltar, guardian of the Mediterranean's gate.

Once we were past the rock, the U-boats of the Atlantic would be behind us. The only submarines we would need to worry about were the desperate U-boats of the Mediterranean.

■

Half our convoy passed through the Strait of Gibraltar, probably bound for our North African bases. The rest of us entered Gibraltar Bay. There were thirty merchant ships at anchor, probably waiting for us to join them in forming a new convoy.

The rock, two miles wide at its base, towered fifteen hundred feet above us. Its steep face, lined and tiered with gun emplacements, made it the mightiest fortress in the British Empire. The English town of Gibraltar clung to the rock. At the edge of the bay was the Spanish port of La Linea, where Franco first landed his rebel forces armed with Mussolini's tanks and Hitler's air force. It had been the start of the tragedy of the Spanish people and the prelude to World War II.

Jack Lipton, my next-door neighbor in the Bronx, was killed somewhere beyond La Linea, fighting with the Lincoln Brigade. When news came of his death, his mother covered all the mirrors, and we sat on the floor, without shoes, as the Jews have done for 5,000 years. My mother cooked the hard-boiled eggs that the mourners ate for seven days.

Beyond La Linea, the barren Spanish mountains recede toward the north.

Along the bay's shore we could see five or six beached Allied ships. "That fucking Franco!" Pete Harmon pointed to the crippled ships. "He lets the Nazi frogmen blow up our ships." Pete, who had been to Gibraltar before, explained that at night the German frogmen came from the Spanish side of the bay. They would walk the bottom of the bay and place sticker time bombs on the keels of our ships.

Our anchorage was less than two hundred yards from the Spanish shore, so close that we could smell the orange blossoms. Before we dropped anchor a dozen rowboats swarmed around us. "Brandy! Brandy!" their occupants shouted up to us in broken English. "One carton cigarettes, two bottles brandy!" There would be no shore leave while we were at Gibraltar. Down went the lines baited with cigarettes, and up came the brandy. It was good brandy, thick and smooth on the tongue.

That night, under the stars, we celebrated our safe crossing with the biggest and drunkenest party yet. Woody was the main attraction, Cisco was second, and I accompanied them with my three poor chords, which after several brandies began to sound pretty good to me. Charlie from Ohio took over during our breaks. The men danced hoedowns to Woody's music and jitterbugged to Charlie's.

I had one solo, a Spanish Civil War song, "Ay Manuela," about how the International Brigade, without tanks or planes, covered itself with glory. Drunk as I was, I sang it in Spanish, shouting my angry words toward Franco's shore as loudly as I could. "That was pretty good," Cisco said, "but you were singing in the wrong direction. The Spanish shore is over there. You sang your song to the English shore."

It was very hot, but the night was beautiful, the brandy was beautiful, and the British patrol boats watched over us, dropping their depth charges soon after sunset. The charges weren't big enough to hurt a ship — just big enough to kill any German frogmen lurking about. "Don't anybody get any ideas about swimming off the side of the ship," Cisco warned our audience. "Just one of those little depth charges'll turn you into mashed potatoes."

It was a great party. Nobody swam and we danced till dawn.

The next day more ships anchored in the already jammed bay. There was no doubt that we were going to be part of an invasion fleet. The question was, what invasion?

Churchill favored landing in Greece, which he called the soft underbelly of the Nazi "Fortress Europa." The Russians wanted the Allies to invade northern France. Others wanted to attack in the north of Italy to trap the German armies already in the long, narrow peninsula. Invading Sicily was out of the question because although Sicily was only a stone's throw from our African bases, our armies would have to fight every inch of their way up the Italian boot. One well-placed German division would be able to cut up ten of ours. Only Mike Sala wanted us to invade Sicily; the rest of the world knew that it would be idiotic. That morning — the 10th of July — our ship's radio announced that the Allies had invaded Sicily.

Woody shook his head. "Mike Sala must have an awful lot of influence with the Allied chiefs of staff."

Heavy static made it difficult to catch everything the announcer was saying, but it was clear that our forces had landed in the south and the east of the island. The main German forces were at the other end, near Palermo.

"What's the name of Mike's mother's town?" Cisco asked me, while he kept his ear close to the radio.

"Altofonte — near Palermo."

"Patton's army is headed for Palermo!" Cisco called out.

"Now wouldn't it be something if we got to Palermo too?" Woody took a swig of brandy.

I grabbed the bottle from him. "Well, Mike said that's where we're going, so I guess that's where we're going."

The betting was two to one that we would sail the next day, but one week later we were still in Gibraltar. We didn't mind the wait. In fact it was a real vacation. The weather was great, and we could swim off the side of the ship, since the British dropped depth charges only at night. We sunbathed, read, listened to records, practiced guitar, played chess, and wrote letters.

Woody wrote for several hours a day, either working on his novel or writing ten-page letters to Marjorie. "Hell, how can you write so many pages?" asked a gunner sitting next to Woody, who was scribbling away on number-five hatch. "I've got to use big letters to fill up one lousy little page. How can you fill so many?"

"Easy, just keep writing."

"What about?"

"Everything. Look at those birds." Woody pointed to dozens of screeching seagulls beating the air over the afterdeck, where Roberto the cook was feeding them choice bits from our leftovers. The gulls jostled and bit each other as they dived to catch the morsels in midair, and hardly ever did a piece hit the water. The fastest gull was an old one with one leg. He would dive through the screeching crowd and snatch the food an inch away from an open mouth. Roberto tried to outwit him, but the old bird got far more than his share.

"What do you think of Old One Leg?" Woody asked the gunner.

"He's about the fastest and smartest thief I ever did see."

"Then why don't you write about him?" Woody tore off some sheets from his pad. "And here's a pencil. Start writing, and when you finish with the gulls, tell your folks about the brandy boats and about Roberto's good grub, and how Charlie from Ohio hits those six-string chords."

"No — I think I'll tell 'em about the wind machine first."
"Okay, then I'll write about the seagulls." Woody started to write,

TALKING SEAGULL

Here on my ship deck standing at the rail
Watching that seagull wiggle his tail
Throw him a little bread out of my hand
(Ain't no bird can fly like a seagull can).
Easy rider. Easy glider. Really handles his business.

Look all around. Not a gull in sight.
I throw a piece of bread and I see a sight.
Little gulls flop and the big ones tear
Catching that bread in the middle of the air.
Easy up. Ease over. Catch it. Wing over and gone again.

I went to the garbage can and got some meat
Them gulls come a running. Gonna have a treat
Ten pound of meat in a two-pound gull
And he still didn't have his belly full.
Rubber belly. Him a sailing. Really packing a load.

Little baby seagull there in the deal
Big ones they all grabbed them a meal
Little one pecked at everything in sight
But the sun went down and he didn't get a bite.
Flying all around us. Begging. Squawking . . . raising hell.

Four men made a run for the kitchen then
And we dumped over the side a garbage can
Little baby seagull filled up his beak
Got enough to last him till about next week.
Mama called him. He flew home. We all stood around there on
    the rail of our ship feeling good.

We looked out across the ocean foam
Talked about our women and our kids back home
Talked about the war and the freedom fight
Fighting to get all of the little ones a bite
Seagulls. People everywhere. Every color you can think of.

Clouds come along and covered up the moon
We heard the cannon roar and the depth bombs boom
Big storm broke and the rain it rained
Waiting for the sun to shine out again.
Maybe bring some more seagulls. Whole families of them.

Along in the morning towards eight o'clock
Yonder come the seagulls. Great big flock.
One tough guy said, "You're a silly bunch of fools!
Wastin' yer time feedin' goddamn gulls!"
Work your heads off feedin' 'em bread.
Feedin' 'em meat.
What in the hell did them gulls ever give you?

One old boy there really got red
He cussed out at this feller and he shook his head.
"Man! If you had the least ounce of brains,
You'd know them seagulls give us our Spitfire planes!"

After a few days of lazing about, time began to drag. On the fourteenth of July we celebrated Woody's thirty-first birthday; on the twenty-fifth Mussolini was deposed; on the twenty-sixth the Allies took Palermo; on the twenty-seventh we were still stuck in Gibraltar; and after more than two weeks of no shore leave, the crew began to get very restless. "A man could be at sea for two months without grumbling," Cisco said as he faced the near shore, "but to be less than two hundred yards from land for two weeks without shore leave is a heavy load to bear." He sniffed the air.

The mere sight of a girl strolling along the shore brought forth moans, wails, endearing shouts, and furious cursing. To make matters worse, Newington had cornered the market on girlie magazines. He sold the pages singly at exorbitant profit.

"You guys got any magazines you want to sell?"

"You can have those free." Woody pointed to some on his bunk. "There's *Time*, *The Atlantic*, and the *New Masses*."

Newington looked around at our pinupless walls. "Jesus, in addition to being Reds, you guys must be a bunch of homos!" He slammed the door behind him.

The tension on board mounted with each waiting day. The drinking got heavier and the gambling became more reckless. Fly killing got a lot of betting action.

Killing flies was a necessity as well as a sport, for there were millions of them in Gibraltar Bay. Cisco was the ship's champ. The fact he couldn't see beyond three feet didn't matter. He would quietly get within a foot of the fly and then wham! He never missed. He made a small fortune until the men realized that he had a secret technique and stopped betting with him. Woody and I got him to tell us his secret: face the fly head on and aim for its ass. It never failed. Flies fly backward when attacked from the front; aiming at the ass traps them every time.

From fly killing the men turned to boxing matches. Again Cisco quickly established himself as the ship's champ. He had a simple strategy to compensate for his bad eyes. When his opponent danced around, Cisco couldn't see him clearly and therefore couldn't tell where the punches were coming from. So Cisco would wait for his opponent to throw the first punch; then he would pin the man's glove with one arm, and with his free arm he would beat at the other man's ribs with amazing speed and tremendous power. He could easily have hurt his opponents badly, but he was careful to never hurt anybody.

Cisco also made time pass for us when he would sit on a hatch cover and start singing for himself. In no time the crew would gather around him, and at Woody's urging he would sing the songs he loved best, lonesome ballads like "Tumbling Tumbleweed" and "Bury Me Not on the Old Prairie." But sometimes he would switch to a funny song, like the one about a drunken mouse who came out of his hole to fight a cat. For a quiet man, Cisco had a surprising comic ability.

When he was in the mood he would tell jokes by acting out all the parts with such talent as to turn the joke into a little theatrical production. The crew's favorite was Cisco's joke about a German Egyptologist who was duped into buying six ancient petrified vaginas, of which half turned out to be rectums. But Cisco's talent and Woody's talent could not distract the crew from its boredom for more than an hour at a time, and as the waiting lengthened, tempers got shorter.

To make the time pass faster the three of us conducted mental telepathy experiments. Cisco was very cynical about the project, but having nothing else to do, he participated. We tried card guessing first. Woody got a markedly higher score than anybody, and he got it consistently. "Luck — shit ass luck," Cisco grumbled.

The next day we put Woody in one messroom and we stayed in the other. Cisco and I were to draw anything that came into our heads and Woody would try to guess it. We drew a cigar box. In the cigar box I drew a monkey. Cisco drew a ball in the monkey's hands. Woody guessed that we had drawn a cigar box with a monkey in it playing a game. Cisco still thought that it was just an extraordinary coincidence. Most of the crew thought otherwise — much to Bananas's chagrin.

"Aah, just observe how the, aah, gullible masses fall for mystic bullshit!"

Although Woody could not duplicate the amazing success of the cigar-box monkey, he did get a consistently higher score than the rest of us. But that wasn't dramatic enough to hold the crew's interest, and after a day or two tempers went back to trigger point.

Newington was in a particularly bad mood because somebody had stolen the remainder of his pinup girl stock and distributed the pictures free. "If you're so fucking clairvoyant, Brother Guthrie, why don't you tell us when this ship is gonna get out of this fucking bay?"

"All in good time, Brother Newington, you'll get your share of the action — all in good time."

That night, while we were playing poker, the radio man burst into the crew's messroom. "We're leaving! We're leaving tonight! As soon as we get the code word!"

"Wait a minute, Sparks!" Cisco held up a brandy bottle. "Seein's how you were kind enough to come tell us, have a drink."

"I don't drink." The nineteen-year-old radioman blushed. "But I sure would like to hear you guys sing. I've got time till midnight."

The three of us and the radioman went out on deck, where we sang and drank, and Sparks took his first drink. It was a hot night, and the more we drank, the hotter it got.

Woody took off his trousers. "I know I can't go swimming on account of them depth charges, but there's nothin' says I can't go diving." He jumped up on the rail just as a depth charge boomed.

"Stop, you drunken bastard!" I yelled, but before we could grab him, he was gone. We rushed to the rail. Woody was hanging from a rope that dangled four feet away from the ship — one end of it was tied to the rail, the other to a lifeboat on the deck above us.

"Wheeee!" Woody was swinging like a monkey, twenty-five feet above the deadly depth-charged water.

"Come on — follow the leader!" Woody worked his way back to the rail.

He looked dead sober, but he was obviously dead drunk — as was Cisco, because the next thing I knew, he too was undressing. Another depth charge boomed. I thought I wasn't drunk, yet I did nothing to stop Cisco; instead, I started to undress. Sparks shouted something and began to weave his way back to midship. I turned to Cisco, but he was gone. I climbed onto the rail. Cisco was swinging on the rope, dead serious. Another depth charge boomed. He made his way back, and I jumped. I do not remember swinging over the water, nor do I remember getting back. I do remember philosophizing later about human nature, drunkenness, and how this was the closest we had been to death on this trip. I also remember Sparks weaving his way back to us and crying. He sat down on the hatch cover, put his hands over his face, and wept.

"Come on, Sparks," Cisco said. "What the hell's wrong?"

"I knew I shouldn't have drunk! All I keep hearing on the radio is 'Whiskey! Whiskey! Whiskey! Whiskey!' I tell you, I'm crazy!"

We followed Sparks up to the radio room, and sure enough, that's what the radio was saying, "Whiskey! Whiskey! Whiskey! Whiskey!" That was the codeword our captain was waiting for! Ten minutes later we were on our way out of Gibraltar Bay, headed for Palermo.

10

The ships in Gibraltar Bay were assigned to several convoys. Our Palermo-bound convoy consisted of twenty-five ships formed in five lines, five ships to the line. We were the fourth ship in the middle line.

The Mediterranean was as calm and blue as the books say, but the three of us were too hung over from the previous night's drinking to enjoy it. Immediately after dinner we went to sleep, even though the sun had not yet set.

DRRRINNNGGG! The general-alarm bell blasted me out of my deep sleep. Cisco was already through the doorway; Woody, wearing just his underpants, stumbled after him. I pulled on my trousers, grabbed my life jacket, and tore after them. Men were running helter-skelter through the alleyways.

"Don't run!" Cisco shouted, as he walked down the alleyway with his arms outstretched. "Take it easy! Don't run!" Woody and I couldn't get past him.

"Point the gun at the sun! At the sun!" the lieutenant commander shouted from the boat deck as we got to the gun turret, "Watch out for planes! They'll come out of the sun!" The blinding sun was setting into the sea, directly behind us. The Nazi planes would be coming from the Spanish bases with the sun behind them.

Whoom! Whoom! Whoom! The thud of depth charges reverberated against our ship. Depth charges from three destroyers up ahead were throwing up columns of water. And then we saw a giant flash of bright orange coming from the first ship on the right outside line. The flame was already a hundred feet high before we heard the dull boom of the explosion.

"Submarines! Submarines!" a gun-crew kid shouted to the ensign, who already had his binoculars trained on the burning ship.

"Ensign," I asked as calmly as I could, "can you see anything?"

He handed me the binoculars.

The burning ship was sinking in the middle — her back was broken. She must have caught the torpedo in her engine room. She was going to sink in another minute. Then my view was interrupted by intervening ships. I picked up the flaming ship again, just in time to see another explosion of flames from her sinking hulk, then more intervening ships, and finally she was behind us. The flames were lower in the sky; she was sinking fast. Men were jumping from her. There were no lifeboats that I could see, just funny little figures jumping over the side.

"Goddamn! Goddamn!" the gunner shouted. "She's going!"

I looked through the glasses again. I saw another blast of white steam and black smoke, and then she made a giant V as she broke in the middle and slipped into the sea.

Nobody spoke. I could see her survivors struggling to escape the ship's suction, but for some reason I couldn't feel for them. They seemed ridiculous specks in the sea, unreal compared with the tragedy of the ship itself — that beautiful ship broken in two and lying dead on the bottom of the sea. Her tragedy was an affront to logic and nature. My feeling was for her, just as it had been for the huge trailer-truck I had once seen lying on its side, jackknifed across a highway, her driver next to her, dead. My shock, my embarrassment, was for the helpless trailer. I could not connect with the dead man lying there — he was unreal.

Whoom! Whoom! Whoom! The depth charges were nearer to us now. The destroyers raced up and down the rear of the convoy. They were our only protection. Our cannons were useless, for even if a U-boat did surface, two lines of ships intervened. And what could the machine guns fire at? There were no planes in sight. Still, you had to go by the book, so we manned our guns. You never knew when the Stuka bomb-ers might come screaming out of the sun; and also, the two ships paral-lel to us on both sides would sometimes fall behind or move ahead, leav-ing us wide open to an enemy submarine. What if at that moment a U-boat were forced to surface, ready to slam a torpedo into our belly? A lucky cannon shell might just save us. I prayed for the outside ships to keep in step with us.

The three destroyers were now circling and sending up an ever-nar-rowing circle of water. Whoom! Whoom! Whoom!

"They spotted a sub! They spotted a sub!" several men yelled at once.

"They got one!" A gunner jumped up and down as he pointed to a large circle of black oil that was spreading over the target area.

"Where?" Cisco asked.

"There! Oil!" I pointed. "Beautiful, black oil!"

"Sometimes the subs let out some oil just to fool you." Cisco squint-ed toward the circle. "How big is the slick?"

"Big! Big! They're not playing dead. They're bleeding to death. It's all over the goddamned ocean!" The spreading black circle cheated us from seeing anything below the water's surface, but I could imaging the monster submarine with a hole in its side, spilling out its oil, filling up with water, sinking, its steel plates crumbling under the weight of the sea, crushed to death, as it should be. Its swastika marking was an insult to humanity.

Although the survivors of the torpedoed ship were unreal specks in the sea, the U-boat's crewmen who were now choking and drowning were very real to me. The fucking idiots: "The Master Race!" "Every German a Nazi baron!" "Europe today, tomorrow the world!" In the meantime, choke and drown, you poor bastards, choke and drown with nothing but a black oil slick to mark your grave.

The rush of air hit me before I heard the explosion. Another ship up ahead was hit. Its flames roared into the sky, ten times higher than the other torpedoed ship. "She's a tanker," I said to Cisco. "First ship on the outside line to our left."

The way she was burning, there would be nothing left by the time we pulled abreast of her — nothing but flames. The sea around her was al-ready on fire. We could smell the burning oil.

"You think the crew'll get off?" somebody asked. Nobody answered him.

Another explosion from the burning ship shot a wall of flame around her. The ships in her line veered sharply to port. The ships in number-two line were also in danger because the burning tanker was already drifting and lying across her sea-lane, exploding fire all around her. The ships in number-two line could avoid the tanker's fire only by cutting into our line, at the risk of collision. But what a collision — two ten-thousand-ton ships sideswiping at twelve knots. Twenty thousand tons crushing together at that speed could smash open both hulls and sink both ships in a few minutes. For the ships in the second line, it was either that risk or plowing into the exploding tanker.

The ship next to us, in the second line, veered toward us. We had no choice either. If we veered to starboard, it would cause us to collide with the ships in number-four line. It had to be full speed ahead and pray that we could outrace the encroaching ship before we reached the inferno ahead.

We were neck and neck, coming closer and closer together. I could read her name: *Sea Fury*. Why didn't her captain cut her speed? Was he hysterical? We were now hardly twenty-five yards apart. Her crew screamed at us, "Move over, you dirty bastards! Move over!" We watched, petrified. At that angle and speed it was a collision course. Our ship trembled as she responded to the full-speed order.

The men around us began shouting, "Come on, baby! Come on, baby! You can do it! You can do it!"

We began to pull ahead.

Woody shouted, "Two to one the *Willy B.* makes it!"

Cisco peered at the approaching ship. "How close is she?" he asked quietly. My poor Cisco, he couldn't even see a two-block-long ship at twenty-five yards.

"We're ahead." I answered quietly. "We're ahead by half a length."

But half a length was not enough. We were coming up on the burning tanker, which was drifting into our lane, and the *Sea Fury* was only fifteen yards away from us. The cheering stopped. You could feel the prayer. "Go, baby, go!" The *Willy B.* shook so hard she seemed about to tear apart.

"Are we gaining?" Cisco asked.

"We're three-quarters of a length ahead."

I could feel the heat of the burning ship, with the *Sea Fury* only ten yards from us. The *Willy B.* shook harder and leaped ahead just in time to clear the *Sea Fury*'s bow, which now loomed over our stern. In a few seconds we were abreast of the burning tanker, separated from her by less than a hundred yards of burning water. The tanker was unrecognizable except for her skeleton, barely visible through the flames that consumed her from stem to stern. In the middle of the fiery lake we saw a life raft with six or seven men desperately paddling; two men were floating face down, and another was helping a burning man onto the raft. I thought I saw a man swimming toward the raft, as fringes of flame kept rising out of the water — if it was a man, he was swimming the crawl, and it looked like he was wearing orange-fringed sleeves. In a few more seconds the flaming tanker was behind us. The trip across that burning lake was the longest of my life.

Three hours later and thirty miles away, the tanker's flames were still visible in the night sky. The general alarm was called off around midnight, but fear of being hit continued. Sleep was impossible. The image of the tanker's burning men was too vivid. The three of us went to the ship's deserted bow, where we worked off our nervous energy by finding weird, lonesome harmonies to the black chain-gang song "Another Man Done Gone." Woody changed the words to

> Another ship done gone,
> Another ship done gone,
> Another ship done gone.
>
> I didn't know her name,
> I didn't know her name,
> I didn't know her name.

When Cisco and Woody were ready to turn in, I lied to them. I said I wasn't sleepy and preferred to stay on deck for a while. Neither of them teased me. When they left, I climbed to the highest spot I could find —as far away from our cargo as I could get. If a torpedo were to hit the bombs in our holds, everybody would be killed. Those closest to the cargo would die without knowing it; those farthest away might have a second of final awareness. I lay down near the smokestack and drew close to it to avoid the chill in the air. I pulled my knees up to my chest and lay there waiting.

Forty-eight hours later we were within sight of Italy. The land off our port bow was my racial home, the soil that shaped my genes. The people who lived there were my people. I felt strongly drawn to them, despite my revulsion for the vileness and stupidity that had made Mussolini possible. I tried to think of Dante, da Vinci, and Verdi.

"You sentimental Wop, I bet you're all choked up." Cisco peered toward the shore. "What do you see?"

Coppery-gold mountains ringed the beautiful bay of Palermo — the Italians called it the Golden Kettle. The city of a half-million people looked white and splendid, but as we got closer, we could see the signs of decay, the bombed-out houses and the jumble of the congested waterfront. Several half-sunken Allied ships, some still tied to their docks, emphasized the warning we had received about Nazi air raids on the port. A dozen ships jammed the few still-functioning docks, while twice that many ships in the harbor waited their turn for dock space. The sounds coming from the unloading ships were the sounds of very hurried unloading. Their overworked winches seemed to be screeching, "Let's get rid of this cargo and get the hell out of here!"

"How long does it take for a ship to leave Palermo?" I asked the harbor official in Italian. He had come aboard in a launch and was hungrily eating the food our captain had told me to serve him.

"Perhaps a month," he said without stopping his chewing for an instant, "if you're lucky."

I felt like pulling the dinner plate from under his wolfish fascist face. I was sure that all Italian officials were true fascists, despite their insistence that they were forced to be blackshirts in order to work and despite the claim of the Allied radio that the Italian establishment was now working wholeheartedly for democracy. The sonofabitch said a month! And with our cargo! If he asks for seconds, I thought, he can drop dead.

"And you are lucky." He kept on chewing. "Because of your special cargo, you have been given immediate dock space — well away from the center of the port."

I never thought I'd bless our cargo. "How long will it take us to unload?"

"About two weeks — our facilities were badly damaged. I pray that the air raids will not come and that you will return safely to your family." He stopped eating and took a picture from his wallet. "This is my son. He looks amazingly like you."

"You flatter me." His son looked a little like Valentino in an Italian army uniform. "Where is he?"

"He was killed on the Russian front." He put the picture away and sighed deeply. "This war is insane. Mussolini's dream was insane." He did not resume eating. Whatever the harbor official's passion for fascism might once have been, I was sure that it was gone now — no actor could have spoken those lines with such tragic conviction.

"You didn't finish your food."

"I ate enough, thank you, but if you can please find an empty can, I will take it home to my family."

I filled two empty coffee cans with beef stew and handed them to him. DRRRINNNGGG! The general alarm went off. I rushed to my gun station.

"There they are!" Charlie from Ohio pointed to two planes circling high above us.

"If the motherfakkers drop one on us, Charlie, it's gonna be, aah, good-bye Charlie," Bananas moaned.

How strange it was to see the enemy planes. It was so personal. The pilots were human beings, and they were actually trying to kill us.

Five of our planes chased the enemy planes away, and the general alarm was called off. An hour later we were approaching our assigned dock. In the dock next to ours, a destroyer escort lay on its side.

"Air raid," the harbor official explained to me. "Her captain is Franklin D. Roosevelt Jr. I don't know how many casualties. This war is insane."

As we got closer to our dock, we saw more than three hundred longshoremen, shouting, waving, and ready to storm us.

"Hallo, Americani!"

"Hey, Joe!"

"Hallo, Coca-Cola!"

Their assault began long before the gangway ladder was let down. The horde climbed the ropes and ladders, and loads of them swung aboard in nets of the dockside cranes. We were overwhelmed. They isolated each seaman and bombarded him with pleas. The seaman fought them off, some with bad language, most of them with embarrassed grins.

"Cigarette, Joe?"

"Please, you got bread?"

"You wanna buy a watch?"

Some said, "Please, please, please," without any specific request as they pushed the seamen down the alleyways.

"One moment!" I shouted in Italian. "Attention!"

The longshoremen stopped immediately, surprised by my Italian.

"So this is the grandeur that fascism promised you!"

The silence was shocking. After a few moments a middle-aged longshoreman standing near me said, "I speak only for myself. There are no words to express my shame. The facts speak for me. I earn a dollar a day — that, plus the little rice you Americans are good enough to give us, is barely enough to keep my family alive. And I'm one of the lucky ones. My cousin has no work and six children. To keep from starving, he pimps for his twelve-year-old daughter. What else is there to say about the grandeur of fascism?"

"But if Mussolini had won the war for you, wouldn't you have cheered him?"

The silence was even deeper. Finally the middle-aged man looked up at me sadly and said, "Yes, and that is the greatest shame — we would have cheered." He turned to the men around him. "All right boys, let's go to work."

I touched the man's arm and offered him a cigarette. He took one.

"Pass them around."

"Thank you, my friend," he said. "I hope we have a chance to talk again."

That morning the crew got shore leave, two-thirds of the ship at a time. The three of us paid some of our steward department mates to cover for us so that we would have extra shore leave in Palermo. Shaved and showered, we went down the gangway ladder and into a maelstrom of clanging cranes, screeching winches, shouting longshoremen, and the roar of U.S. Army trucks. The smell of gasoline and fuel oil filled the air, and a cloud of dust covered everything. I bent down, touched the land of my ancestors, and kissed my fingers.

"God, what a sentimental cornball!" Cisco shouted above the noise.

"Ah, balls!" I shouted back. "What do you Anglo-Saxons know about sentiment!"

"Rabbi Longhi's right," Woody said. "Let's go find Mike's mother."

The burning sun fried the oil-filled air. There was nothing to shield us from its painful rays, and by the time we walked to the dock gates, a half-mile away, we were exhausted, wilted, and covered with sweat. The sweat mixed with the dust that filled the atmosphere, the dust of a bombed city.

"There's an umbrella!" Woody ran to the horse-drawn carriage waiting at the gate; a big umbrella shielded the back seat.

"Signori! Signori!" The skinny, sun-burned driver in a dirty undershirt greeted us like beings just come from heaven to save him and his emaciated horse from starving to death.

"How much to take us to the center of town?" I had heard about Italy's swindling coachmen.

The coachman was overjoyed at my Italian, and in a passionate stream of Sicilian dialect, he raised his head and thanked the Virgin Mary for the great good fortune of my presence and the blessing my comrades and I would bring to him, Giovanni One Ear, and to his hungry children.

"How much, Giovanni?" I looked him straight in the eyes.

"Nothing! Absolutely nothing! For you there is no price, just whatever you say. I belong to you. I will never leave you. I will be with you night and day wherever you go while you're in Palermo. There will be no charge! You will give whatever you think my poor horse and I are worth."

"Will you just tell me how much is —"

"No use talking! I belong to you! Don't worry — you will see — whatever you say, whatever you want to —"

"Fucki, fucki?" A skinny, black-eyed ten-year-old boy looked up at me.

"Get out of here, you miserable bastard!" Giovanni flicked his whip toward him.

The boy darted a look of hatred toward the coachman. "Fucki, fucki?" He looked grimly at the three of us.

"Go away!" Giovanni lifted his whip.

"Jesus Christ, is the little bastard pimping?" I asked Giovanni.

"Yes, for his eight-year-old sister." We got into the carriage. Giovanni cracked his whip above the horse's head. The poor horse strained to pull his heavy load. I looked back at the boy. His hate-filled eyes were focused not on the coachman but on me.

"Signore," Giovanni One Ear said, turning to me, "if you want real women, I will take you to two signorine. They are angels — angels! Both of them are daughters of noble families and they were pure, pure — until the Nazis came."

"What's he saying?" Cisco asked.

"He says he's got a couple of broads."

"Tell him it's too damn hot."

"Cigarette, Joe? Cigarette?" A small gang of boys and girls jogged alongside, unbothered by the heat and dust, easily keeping up with our slow-trotting horse.

"Candy, Joe? Candy?"

"Lira! One lira!"

"Fucki, fucki, Joe?"

"Pay no attention to them," Giovanni called back to us. "They are like the flies of Palermo — there's nothing you can do about them."

We tried to pay attention to the sights. The noisy street was crowded with slow-moving horse carriages, falling-apart automobiles hooting their horns, packed motor buses with passengers hanging out the windows, shouting street-hawkers selling watermelon, and others selling ices.

The sidewalks were as congested as the streets: women in black, carrying bundles on their heads; men in undershirts, shuffling in worn-out shoes or old bedroom slippers; barefoot children; and here and there an American soldier surrounded by a gang of yelling children. Some young women called down to us from their balconies. Most of the buildings were ugly nineteenth-century. Many of them were bombed out; their exposed walls, covered with faded pastel colors, made them almost attractive in a macabre sort of way.

The side streets were narrow alleys of seven-story tenements linked by hundreds of lines of drying wash whose colors were as loud as the noise of the crowds below.

Honk! Honk! Honk! — the car behind us tried to push our slow carriage, its front end nearly touching our rear. "Move over!" the driver shouted. "Move over, imbecile!" Instead of turning around, Giovanni lifted his left arm and hit the crook of it with his right hand, which simply meant "Up yours!" The driver screamed something about Giovanni's mother's vagina. Giovanni, looking ahead imperturbably, merely repeated the arm gesture and then followed it by raising his right index finger and making circles in the air as the car passed us.

"Giovanni, I understand the arm business, but what does the circling finger mean?"

"The arm means up his ass. The circling finger includes his whole family."

"Okay, Giovanni, now let's get out of here. We've seen enough of Palermo."

"Where would your excellencies want to go?"

"Do you know Altofonte?"

"Sure, a village of three thousand, about twelve kilometers from here."

"Can you take us?"

"Only to Monreale; beyond that it's too dangerous. They say that there are bands of German soldiers still roving around in the hills. If you want to take the chance, you'll have to go the rest of the way by yourselves." We decided to go up to Monreale, and from there we'd decide about Altofonte.

Our carriage slowly climbed the orange-fragrant road to Monreale. On the steeper hills we got out and walked, despite Giovanni's entreaties and assurances that Garibaldi was strong enough to carry us. We didn't want to risk having a dead horse on our hands. When we came to a very steep hill, we helped push the carriage. Giovanni raged at Garibaldi. Garibaldi turned, ignored his master's fury, and stared gratefully at the three of us.

Eventually, after walking more than half the way, and half-dead from the heat, we arrived at Monreale.

We drank lukewarm beer in a tree-shaded cafe. A middle-aged man at the next table eagerly entered into conversation with us. He was a lawyer. When he learned that I was studying law, he became more intimate, and when I told him that my father was a socialist, he hesitantly identified himself as a Communist. I translated for Woody and Cisco.

"We Communists have got to be careful. Your military government is so frightened of us that it prefers to work with Fascist officials and the Mafia. Any demonstration or meeting by us is forbidden, and several of our people have already been jailed." The lawyer stood up. "You must excuse me now, but I have to go."

"Please, before you go, can you tell me about getting to Altofonte?"

"That's up in the hills. There are bandits and German holdouts. It would be folly for you to go unless you went with that young man sitting there with those four men."

"Who is he?"

"Nino of Altofonte — he's only sixteen, but he runs everything between here and Altofonte."

"Mafia?" I studied the handsome, thin, dark-eyed boy.

"Yes. Well, good-bye, and be careful."

The young Mafia chief had been watching us since we sat down; as soon as the lawyer left, he rose and came to our table. "I hope you like Monreale."

"Yes, we do, but it's Altofonte we want to get to. I hear you can help us."

"Why Altofonte?"

"My friend's mother lives there."

"Who is your friend?"

"Michele Sala of New York."

The boy grabbed my hand. "Michele Sala is my uncle! You are looking for my grandmother!" He waited for the embrace, which I gave him.

When I assured him that Mike was okay, he said, "Fantastic! Unbelievable that you are here! What can I . . ." He patted his shirt pockets. "What can I . . ." He patted his trouser pockets. "Here!" He pulled out a gun and slapped it into my hand. "Here, take this as a welcoming present from me!"

It was a beautiful twenty-two caliber automatic, tiny and deadly. "Nino, you're as crazy as your uncle Mike!" I thrust it back at him.

"Keep it! Keep it! But be careful; it's loaded." He gleefully showed me how to work it, and then he slipped the gun into my pocket. "Now we go find my grandmother. It's an hour's walk, shortcut, or two hours along the road, which is longer but easier. Or you can wait until this evening, when my car returns from Corleone. I sent it there to pick up certain . . . things."

We decided to take the shortcut because we had to get back to our ship before curfew — we were told that the military police were especially tough on merchant seamen. Nino promptly dispatched a young man to announce our arrival in Altofonte.

I wanted to pay off Giovanni, but he insisted on waiting in Monreale until we returned. Nino had a word with him, but I could only hear snatches. "Of course, Nino, of course." Giovanni took the money Nino was offering him. "I'll be waiting for you tomorrow at the ship!" Giovanni called to us.

"I am taking you home tonight, by car." Nino put his arm under mine. "Let's go."

11

The climb wasn't too hard. We crossed a number of small vineyards and groves of oranges, olives, and lemons.

"Don't touch anything!" Nino called out as we approached a German ammunition dump about fifty feet in diameter. It was piled with rifles, howitzers, and machine guns. "Don't go near there. It's surrounded with mines. When the Germans retreated, they left that pile for us as a little surprise. Come, I'll show you another dump where you can pick souvenirs to your heart's content."

Nino led us up the next hill to an abandoned German army camp for about twenty soldiers. It was evident that the Germans had fled hurriedly.

"I'm afraid we've picked the camp bare except for those." Nino pointed to a pile of letters and photographs.

None of us read German. We looked at photographs of women and some of German soldiers in souvenir poses. I felt again the same embarrassment, the same anger, disgust, and fear, as I felt when I had seen the Nazi planes over the harbor. I wondered if I'd ever see the enemy in the flesh, face to face.

"Nino, do you know what caused the Germans to run so all of a sudden?"

"Yes — us kids. My friends and I surrounded them one night. They thought we were a hundred — we were only twenty-five. Come on, Grandma is waiting. Take what you want and let's go." We took nothing.

As we walked, Nino and I talked about his role in the area. "Somebody has to keep order." He stopped walking. "When the Germans were here, it was bad for us — very little food — and toward the end they left us to starve. Somebody had to find food for the villages. I and my friends found the food. Now the Germans are gone, and the Americans are too busy to worry about small villages. They give us dehydrated soup and a little rice, and my friends and I run things for the benefit of everyone — more or less." He smiled and continued walking.

"What about the antifascists? Aren't they giving any leadership?"

"They are our enemies."

"Do you know that your uncle Mike is an antifascist?"

"Yes, I have heard that."

"What will you and your friends do when Mike comes back to Altofonte?"

"Why — we will become antifascists."

Nino raced ahead, up the last quarter-mile to Altofonte. As we entered the village's narrow, cobbled main street leading to the square, we saw a tiny figure dressed in black, surrounded by a crowd of silent onlookers. Mike Sala's mother was waiting for us.

I could hardly believe it. That crazy Mike — we were actually here!

As I approached Mike's mother, she opened her arms to me, and we embraced. I looked down at the frail, white-haired lady. "Signora, Michele sends this kiss."

"My son, my son." We held each other tightly as she wept silently.

"He's coming, Signora. He's coming soon." I patted her back and looked around at the villagers who had come to see the miracle, the deliverance of a son's kiss across five thousand miles of dangerous waters, through four submarine battles and an invasion of two hundred thousand men.

"From 11th Street and Broadway in New York City, straight to the village of Altofonte near Palermo!" Cisco bent down to kiss Mike's mother.

"Now this is what I call special delivery!" Woody kissed the little lady soundly on both cheeks as the crowd shouted bravos.

For the rest of the day we were treated like kings and feasted with dehydrated soup, boiled rice, figs, and strong red wine. In her joy Mike's mother and Nino invited the entire Sala clan to join the sumptuous banquet, consuming more than a month's rations, "in honor of Michele's miraculous messengers."

There was no shortage of guitars in Altofonte. We borrowed three and put on a real hootenanny. Woody's hoedowns alternated with Sicilian tarantellas until well after sunset.

"It's time to go, Nino." I put down my guitar. "We've got to get to our ship before curfew."

Nino's car had not returned from Corleone, but he assured us that he would get us to Palermo in time. He led us to an ancient three-ton open truck. "The motor is not very strong," Nino said with a smile, "but it is downhill all the way."

"How are the brakes?"

"Half and half. Climb up." Nino laughed. "I am sitting with the driver."

A crowd of men and women had gathered, pleading with Nino to take them to Palermo, where they might find work. Nino told them I was the truck's commander. It was impossible to refuse them.

"All right, but just ten." I was thinking of the half-and-half brakes. In an instant there were forty people packed standing on the rickety truck, and we roared away.

"Slow down! Slow down!" I shouted to the driver as we came to the first curve. The truck's wooden railing nearly gave way as the crowd of passengers swayed against it. "Slow down! Slow down!" I pounded on the cab's roof as we approached another curve. "Slow down!" We braced ourselves to keep from smashing through the rails.

"Mother of God help us!" a woman called out as we came to the next turn.

"What the hell's wrong with that crazy driver?" Cisco shouted.

"Brakes! Too big a load!" I shouted as more women began to pray and one woman began to cry. The men were grimly silent.

The road rose occasionally, slowing us down just enough to keep us from hurtling over the side of the mountain.

"Only ten minutes!" Nino shouted up at us.

"Mother of God!" the women shrieked as we screeched and teetered around another curve.

"C'è la luna mezzo mare!" Cisco sang out at the top of his voice. It was a Sicilian naughty song. Several men joined him on the next line, and several more joined in as we hit the next curve.

"Saint Anthony save us!" the women screamed.

"Iddo va iddo vena . . ." Woody and I joined in as loudly as we could, urging the women to join us. After a couple of more hysterical curves, some of the women began singing with us, and by the time we rolled into Palermo, the whole truckload of wild-eyed Sicilians was shouting the dirty sex song. The military police we passed were too astonished to do anything about it. When the truck finally stopped, the passengers jumped off and disappeared.

Nino got us back to the dock gates in time for curfew. He embraced each of us. "Send word if you need anything, anything at all." We waved to him as the Altofonte Express roared off.

"You crazy bastard." I turned to Cisco. "Why did you sing that dirty song?"

"It's the only Italian song I know."

The next day I finally came face to face with the enemy, but it was not the way I imagined it would be. In my fantasy I would first, somehow, render him helpless, then I would spit in his Nazi face, or smash my fist into his nose, or hit him in the solar plexus, forcing him to bow to me in pain, after which I would stun him with a passionate speech about Nazism that would finally cause him to turn his eyes away in shame. That was my fantasy. In reality I had nothing to do with disarming him. The German soldier standing before me was one of five hundred prisoners of war about to board the ship next to ours that would take him from Palermo to the United States, and instead of turning his eyes away in shame, he stared back at me contemptuously, disdainfully allowing me to study him.

He wore the SS insignia proudly proclaiming him to be a member of Hitler's elite corps. Bronzed, blond, blue-eyed, tall, handsome — he could have been Cisco's brother. The resemblance made the moment all the more bitter. How could a human being become a Nazi SS man? How could he? I searched his eyes. No, my fellow human being, still staring at me, was not insane. My fellow human being was a selfish, calloused, disciplined murderer. *I* turned my eyes away in shame.

Later I looked for Italian prisoners of war. Hundreds of thousands had surrendered immediately after the invasion, and I had heard that a battalion from Foggia, my parents' province, was assigned to the Palermo docks. I found several men from Lucera, my father's hometown, and after effusive greetings and the passing around of cigarettes, they told me about my family.

"Your grandfather was a great lawyer and a great man."

"His funeral was the biggest one we ever saw."

"He could have been knighted, but he refused it."

"Do you know why he refused it?" I knew why, but I wanted to see if they knew.

"Yes, he wouldn't accept the knighthood from Mussolini."

"Then why was his funeral so big? Were there that many antifascists in Lucera?"

"No, but we all respected your grandfather."

As I walked back to my ship, I thought about my grandfather's funeral and I was happy that I was named for him.

Palermo's unbearable heat made it impossible for us to acquaint ourselves with whatever charm that pathetic city might have held for us. But even if it had been cool, the poverty and the besieging kids made it easier for us to stay aboard. The problem with staying aboard was boredom. The three of us fought it as best we could, with poker, reading, writing, singing, and more experiments in mental telepathy. One day when we couldn't stand the ship anymore, we decided to visit a U.S. army camp outside of Palermo. At least we'd see a movie.

We got a lift on one of the army trucks unloading our ship. The heat in the truck's cab was over a hundred. It was so bad we had to close the windows to keep out the hot air.

At the camp we identified ourselves to the sentry, and he let us in, but he warned us that everybody was sleeping because it was too hot to work in the middle of the day. It was an eerie thing to see an entire camp — ten thousand men — sound asleep, nothing stirring, in the middle of the day. Yet we had to wake somebody. We couldn't wait three hours in that heat, and we had come too far to turn around and go home.

The camp was divided into two sections — I chose the left section. Each section was divided into rows of streets containing fifty Quonset huts on one side and fifty on the other. I chose one of the streets, and we walked between the two rows of huts. I chose the row on the left and stopped in front of one of the huts. I opened the screen door. Everybody was sleeping. There were twenty-five beds on one side and twenty-five on the other. I chose the beds on the left. Each bed was covered with mosquito netting. I stopped in front of a bed, pushed the netting aside, and gently shook the sleeping soldier.

The soldier opened his eyes sleepily, looked at me, and said, "What the hell do you want, Enzo?" It was Tommy Pugliese, an old neighborhood buddy, calling me by my neighborhood name.

I didn't answer him because I was stunned. When Tommy realized that he wasn't dreaming, he leaped from his bed shouting, "It's Enzo! It's Enzo!"

The whole hut woke up, and everybody thought Tommy had gone crazy from the heat, until I was introduced.

Nobody went back to sleep. Everybody insisted on celebrating the little miracle with can after can of ice-cold beer and all kinds of good chow, with Tommy clutching my arm during the whole proceeding until nighttime, when, after the movie, he got a lift for us and we said goodbye.

In the truck I said to Cisco, "You see what I mean by other dimensions we know nothing about? Didn't I go straight to Tommy like a homing pigeon? Did you ever see such mental telepathy?"

"Mental telepathy my ass. It was just plain luck." He lowered his head and promptly fell asleep.

"What do you say, Woody?"

Woody said nothing.

■

It took three weeks to unload our cargo. During that time the Germans didn't bomb the port once; the Allies took all of Sicily; the Red Army drove the Nazis back toward the German border; Giovanni One Ear drove half the crew to his noble signorine; half of that half got the clap; half of that half recovered; Woody wrote a hundred pages of his book, plus fourteen songs; Cisco finished Darwin; and I finally mastered the F chord.

As soon as the last bomb was removed from our holds, we moved out to the middle of the bay to wait for sailing orders. Three weeks later we were still there. During that time the Italian government surrendered to the Allies; the Red Army drove the Nazis closer to Germany; Giovanni drove the other half of the crew to the two signorine; half of that half got the clap; half of that half recovered; Woody wrote another hundred pages of his book, plus sixteen songs; Cisco reread *Martin Eden*, and I went nearly crazy thinking of Gabrielle and wondering when the hell we were going home.

On the twenty-first day of our anchorage, we got our orders to sail — to North Africa. That evening we took on passengers, forty American military police. Destination: Tunis, seventy miles across the Mediterranean at its narrowest point. At ten o'clock we lifted anchor and began moving toward the open sea, alone, without any naval escort.

"Alone?" One of the soldiers turned to me. "How can they send us alone? I can't even swim!"

"Don't worry, we'll be there by tomorrow morning."

To Cisco I murmured, "We should only live so long."

"What's the weather like?" Cisco sniffed the air.

"Perfect — for submarines," I muttered.

12

The sea was a flat black mirror reflecting the biggest moon I'd ever seen. We were a well-lit sitting duck.

"Well, Reb Longhi, what did you think of the land of your ancestors?" Woody asked.

What I thought was: good-bye heat, dust, diesel-oil fumes, noble signorine, ten-year-old pimps, eight-year-old whores, and dead sons on the Russian front, good-bye to the stupidest campaign and the dumbest waste of American lives ever thought of in all the combined history of the Allies. But all that was too much to say. What I said was, "Fuck you, Guthrie."

"What are you guys doing?" Cisco called to some soldiers who were spreading their blankets on a hatch cover's canvas.

"Tell you the truth, sailor," one of them answered. "We're too scared to sleep below deck."

"I can understand that," Cisco said, "but if we catch a torpedo in that hold, the air pressure has no place to go but up. It'll blow the hatch covers and you halfway up to heaven."

"Okay, sailor, thanks — we'll sleep on the deck."

After we warned the soldiers on the other hatches, we turned in.

I couldn't sleep. I kept seeing our ship cutting through the glassy sea, all alone, spotlighted by the big moon, making us the perfect target. The U-boat wouldn't even bother to submerge. But at least we were rid of our cargo. If we were hit now, I wouldn't die ignominiously, without knowing it — unless we caught a torpedo directly under our cabin. As I fell asleep, I thought: Dear Supreme Intelligence, which for lack of a better name Einstein calls God, if you are at all interested in me, please don't let me die without at least hearing the explosion.

Ten minutes after falling asleep, my prayer was answered. BOOOMM! The torpedo's explosion blasted me out of my unconsciousness. *My God, we're hit!* Tremendously hit! The blast expanding inside my brain is going to blow my head apart! The air is squashing me! I can't breathe! I can't see! It's so black — I'm so cold — this is my last second! Why am I standing? Because the ship is on its side — she's teetering on her side. Then the blast went through my skull, and the air pressure suddenly released me as the ship threw herself backward and flung herself from side to side, violently, agonizingly, her death throes accompanied by the crash of steel against steel from her torn innards, the crash of pots, pans, of everything smashing against everything else from side to side, until the ship lay still. Then men began shouting. In the pitch dark I couldn't tell if Cisco and Woody were dead. I jumped from my bunk and collided with both of them.

"Hold onto me!" Cisco shouted as he found the door and led us through the confusion of the blacked-out alleyway, out onto the afterdeck. Men shouted as they dashed to the lifeboats. The three of us made for the life raft and looked up at the boat deck for the captain's signal to abandon ship. The ship's horn gave four forlorn-sounding blasts.

"Is that it?" I asked Cisco.

"No, that means we've been hit."

"But there's nobody to hear us."

"It's standard procedure."

From the boat deck, a red rocket shot high above us.

"And nobody to see us. Look!" I pointed to the bow. "We're sinking up forward!" The moonlight made everything almost as clear as day.

"Christ, we can go down in a minute!" somebody cried out.

"Swing those boats out! Swing them out!" the second mate shouted.

"Shall we let the rafts go?" somebody shouted to the mate.

"No! Wait for abandon-ship order!"

"It may be too late!" somebody shouted. "We may be sucked down with the ship."

"Take it easy!" the mate shouted back. "The captain's checking the damage."

"It's the number-three hold!" Some black-gang men stumbled onto the deck. They were covered in oil. "We caught it in number-three hold! She's filling up with oil and seawater!"

"Anybody hurt?"

"No, we all got out!"

"Two of my men are gone!" an army sergeant cried out. "They were sleeping on the hatch covers!" He turned to Cisco. "I told them to listen to you."

"What year is this?" a gun-crew kid asked me.

"What do you mean, what year?"

"What year is it? Jesus, I can't remember what year this is!"

"Come on kid, take it easy. It's 1943, September 13 — our lucky day. Thank God we got rid of our cargo."

"Hey, Cisco!" a crew man on the boat deck shouted down gleefully. "Torpedo cancels all poker debts!"

"Hell, no!" Cisco shouted back. "Ship's got to sink!"

"Then let the motherfucker sink!" he called back.

"Float, baby, float!" the winners began shouting.

"Sink, you bastard, sink!" most of the losers shouted back.

Woody and I, both losers, kept our mouths shut as the shouting increased.

"You goddamned idiots!" The bosun silenced everybody. "You're all hysterical. The submarine that got us is still out there. They'll stay out of our range until we get into the lifeboats, then they'll machine-gun us. Now, you losers still want the ship to sink?"

The ship shuddered, and her bow sank deeper.

"God bless the Red Army!" Woody called out.

Newington swung and hit Woody on the nose. Cisco and I jumped on Newington.

"What did you do that for?" Woody held his nose.

"Why did you ask God to bless those atheist communist bastards?"

"Because those atheist communist bastards are chewing up the Nazi army, and if I get machine-gunned, at least I'll die knowin' that the Red Army is going to finish the job for us."

"Man the guns," the lieutenant commander called down from the boat deck, "and watch for the submarine!" The navy kids jumped to their stations.

"You men stand by the lifeboats," the second mate called, "and if the captain orders abandon ship, you better move fast! Bosun, take three men and search for casualties."

The ship gave another shudder, and the bow dropped lower.

"I've got to get my guitar anyway." Cisco stepped toward Bosun. "I'll go with you."

"Me, too." Woody went to the bosun.

I had no choice. "Okay, but let's do it fast. Let's go!"

Bosun turned on his flashlight and led the way down the black alleyway. We banged doors open. "Anybody here?" we shouted, louder than was necessary. Bosun led us to the ladder going down to the 'tween deck of number-three hold. The acrid smell of explosives rose out of the blackness below. Bosun flashed the light around. The 'tween deck was gone, blown up right through the hatch covers. We could see the moonlit sky above us. The center of the hold was filled with oil. We stayed close to the sides, because the steel deck was very slippery. "Anybody here?" we shouted.

Bosun flashed his light around. "God knows what's holding this ship together. Let's get out of here."

"Wait!" Cisco froze. "I hear something."

"Oh God — oh God — oh God —" The moaning came from the pool of oil.

Bosun flashed his light around. "There he is."

A black figure, half-submerged, clung to the hold's ladder. The four of us held hands as Bosun edged out toward the man. He grabbed the man's wrist, but his hand slipped. Bosun quickly pulled off his shirt, wrapped it around his hand, grabbed the man's wrist, and pulled him up. The man's face was covered with oil. Blood was coming from his nose and ears. He was incoherent. His oil-soaked shirt was army. We carried him by his arms and legs.

"He's got to be one of those two soldiers who slept on the hatch covers," Cisco said. "His buddy must have been blown overboard, and this guy fell back into the hold."

When we got the soldier topside, the purser took over from us. I looked up at the sky. How wonderful it was to be in the open again. "What's been happening?" I asked Chips, as though we'd been gone for three weeks instead of three minutes.

"Nothin', except that the bow is a little lower."

"Shit!" Cisco shook his head. "We forgot the goddamned guitars!"

This time we were gone only twenty seconds.

"What fakking good are those, aah, instruments gonna do you?" Bananas asked. "If we take to the boats, the motherfakking Nazis are going to machine-gun us. If we don't take to the boats, we drown when the ship goes down. So what fakking good are those guitars?"

"A little music may help to soothe you in your last few moments, Old Banana Peel." Woody started picking out a talking blues:

> Down in the henhouse on my knees,
> Thought I heard a chicken sneeze.
> Nothin but a rooster sayin' his prayers,
> Thankin' God for the hens upstairs —
> high-protein feed —
> Jamaican rum — the Red Army — an' things like that.

"All right, men!" the first mate called from the boat deck. "Captain Sandburg thinks we might be able to make it to port. Stand by the lifeboats and keep your fingers crossed." We held our breath as the engine started and the ship began to move slowly, feeling the weight of the sea against its ripped-open hull, slowly picking up speed. It was two o'clock. The African coast was at least six hours away.

"Can anybody see the submarine?" somebody called out.

"The light's not good enough."

"You think it's following us?"

"It's following us all right."

"Why don't they hit us again?"

"Why waste a torpedo? You heard the bosun; they think we're done for. They're just waiting for us to get into the lifeboats."

"What if we don't sink?"

"They'll put another torpedo into us at the last minute."

Cisco picked up his guitar and began to sing about a drunken cowboy tying a knot in the devil's tail. A silence fell over all of us. There was nothing to say or do except wait and listen to Cisco's singing. He sang other songs — mostly cowboy ballads — his voice blending with the soft air and the moonglow. The night was as beautiful as we were ludicrous, sitting around in our underwear waiting for the German shark to finish us.

Four hours later the sun rose out of the sea, and the rust-colored coast of Tunisia appeared before us. Our bow was way down, but it looked like we were going to make port unless the U-boat put another torpedo into us. As the sun rose higher, we saw that the U-boat had abandoned us to our fate.

"We're gonna make it! We're gonna make it!" The men came alive. "Hey, we're gonna make it!"

The ship's horn gave three joyous blasts. "What's that for?" I asked Cisco.

"That's the captain giving three cheers for the *Willy B.*"

"Why didn't the Germans hit us again?"

"Probably ran out of torpedoes."

There were four more blasts of the ship's horn and two red rockets fired from the bridge, only this time there was somebody to see and hear the ship's signal that she was dying and might not reach port. A tugboat came racing out to stand by. We lowered the wounded, unconscious soldier down to the tug. The tug then sent up a pilot, who guided us to a shallow spot in the Lake of Tunis where our tired ship slowly began to settle onto the lake's sandy bottom.

A diver was sent down to inspect our damage. When Captain Sand-burg got the report, he told the first mate that he would have abandoned ship and taken his chances with the Germans if he had known that the hole in our side was twenty feet in diameter.

We stayed aboard for a couple of days until arrangements could be made to repatriate us. When it was time to leave the *Willy B.*, it was like saying good-bye to a dead friend.

The trip home was a horror, twenty-eight days of franks and beans on a non-N.M.U. Liberty ship. We had storms all the way, dirty blankets on the floor of the 'tween deck for beds, and a union-hating chief steward. But that evil ship did take us home.

When we were within sight of Coney Island, Woody waved and shouted, "I'm a'comin' Momma Marjorie! I'm a'comin' Missie Stack-abones!"

As our convoy filed through the narrows and into New York Bay, we were saluted by a brass band on a destroyer. The welcome was confirmation that we had, indeed, been to war. War! We had actually been to war!

We tied up at a downtown dock. Crowds of well-fed, well-dressed people filled the sidewalks, taxis blared, and buses moved down the street. Nobody looked like they had ever heard of a general-quarters alarm.

The first thing we did was phone our girls; then I called Mom and Mike Sala. After that we went to the shipping office to get paid off.

The trip had taken four months — it seemed four years — and we got about eight hundred dollars. My gambling debt of two hundred dollars was canceled because, after all, the *Willy B.* did sink.

We said good-bye to our shipmates. It was amazing that our crew had suffered no casualties apart from a few cases of clap, and nothing would have happened to the two soldiers if they had taken our advice. We never found out whether the wounded one died.

We signed the discharge papers, and my first trip to sea was officially ended. Now it was time for the three of us to go our separate ways. Each of us waited for the other to say something.

"Now that you know what it's like to ship out," Cisco said to me, "I wouldn't blame you if you went into the army."

"No, I'm shipping out again when my thirty-day shore leave is up."

"I hope we have better luck next time." Cisco said.

Leave it to Cisco. Without either of us having to go through the embarrassment of asking the other, he just took it for granted that we'd make the next trip together.

"What about you, Woody?" I asked. "You've got a family. You've paid your dues to this war. You don't have to ship out again, right?"

"Wrong. Job's not finished yet. Furthermore, t'ain't easy to build a good trio." He slung his seabag over his shoulder, straightened the guitar on his other shoulder, and picked up his fiddle case, his mandolin case, and his stack of books. "Call me tomorrow," he said as he walked away.

"I'm glad you're coming too, you crazy bastard," I called after him, "because to tell you the truth, I don't think we'd of made it without the wind machine!"

Cisco went to find Bina, and I went to meet Gabrielle.

The *The* **FLOY-FLOY**

13

My month-long leave was over in a flash. Although Gabrielle and I had been married for three weeks, it felt like three days, and I couldn't bear to part from her. The pain of my leaving her was made worse by my guilt. Shouldn't we have postponed our marriage until the end of the war? What if I were killed or came home a cripple? And to make matters sadder, Christmas was approaching. My leave would be over on December 2. I had only a few days left.

I also felt guilty because Cisco and Woody, too, would miss Christmas at home. Since they were exempt from service, they could have shipped out after Christmas, but they insisted on coming with me. I tried to talk them out of it. I even talked with Marjorie and Bina.

"It's no use, Jim. That's the way Woody is," Marjorie said as she dressed little Cathy Stackabones. "Even though he doesn't have to go, he wants to fight this war according to the rules. And furthermore, he's grown very fond of you. Don't worry about Christmas. Miss Stackabones and I are going to be okay." Beautiful, wise Marjorie, holding Miss Stackabones on her bony dancer's hip, smiled up at me with her crinkly eyes. "Don't worry."

Bina said more or less the same thing about Cisco, although she put it a little differently. "That blind son of a bitch is going to get himself killed one of these days, just like his brother." The tears in her blue eyes accentuated her blonde beauty. "He's a nut about this war, God bless him, and even though the holidays are coming, he insists on shipping out with his two buddies. So do me a favor will you? Find a way to stretch your leave, like break a leg or something!"

The next day I went to Ferdinand Smith's office to see what he could do for me. He knew about my being torpedoed and listened sympathetically to my complaint about my ears, which in fact had been affected by the torpedo's explosion. I asked him what my chances were for a thirty-day extension of leave.

"Brother Longhi, it's too bad you waited so long to make a complaint. The authorities'll pay no attention to your request, and furthermore, the opposition heard all about how you and your buddies put down that Newington crowd on the *Travis*. Man, they'll be happy to turn you over to the army if you overstay your leave by one second."

I took my misery to the crowded bar across the street from the union, where the drinks were twenty-five cents.

"Hey, Jimbo!" The bosun from the *Travis* greeted me with open arms. "Have a drink with us! Have a drink!" He turned to his drinking companion, a villainous-looking, fiftyish burly seaman with a red-blotched, unshaven face. "Kel, this is Jim, one of the Woody Guthrie trio I was telling you about!"

"Ah yes, yes indeed, it's a pleasure to meet with a fellow worshiper of the muse of music!" His breath staggered me; another whiff would have made me drunk. "I too am an aficionado of the guitar." His nose practically glowed as he watched Bosun pour enormous whiskies. "And so, gentlemen, I raise my glass to the gods of the guitar, Segovia, Django, Eddie Condon, and Josh White!" When he downed the drink in one gulp, I realized that he was the perfect stand-in for W. C. Fields.

Bosun put his arm around me. "Jimbo, I want you to meet Courtroom Kelly!"

"Courtroom Kelly?" I stared in disbelief. "Are you really Courtroom Kelly?" I could hardly believe that I was in his exalted presence.

"At your service."

"Courtroom! Courtroom Kelly!" I pumped his hand as I studied every feature of his bloated face. "I sure am honored to meet you!"

Talk about living legends! To the men of the sea, this simple seaman was Clarence Darrow, Robin Hood, and Paul Bunyan all in one, the supreme defender of the hard-won rights of the maritime proletariat, the genius who had outwitted the most Machiavellian masters of the seven seas, the savant who knew the letter of the sea law a hundred times better than those who wrote it. Courtroom was the sea law's equivalent of Oliver Wendell Holmes and Benjamin Cardozo, the invincible advocate who turned every unfair employer's clause into a double-edged sword of justice. No lawyer ever had a more glorious career: undefeated after thirty-five years of going to sea, battling against the toughest, shrewdest captains of his time without even once being fined or punished. It was said that the greatest ambition of every sea captain in the American Merchant Marine was not to become commander of the largest ship afloat but to become the first captain to ever "get" Aloysius Courtroom Kelly.

"Please, Courtroom, let me buy you a drink! You too, Bosun!"

"Why, thank you, Brother Jim," Courtroom said, beaming.

"Jim's a student of the law too." Bosun patted my back.

"Yes, and I study your cases as closely as I do those in Blackstone." I lifted my glass to Courtroom.

"I drink to charming exaggeration." Courtroom gulped my offered drink.

"Courtroom, now that I've got you here in the flesh, would you mind talking about the case of the carved initials?" The case of the carved initials — a recent case — was the first and only time that Courtroom was logged (fined). The waterfronts of America shook with the news. Courtroom had carved his initials on the ship's steering wheel, and the captain had caught him in delicto flagrante. Since he was caught red-handed, Courtroom pleaded nolo contendere; that is, he took the rap without any argument. The captain, delirious with joy, flung the book at him in the name of all his fellow captains who had been frustrated to near apoplexy by this monster master of legal perversion. He logged Courtroom the most the law allows — the value of the wheel, which was one hundred dollars.

The shocking news of Courtroom's downfall spread to every port and preceded the ship's arrival in New York. Courtroom said nothing to the jeerers who torment every defeated champion, nor did he acknowledge the condolences from his saddened friends.

In a few days his ship was reloaded and ready to join her convoy. Two hours before sailing time, two federal officers came on board and served the captain with papers demanding the repossession of the steering wheel. The demander was Courtroom; the law says that if a man is logged the value of a defaced article, the defaced article becomes his.

The ship couldn't sail without the wheel, and there was no time to replace it. After long and furious telephone consultation with the ship company's lawyers, the shipowners decided to purchase the wheel from Courtroom for one hundred dollars. Courtroom's price was five hundred, but he settled for four hundred because it was wartime.

It was rumored that the captain was taken to a hospital and that the ship sailed without him.

"Courtroom, may I ask you one question about the case."

"Proceed, Counselor."

"When you carved your initials on that wheel, did you know how it was going to turn out?"

"Objection, your honor! The question is in violation of the Fifth Amendment of the Constitution of the United States and to the republic for which it stands, one nation, indivisible, with liberty and —"

"Easy, Kel." Bosun grabbed Courtroom as the great man's knees began to sag. "I think we may have had one too many."

"Don't be ludicrous!" Courtroom straightened himself with fierce dignity. "I'm still a member of this bar in good standing! Proceed, Counselor."

We went on to discuss some other of his more famous cases, such as the one where he was accused of stealing a grand piano from a luxury liner. Courtroom's defense was that he had not broken in or done anything criminal like that. He had simply come on board with three white-overalled assistants and carried the piano to a waiting van without any of the ship's officers saying anything about it. He then took the piano to the union hall, where it was desperately needed for a wounded seamen's relief party to be held that night. When the shipowner heard Courtroom's defense, he contributed the piano to the seamen's relief fund.

In a similar incident Courtroom managed to obtain a flag mast from another luxury liner. It was rumored that the mast was the one atop our union building.

"Courtroom, have you any cases pending now?" I offered him another drink.

"As a matter of fact, yes. On my last trip I was torpedoed — shook up my nerves something fierce."

"I can imagine, but what can you do about it?"

"Well, to begin with, I'm thinking of suing Hitler." He downed his drink without blinking.

I decided to ask Courtroom for his advice on the problem of extending my shore leave before he became too drunk.

"Courtroom, may I consult you on a legal matter that involves me personally?"

"Certainly, and because you're a fellow counselor, I waive my fee, which is usually paid in Haig's Pinch. I'll just take a Black and White."

I told him about my recent marriage and Christmas and the opposition ready to turn me over to the army if I overstayed my leave for one second. What the hell was I going to do?

"Elementary, Counselor!"

"You mean you can get me a thirty-day extension?"

"Not only can I get you one, but I'll see that you get paid for it, too."

"Now you're kidding me."

"Not at all. Tomorrow morning you and I are enrolling in the Cook and Bakers School of the Maritime Commission on 13th Street. The government's pleading for men to learn to be second cooks and bakers. It's a one-month course, and they pay forty dollars a week, which I can use while I'm recuperating from trauma to my nerves."

"Wait a minute, Courtroom, there's a terrible flaw in your plan. I'm not going to ship out as a second cook and baker! That would be impossible! They can't teach us how to be a second cook and baker in only thirty days! We'd know nothing — the crew would throw us overboard!"

"Who said anything about shipping out as a second cook and baker? The regulation only talks about training us. There's nothing in the law that says we're compelled to ship out as second cooks and bakers. So I take it that as of tomorrow morning, you and I are going to be classmates."

I kissed Courtroom on both cheeks and ordered a whole bottle of Haig's Pinch.

That night the three of us and the girls celebrated our reprieve with a party in the furnished studio Gabrielle and I had rented on 70th Street near Riverside Drive. Woody and Cisco — well oiled with Myers's Rum — were in great form, and the party would have gone on till late, but I had to get up early to enroll at my new alma mater.

The Cook and Bakers School was across the street from St. Vincent's hospital. I should have known that was a bad omen, but I promptly put it out of my mind; I was not superstitious. The school looked like a grim Victorian prison — another bad omen — but that bad thought was eclipsed by the sight of Courtroom's beaming grin. He had just fallen out of a taxi that had dumped him and five boozy buddies onto the sidewalk. They were unshaven, unkempt, and semiconscious. It was obvious that they had been on an all-night fling before the commencement of their new school term.

"Top o' the mornin' to you, old classmate!" he sang out to me. "Meet my fraternity brothers!" He waved toward the five stumblebums. Then, his arm still extended, he called out, "All right, brothers, let's hear it for Jimbo!" The five hoarse boozers, led by Courtroom, shocked and frightened the passersby as they sang:

Boola, boo-la
Boola, boo-la
We'll make some moola
As we go to schoo-la!

"What the hell was that?" I asked Courtroom.

"Our fraternity song. Last night we founded the first fraternity of the Cook and Bakers School of the United States Maritime Service — we named it Eta Beta Pi. Come along, brothers!"

Courtroom swept through the entrance door, followed by the six of us, down the corridor and into the registrar's office, where we were confronted by a startled Coast Guard lieutenant who jumped up saying, "I'm afraid you men have made a mistake. St. Vincent's hospital is across the street."

"It's not St. Vincent's we're looking for, my good man. My companions and I are devotees of Escoffier and Brillat-Savarin, and we have come in answer to your appeal for some stout-hearted fellows to follow in the footsteps of those culinary kings."

The lieutenant stared at Courtroom in disbelief. "You mean you want to enroll in the cooker and baker's course?"

"Yes."

"Are you guys kidding?" The lieutenant glared at the bedraggled boozers. "This is the Merchant Marine, not the Bowery Mission!"

"Sir." Courtroom clapped his eyes on the lieutenant. "We are licensed members of the United States Merchant Service, and we are ready to take up your offer to train us as cooks and bakers. Your duty is to enroll us. Do your duty!"

The lieutenant glared, gritted his teeth, and turned red. Finally he shoved some forms at Courtroom and growled, "Fill these!"

"Yesss Sir!"

We filled in the forms under the lieutenant's silent stare. Courtroom handed his in first. The lieutenant picked it up. "Aloysius C. Kelly," he read disdainfully. "What's the *C* for? Cookie?"

"No," Courtroom answered calmly, "the *C* is for Courtroom."

"Courtroom? You're — you're not Courtroom Kelly?"

"The same, sir."

"Oh, my God!" the lieutenant dropped the form and exited hurriedly.

He came back with a lieutenant commander. "Mister Kelly," the lieutenant commander began, looking as distraught as his junior was, "let's get one thing straight. We're not going to stand for any trouble. Classes start at eight and end at four, and you're to be clean and tidy at all times. Now, you either toe the line or else! Are there any questions?"

"Yes," Courtroom answered, "when is payday?"

Without a word the lieutenant commander turned us over to a man in a white uniform who led us into a big locker room. We were each given a white apron and white jacket. Courtroom tied his apron around his great beerbelly and put on his jacket. Then, with a magician's grand flourish, he pulled a tall chef's hat out of the air. With the hat tilted like a streamlined smokestack and his belly protruding like a bow, I couldn't help crying out, "Courtroom, you are grander than the *Queen Mary!*"

"Well then, we're off!" Courtroom broke into his hoarse, howling laugh, stamping his foot, holding his belly with one hand and his hat with the other. "We're off on the best deal I ever heard of: forty bucks a week, all the chow you can eat — and McSorley's Saloon not a furlong away!"

Actually there was no food for us to eat. In fact there was hardly any food in the school. Because of the general wartime food shortage, our education was going to be mostly theoretical. Except for a few items that our teachers used for demonstration purposes and some baking products, food in that school was an abstract term.

"The gall of those Washington politicians is beyond belief!" Courtroom bellowed when he heard about the "no-chow" situation. "But that only confirms their pompous presumption — imagine thinking that they can turn out a ship's second cook and baker in four weeks."

A Liberty ship has one cook and one second cook. The second cook does the breakfast and all the baking. A ship's personality is molded by those two men more than by anybody else. A good-feeding ship is a happy ship. She smells clean. Her galley is spotless, her messrooms shine, and the men take their places at table well before the chow bell sounds.

Variety is one of the necessary characteristics of a good feeder. A good cook has to have a hundred recipes for beef, pork, veal, lamb, fowl, fish, and all the organ meats. A second cook and baker, which is what we were supposed to be by the end of our four-week course, has to be just as versatile. In addition to making breakfast, which includes porridges, flapjacks, and twenty ways to make eggs, he has to do all the baking, beginning with good bread. The best dinner is spoiled if the bread is bad.

Then, after baking forty loaves of bread each day, he has to turn out good rolls of various kinds, biscuits, scones, toasts, puddings, and pies, plus a wide variety of cakes and cookies.

After dinner the tables on a good feeder are quickly cleared and the messrooms become living rooms. The men settle down to checkers, chess, cards, or letter writing, and at the end of a cold watch a man can always come in for a good cup of coffee and something to go with it. A good feeder is a good ship. A bad feeder is a prison.

The menus of a bad feeder have no variety. Day after day it's greasy pork chops, smelly meatloaf, and tough swiss steak. Even the best beef stew becomes poison if it is served more than twice a week. Bad food and monotony breed misery. The men come in late for their meals, half the food is left untouched. and there is always one joker who concocts "goo plates" — a messy combination of every dish on the table, covered with milk, mustard, soggy apple pie, and vinegar, all churned together and shoved under the messman's nose, with instructions to dump it on the cook's head. The tables and decks are slopped over with uneaten food, and the messman needs an extra hour to clean up before the men can start their social activities. Tempers are short, letters go unwritten, and the crew's anger is lumped into a ball of hatred for the cook. No cook or baker on a bad feeder can turn his back on the crew, for fear of getting hit with a plate of hash or a loaf of water-soaked bread.

When the food is very bad, it is not uncommon for the crew to invoke the dreaded "Pee Call" against the offender. This torture is simple: the victim is repeatedly wakened from his sleep by solicitous inquiries regarding the condition of his bladder. No matter where the victim hides, be it the chain locker or the crow's nest, the hunters find him and wake him with the question, "Cookie, dontcha have to pee?" A bad cook or baker has no business going to sea.

Our laughter over Courtroom's remarks about the government's presumption was especially loud because we knew that not one of us experienced seamen would be stupid enough to ship out as a cook or baker after only four weeks' training.

Courtroom tightened the apron string around his belly, adjusted his tall cap, and called out, "Let the comedy begin!"

The students were divided into groups of fifty. The course was divided into two weeks of baking, one week of cooking, and one week of butchering. Our group was assigned to Baking One. The big room had five long tables, with ten students to a table and one instructor. One wall of the room was lined with beautiful aluminum electric ovens of the most modern, commercial kind. At sea the stoves were old coal ovens whose temperatures varied with each roll of the ship. The instructor said that although a ship's baker would have to turn out forty loaves of bread a day, we students would be limited to making one or two loaves at a time, for reasons of economy. He assured us, however, that multiplying the recipes from one to forty would be easy. At the beginning of the week I started taking notes, but I soon gave up.

Baking Two was an art class. Two days were spent learning how to decorate birthday cakes with lovely rosettes and beautiful whipped-cream angels. Courtroom was very adept at this — he had once been a tattoo artist. In the next two days each of us took turns poking a stick at some doughnuts frying in a large kettle of boiling oil. On the last day we learned how to make striations in marble cake.

The third week was spent in cooking class. The work was all theoretical, except for the preparation of a salad, which I actually made by myself.

The last week was spent in the butchering class, where everything, of course, was theoretical. We learned from charts. Our teacher was Joe Cohen, the president of the butcher's union, a nice guy who donated his time to teach us his art. Because of his influence, he managed to bring a large piece of meat on the last day of the course as a farewell gift. We gathered around Joe like students in an operating theater as his knives, saws, and cleavers flew in a blur around the butcher's block. In less than fifteen minutes he produced his masterpiece, a crown roast. It was a beautiful thing to see. It consisted of a whole row of lamb rib chops shaped into a king's crown, its interior stuffed with a rolled roast topped with chopped meat. We broke into thunderous applause as Professor Cohen faced us with a graceful bow.

Our graduation ceremony took place the next day in the school auditorium. Neither the lieutenant commander nor the lieutenant were present. A young, immaculately uniformed ensign presided over the ceremony. His yeoman assistant sat near him at a table covered with a neat stack of rolled diplomas. When the class of two hundred was seated, the ensign began his speech. We listened with pretended enthusiasm. He spoke for a few minutes about the government's need for cooks and bakers and how "you men are the bellybone of the Merchant Marine."

The ensign seemed unaware that his joke received much more laughter than it should have, and when he concluded his speech with "no matter how tough it is to make a living, you men will always be in the dough!" he seemed very pleased with the exaggerated ovation we gave him.

One by one we filed onstage, where the ensign gave each of us a diploma, a handshake, and a check for our wages. When the last student received his diploma, we flung our hats into the air, just as they do at Annapolis. The gothic script of my diploma proclaimed me to be a second cook and baker in the Merchant Marine of the United States of America.

"Listen, Courtroom," I said as I gave him a farewell handshake, "by the Merchant Marine of the United States of America I'm a second cook and baker, and by that nice ensign I'm a second cook and baker, but by a second cook and baker am I a second cook and baker?"

"What are you worried about, Counselor — is there anything in the law which says you *have* to ship out as a second cook and baker?"

Thanks to Courtroom, Gabrielle and I had a wonderful Christmas and New Year. When it was time to ship out, I hurried to meet Cisco and Woody at the union hiring hall. Because I got there late, I paid little attention to the ambulance that was pulling away from the curb. Cisco and Woody had already spotted three steward jobs for us on a ship called the *William Floyd*.

The dispatcher was trying to sell a second cook and baker job on the same ship. "She's a great little ship on a short trip. I guarantee you she's only going to Hoboken and back. Now who's the lucky second cook and baker? Who's gonna . . ." The dispatcher was getting no response. "All right, you guys, we gotta fill this goddamned job. There's a war goin' on! Now let's go, who's gonna . . ."

"Why should I feel guilty?" I said to Cisco and Woody. "I'm not a second cook and baker. We didn't learn a thing at that school."

Cisco took out his shipping card. "Come on, let's take those three mess jobs."

Cisco and Woody turned in their cards to the dispatcher and got their job slips. I turned in my card. The dispatcher flung it back at me. "You can't ship out as a messman. Your card says second cook and baker."

"What are you talking about? I'm a messman." I tried to keep my calm. "I don't know the first fucking thing about cooking *or* baking."

"Then I would say you're up shit creek without a paddle, buddy, because as of this morning we've got new orders. A man has to ship out at his highest rating, and your highest rating, brother, is cook and baker."

A torpedo exploded in my brain. "Take it easy!" the alarm system in my head signaled. "You've been torpedoed before. Look around — what's the damage? What are your alternatives?"

The first thing I thought of was to blow up the Cook and Bakers School, but what good would that do me? Kill my wife? Ridiculous. What I needed was a lawyer! Courtroom Kelly! Courtroom got me into it; Courtroom would get me out of it! "Cisco! Woody! Have you seen Courtroom Kelly?"

"What are you shouting about?" Cisco asked.

"The dispatcher says I can only ship out as a second cook and baker! Please, have you seen Courtroom Kelly?"

"Take it easy. Yes, we saw him. He was just taken away in an ambulance."

"An ambulance! What for?"

"I don't know. He was arguing with the dispatcher about not wanting to ship out as a second cook and baker. Suddenly he collapsed — couldn't breathe. When they carried him out on a stretcher, he was babbling something about a flour allergy."

"Flour allergy, my ass!" I shouted. "That selfish son of a bitch! He figured out a way to save *his* ass and left me to the wolves. Left me to hang!"

"Well, calm down and figure a way out too. You can't blame Courtroom."

"Cisco's right," Woody added. "You couldn't both have collapsed from flour allergy. Let's try to figure a way for you to —"

"What's there to figure? I've got no choice but the army."

"Reb, we've got a pretty good trio going." Woody offered me a cigarette. "We're doing a good job entertaining the crews, keeping up morale and things like that. Now you can't give that up without some serious reflection."

"Okay, fine, sure, go ahead — let's reflect!" I lowered my head between my knees. Cisco put his hand on my shoulder. "Maybe you're exaggerating. The job may not be as hard as you —"

"Look," I said, raising my head, "I appreciate that you guys want me to ship out with you. I want to be with you, too, but if I ship out as a cook and baker, the crew'll lynch me!"

Woody and Cisco led me to the bar across the street.

14

"Well, let's see." Cisco stroked his chin. "Did you learn anything at school?"

"Yeah: how to make one loaf of bread — theoretically."

"Well, that's a start," Woody added. "Now if we can sorta build on that we —"

"How much practicing would you need to make bread?" Cisco took out a pencil and a piece of paper.

"At least a week. What the hell do I do in the meantime?"

"You feed 'em store-bought bread! We'll be in port a week. You buy what you need every day, then on the last day you buy a whole week's supply of bread and cakes. That gives you two weeks time to learn! And you can probably pay the chief cook to teach you. Let's figure out the minimum you need."

"You're crazy! We use forty loaves a day!"

"We'll cut 'em down to twenty, put on a campaign to save bread for starving children or something like that."

"Twenty times fourteen — I'll need to buy two hundred and eighty loaves of bread, and what about cakes and pies and cookies? It's crazy."

"It's not crazy; it's just a bit bizarre." Woody took out his wallet. "I can lend you twenty dollars."

"And I can lend you twenty-five. How much have you got?"

"All I've got is about twenty-five."

"Okay, go take the job. With seventy dollars worth of baked goods in the chill-box and your brains, you'll make it!"

Cisco and Woody escorted me to the dispatcher's window. "Go ahead," Cisco said, nudging me, "tell the man you want the job."

"Okay, I'll take that job." My voice was barely audible.

"What did you say?" The dispatcher leaned toward me.

"He said he'll take the job," Woody answered for me. I gave my union card to the dispatcher, but I felt as though I were surrendering my passport to life.

The *William Floyd* was a Liberty ship, an exact replica of the *William B. Travis*, including the smell of a good-feeding ship. All the worse for me. Woody tried to cheer me up, saying the ship talked to him, that she would be good to us, and that he was renaming her — from now on the *William Floyd* would be the *Floy-Floy*.

While Cisco and Woody looked for the chief steward, I entered the galley. It was immaculate. The stove was shiny black, the red-tiled deck glistened, the neatly hung pots gleamed, and a fresh white towel hung near the big bread-making trough.

"You new second cook?" A young, neatly dressed Chinese man stood smiling in the doorway, a suitcase in his hands.

"Yes — you the one that's signing off?"

"Yes, me stay home one month now." He put his bag down.

"She's a good-feeding ship, isn't she?"

"The best number one okay first class. I sign off because my wife have a new baby."

"You keep a beautiful galley."

"Number one, but you watchee big oven very much. No thermometer. You put hand in one, two, three, four, five — too hot, you pull hand out, put bread in. Understand?"

"Your English is perfectly clear, mate, but I don't know the first god-damned thing about baking."

"Oh-oh! You come from fuck-up Cook and Baker School?"

"You guessed it."

"Goodbye and good luck, Charlie." His picked up his bag.

"Wait a minute — wait! What's your name?"

"Murphy. My Chinese name too hard."

"Listen, Murphy, you can save my life. Do you live in Chinatown?"

"Yes, Mott Street."

"Murphy, please, I beg you, put down that suitcase and listen." I told him my story.

"Please, Murphy, only you can save me from being murdered by the crew. I'll pay you my week's wages if you come every day for two hours to teach me how to bake. It'll only be for a week. If you don't help me, Murph, I'm a dead man."

Murphy looked at my hands held before him in supplication. "Okay"

I wanted to hug him, but I didn't know how a Chinese man might feel about that. Instead I said, "You're a great good man."

"I go home now, but I be back tomorrow morning. You got enough pudding and bread for today. Don't touch anything in the galley. I see you tomorrow morning." I hastily pulled some dollar bills from my pocket, but Murphy pushed them aside. "Don't worry. I be here in the morning."

The chief steward was a heavy-set fifty-year-old Puerto Rican. He had a nice twinkle in his eyes and the sweet smell of rum all about him. Cisco introduced me as the new second cook and baker. The chief stared at me blankly for a couple of seconds and then blinked and said, "This is your first trip as cook and baker?"

"You can tell from just looking at me?" I was glad he knew. Now I could appeal to him for some instruction and some sympathy.

"One of them thirty-day wonders from 13th Street?"

"Yes, Chief, but Murphy's going to teach me for a couple of days and —"

"Santa Maria!" he mumbled.

"Don't worry, Chief," Cisco said. "In a week he should be able to —"

"In a week? Santa Maria . . ."

"Well then, maybe after we put out to sea you could teach me. I'd be willing to pay you and —"

"Me? I don't know anything about baking. If you fuck up, I wash my hands and turn you over to the fucking crew!"

I realized he was quite drunk and definitely not in the mood to face my problem.

"But if you do your job, we be buddies. So long, amigo." He shuffled down the alleyway, leaving a sweet cloud of rum behind him.

When I told Woody and Cisco about my deal with Murphy, they both assured me that I had it made, and then to distract me from my problem, they said it would be better if we grew beards. Cisco said beards would make it easier for us to pass into off-limit zones. The MPs were more likely to mistake us for natives, especially if we were in Arab countries.

That afternoon we were ordered into the officer's saloon for the signing of the ship's articles. Here was my last chance to back out, but with Murphy's coming instructions in mind, I gulped and signed. The captain waited for the last man to sign on before announcing that the ship was sailing to Philadelphia at midnight.

Good-bye, Murphy!

I examined my alternatives: desert ship at once and face whatever the consequences might be or try to get the chief cook to give me paid lessons. I could also use the bread-purchasing plan. I decide to continue in the service of the Merchant Marine.

The chief cook was an austere Jamaican of about sixty, tall and powerful, with pure black skin and a bearing that was altogether regal. Nobody called him Cookie; he was Mister Johnson. When I entered the galley, he studied me for a moment contemptuously and then turned away as though it pained him to have me in his presence. I had seen that look before on some of the black longshoremen, the Garveyites, who dreamed of going back to Africa.

"Mister Johnson, I need your help." I told him my story and made him my offer to pay for lessons. He listened wordlessly. "Will you do it, my friend?"

"No white man is a friend of mine. You mind your business and I mind mine — and every morning I come into this galley, I want to find it exactly the way I left it. Do you understand?"

"Okay, Mister Johnson." I backed away.

That left me with the bread-buying plan. But the bread-buying had to be done in Philadelphia. There was to be no shore leave in New York.

Although there was enough bread and dessert until the next day, the campaign to save bread for the starving children of the world began with the evening meal. The crew might as well get used to it as soon as possible. I issued two loaves of bread to each messroom instead of four, with strict instructions to the saloon messman. "Don't for Christ's sake overload the bread trays, okay?"

Cisco would ride shotgun on the regular-crew mess. Woody was again working as a dishwasher, but he was in an advantageous position to help me, because from his galley doorways he could oversee both the regular and the gun-crew messrooms. Periodically he would surprise the diners with a short speech delivered from the galley doorway, his arms covered with soapsuds up to his elbows. "Men, just think of them pore little starving children dying for the want of a single slice of bread!" He would then withdraw into the galley, only to emerge again two minutes later. "Just think — one slice of bread can keep an innocent little baby from starving to death!" Then he'd come back a minute later. "Every extra slice you eat, you're eating the life of a pore little child!"

His propaganda had a marked effect on the gun-crew kids, but in the regular-crew mess the bread was still going too fast. Despite Cisco's efforts, two loaves were gone before the meal was two-thirds over. I brought up half a loaf, slapped it onto the table, backed into a corner, and stood there glaring at the biggest eaters. Nobody said anything. They just gave me puzzled looks and went right on chomping away at the bread. Half of them were old hands, tough guys better left alone.

A young wiper was about to bite into his third slice. I leaned across the table and snatched the slice from his hands. "Conserve, boy! Conserve! Doncha know there's a war goin' on?" The wiper blushed and apologized. Probably a first-tripper.

We got through the meal with my consumption quota almost achieved.

After dinner I phoned my mother from the dock telephone booth to ask her who was the patron saint of bakers. My mother has a saint for anything imaginable, but she couldn't think of the saint. It's not that I was superstitious; it was just more of my lousy luck. "But don't worry, my boy. I'm gonna find out, and I'm gonna light candles for the saint everyday!"

My last good-bye call was to Gabrielle. I explained my predicament and urged her to pray for my ship to get torpedoed immediately. That way I'd at least have a chance to come back alive.

We sailed for Philadelphia at midnight. I stayed up half the night doing mathematical problems — mostly division — such as how to divide a loaf of bread among sixty men. When I woke up, we were in Philadelphia.

The campaign for the preservation of bread for the starving children was intensified at breakfast, but it brought diminished success — two meals and already the law of diminishing returns was working against me. I helped Cisco and Woody with their chores so that we could all the sooner make a concerted raid on the nearest bakery shop.

"All right, how much have we got altogether?" Cisco handed me twenty-five dollars.

"Here's mine." Woody gave me his twenty.

"We've got seventy-two dollars and twenty-three cents. Figure the two dollars and twenty-three cents for cab fare and tip — that leaves us only seventy dollars."

"Cheer up, Reb." Woody put his hand on my shoulder. "At twelve cents a loaf, seventy dollars is a lot of dough."

"Listen, buddy, this is no time for jokes."

A cab took us to a bakery about a mile from the docks; we told the driver to wait. There were three women customers in the store and a young woman behind the counter. The shelves held about thirty loaves of bread, and the counter case had a variety of buns and small cakes. I watched begrudgingly as the women each bought a loaf of bread.

"Next." The young salesgirl looked at me.

"We'll take everything."

"Oh, my God." The girl turned pale. "Is this a holdup?"

"Don't be silly. We just want to buy everything you've got."

"Are you kidding me?" She wasn't at all pleased. "What about our other customers?"

"Listen, miss, this is a democratic country! Your goods are for sale, and I've got the money to buy them! Are you discriminating against me because I'm Italian?"

She stared at me. "Please wait a minute." She backed away and disappeared into the rear of the store. We heard hurried mumbling, and then the baker came out with a rolling pin in his hand. The girl cringed behind him.

"Whatta you guys want?"

I told him. He looked at the money in my fist. "Okay, Sophie, give the man what he wants. Then you can go home early."

He gave us some cartons to pack the bread and cakes. "Can I ask you what all this is for?"

"Sure; it's to save my life." I didn't have time to explain. We had to hit a few more bakeries.

We emptied another bakery and three grocery stores before we got what I needed: two hundred loaves of bread and eight cartons filled with buns, cupcakes, cookies, coffee rings, and cheap Danish pastry. It took three taxicabs to carry the load. Each of us rode in one, and I couldn't escape the feeling that it was a funeral cortege — mine.

A crowd of our fellow crewmen gathered at the gangway to watch us load our cargo from the taxis onto the ship. Some of the boys came down to help us. The chief steward shook his head as he watched us from the boat deck. I couldn't hear what he was saying, but I could read his lips clearly, because he was repeating the same thing. "Santa Maria!" he kept saying while shaking his head. "Santa Maria!"

We managed to store everything in the chill-box by piling the cartons up to the overhead in the limited space allotted to me by Mister Johnson. Billy, the saloon messman, one of the men who helped us, was dying to know what I was doing. I told him about my problem and explained my plan. I'd start my baking experiments that night. I'd probably have a week in port. The day before sailing, my buddies and I would sortie again to replenish our supplies, which would give me an additional week's grace at sea. With two weeks' experimenting, I might just manage to save myself.

"It makes great sense, Baker." He was the first person to call me Baker. It had an awesome ring to it. The title carried an enormous sense of responsibility. Given the position I was in, I felt as Lincoln must have felt the first time he was addressed as "Mister President" — just before the Civil War broke out. "But Baker, there's only one thing wrong with your plan. You won't have a week in port."

"Why not — we're not fully loaded yet."

"I know, but I guess you haven't heard. There's no more shore leave after today."

I rushed up to the main deck to find an officer or somebody who could tell me something. The ship's bosun was standing at the gangway looking down at the dock. He swung his arms and stamped his feet to keep warm. "What's the score, Bosun?" I tried to appear calm. "Why no more shore leave?"

"I dunno, Baker. They didn't order me to rig the booms, so it's a cinch we're not taking on anymore cargo, yet we've got plenty of space down below. I dunno what —"

And then I heard it: the sound of singing, the sound of massed voices singing "The Eyes of Texas Are upon You." The singing was coming from the darkness of the dock shed and getting closer and closer. Then, out of the darkness into the bright sunlight, there came a sea of ten-gallon hats atop a battalion of giants marching and singing, "The eyes of Texas are upon you. You cannot get away!"

There was another ship tied up alongside of us. "Please, God, let them board another ship!"

"What did you say, Baker?" the bosun asked without taking his eyes off the approaching crowd.

"I said, please God —"

"Here they come!" somebody shouted as the singing horde charged up our gangway.

"Bosun!" the third mate called out, "we're taking on two hundred oil workers bound for the Persian Gulf. We're taking them as far as Oran, Algeria."

"Bosun!" I grabbed his arm. "Am I dreaming? Did I hear right?"

"You heard right, Baker!" he shouted above the singing. "Two hundred Texans all the way to Oran, and one helluva trip it's gonna be!"

"Baker!" somebody called. "Hey, Baker!" He shook me.

"Yeah, buddy." I smiled stupidly.

"The chief steward wants you in his cabin right away."

As in a slow-motion dream, I walked indoors and down the alleyway past a crowd of red-cheeked Texans jamming the area in front of the galley. They were peering at the busy cook through the mesh-wire fence and sniffing at the smells from the steaming pots as they stomped their feet and snorted. "Hongree, man! Hongree!"

The steward lay sprawled on his bunk, a bottle of rum in his hand. "Baker, I'm gonna give you four hours overtime every night, and you gonna give me what I need — right, amigo?"

I stared at him blankly.

"Right!" he continued. "Cut the crew to twenty loaves a day and make sixty loaves for the Texans — that's eighty loaves a day and twenty pans of cake and six kettles of pudding. And Baker —"

"Yes?"

"I'm gonna stay drunk until you finish tonight's baking." He put the bottle to his lips and waved me out. I closed the door thinking if he's going to drink until I finish tonight's baking, he's going to wind up drinking himself to death.

As I descended to our cabin, my sanity returned. I shouted "Cisco! Woody! You lousy bastards, where are you?" I tried the cabin. The door was jammed. "Open up, you bastards! Open up! Courtroom put me in my coffin, and you two nailed down the lid! Open up, I'm getting off this fucking ship!"

"Now take it easy!" Cisco opened the door. "Let's think a minute!"

"What's there to think?" I started gathering my things. "Sure, our supply would have lasted a week, but that mob of monsters'll snap it up in two days! You guys meant well. I wish it could have worked out, but I've got no choice. Let the army grab me!"

"I don't blame you," Cisco said. "We'll see you when we get back or something — I don't know — we'll find each other." We embraced.

"Sorry, Reb. Keep practicing your F chord." Woody embraced me. "We'll be seeing you."

I dashed out to make sure I'd get to the gangway ladder before it was pulled up. The gangway watch spread his arms. "There's no more shore leave."

"I don't want shore leave. I'm getting off for good!"

"Sorry, bud, you gotta have a pass from the captain."

The ship's horn gave two long blasts. I dropped my sea bag and ran to find the captain. He was on the bridge. "Sir! Sir, I've got a terrible pain in my right side. I've been warned before — it's appendicitis. I think it's best if I went to a hospital."

The captain stared at me. He was a seventy-year-old white Jamaican. "What the bloody hell do you mean, 'appendicitis,' just as we're about to sail? What's your job?"

"Second cook and baker."

"Baker? What, lose my baker? My good man, I assure you it's not appendicitis!"

"But sir — my side!" I winched and started to double up.

"Don't worry, my boy, it'll probably pass. Anyway, we've got a doctor on the convoy commodore's ship, in case you need one. Now get out of my flaming way! Cast off!" he shouted to his first mate.

I turned and ran back to the gangway. I was going to get past the watch even if I had to slug him. But the watch wasn't there. The gangway was up, and the ship was already drifting away from the dock.

15

I stood riveted to the deck, indifferent to the bitter cold, as the City of Brotherly Love disappeared in the icy mist. Slowly I began to assess my situation. The steward couldn't help me, and Mister Johnson wouldn't; therefore the men would have to go for months without bread and desserts. I would not only be logged for my wages; I'd probably be tried for impersonating a baker or for sabotaging the war effort. But far worse was the punishment the men would devise and mete out, unrelentingly, for each moment of my life on board — an eternity.

My fate is written, I thought. Now just have the courage to play the game to the end — try to carry out the steward's order no matter how ludicrous the idea. Let my mates see that at least I had the courage to try. I had nothing to lose. I was a dead man anyway.

The baking was done at night, after the cook was finished with dinner. At ten o'clock I would have to face my doom. That evening I ate a hearty meal. When it was time, Cisco and Woody accompanied me to the door of the galley.

"We'll stay with you." Cisco looked grim.

"Maybe we can help you," Woody said unconvincingly.

"Thanks, but I'd rather face it alone. I don't want you guys to see."

"Okay." Cisco shook my hand. "We'll be down below, with the Texans."

I closed the galley door behind me and turned on the light switch. The galley gleamed. Everything was in its place. I felt like a defiling unbeliever in a holy place. I approached the radiant bread-baking oven. It was six feet high and had four tiers. I pulled open one of the doors and looked into the oven's mysterious depth. I closed the door gently. Then I went to the dough trough and ran my hand over its spotless wooden cover. I lifted the heavy cover and looked inside the immense tublike basin. If only I knew what to put into it.

Luckily I had brought my practically unused cooking and baking school notebook with me for use as a general notebook. I opened it to the page on bread. It was blank except for some gibberish: 3 c. milk, 3 c. ht. wtr., 8–9 tbs. sht., 6 tbs. sg., 6 ts. slt., 5 c. fl., 3 cks. yst. It took me only half a hour to decode and understand the recipe. I was slightly pleased with myself. The only thing I was unclear about was the yeast. I knew "cks." meant cakes, but I couldn't remember how heavy a cake was. The yeast cakes on the ships weighed two pounds. The recipe called for three cakes, but three two-pound cakes, or six pounds of yeast, for one loaf was obviously ridiculous. I decided on the commonsense approach and thought that eight ounces of yeast for a loaf of bread sounded right. There was another thing I wasn't clear about — whether the recipe was for one or two loaves. I opted to err on the side of generosity and called it one loaf.

I then began to multiply everything by eighty. The results were astounding: 720 tablespoons of shortening, 400 cups of flour, 280 cups of milk, ditto for water, 480 tablespoons of sugar, 520 teaspoons of salt, and 40 pounds of yeast. To the attack!

I found everything I needed in the storeroom, and after working like a donkey to carry up four fifty-pound sacks of flour, four big cans of shortening, big cartons of powdered milk, and twenty two-pound cakes of yeast, I was ready. I took a clean white apron from a peg, and with considerable difficulty I managed to tie the apron strings behind me. Then I stood before the closed dough trough, said a silent prayer to the anonymous patron saint of bakers, and lifted the heavy lid.

Big as the tub was, it was too small to accommodate the mountain of ingredients needed to make eighty loaves of bread, so I decided to divide things in two. I remembered that it would take between forty-five minutes and an hour to bake a loaf of bread in an oven of 450 degrees. I would prepare the first batch of dough, and while waiting for it to rise, I would light the oven; then, while my first batch was baking, I would prepare the second batch.

I divided my original figures in half and started measuring 200 cups of flour, using a tin quart measure. That took a bit of time. Then I put in 70 quarts of water and milk. Then the shortening. Seven hundred and twenty tablespoons of shortening divided by two was still a lot of tablespoons. I measured to see how many tablespoons made a cup, and then I used a cup to scoop up the required shortening. I did the same with the sugar and salt. And then came the yeast. According to my calculations, I should put twenty pounds — ten two-pound cakes — into this one batch. After some hesitation and more than a little anxiety, I said to hell with it and threw all ten cakes into the trough.

To mix the ingredients, I used a four-foot wooden paddle that was hanging near the dough trough. The work was very hard, and with each churn of the paddle it became harder and harder. The paddle was becoming helpless against the increasingly solidifying sticky mass. Churning and straining, churning and straining, my back nearly breaking, until the whole mass congealed into an immovable mess of rubbery cement. Then I backed away for a moment's rest.

I remembered that the dough had to be kneaded for fifteen minutes, and tired as I was, I began to punch away at the immense white mass. I broke up the fifteen minutes into five three-minute rounds, with a minute's rest in between. I don't know who got the better of whom, but after the last round I was happy to close the lid on my opponent.

I desperately needed a smoke, but I was covered with flour and dough — hands, arms, eyelashes, eyebrows, hair — and it was half an hour before I could scrape and wash off enough to permit me to light up. I took a deep drag and surveyed my situation. The first battle was over, although the outcome, of course, was still in doubt. What went into that trough went in; what would come out, only God knew.

The thing that amazed me was the state of the galley. That one person alone could bring about such a transformation was astounding. There was flour everywhere. Dirty pots, kettles, buckets, and measuring implements littered the work tables and the stove. The deck itself was unbelievable. I had had an accident in opening one of the flour sacks. I had also spilled a five-pound sack of salt and kicked over a bucket of water, which got mixed in with the salted flour as I moved about the galley, causing almost the entire deck to be covered by a thin layer of sticky dough. All the deck needed was a little tomato sauce and some mozzarella cheese and I'd have a pizza big enough to feed the whole crew as well as two hundred Texans.

I finished my cigarette calmly. The dough would take an hour to rise, after which I was to go a few more rounds with it. What I had to do now was prepare the bread pans and light the oven. I turned on the oven first. Starting the oven's fire would give me pleasure. It was the one thing in that galley I could do with self-assurance — I used to be a Boy Scout.

I started by stuffing the firebox with newspaper and kindling wood. I lit the pile nicely and stepped back to enjoy my handiwork. The paper burned briskly for a minute, but nothing happened to the firewood. I started all over again, only this time I doubled the newspaper and twisted some of it into tight, flammable logs. I lit the pile and watched the paper blaze, but because time was beginning to run out on me, I closed the fire-door and started to prepare the bread pans while the fire took hold.

I laid out the twenty-five aluminum pans. They were eighteen inches long, five inches wide, and five inches high. I began greasing the insides, as I had seen my instructor do. I hadn't finished greasing the pans before I realized that my coughing was due to the smoke that was now escaping from the firebox grating. I opened the fire-door, and a great puff of smoke hit me in the face. The paper logs were smoldering, but the sticks of wood just lay there like slices of lox. My eyes teared, I coughed, I looked at the clock, and I began to get angry.

"Schmuck!" I said out loud. "What it needs is coal!"

I started all over again — a mound of paper, a bunch of twisted paper logs, more wood, three shovelfuls of coal, and a final mound of paper. I lit the pile, closed the fire-door, looked at the clock again, and went back to greasing the bread pans.

Soon black, sulphur-stinking clouds billowed out from the bottom grate, filled the galley, passed through the wire enclosure, and rolled down the alleyways. I coughed and cursed and wiped my eyes. As I yanked open the fire-door, a blast of smoke hit me in the face and continued on up to the overhead. I slammed the door shut and kicked it furiously. "Owwwww!" I bellowed in pain. I had forgotten that I had changed to open-toed sandals.

"All right, you son of a bitch!" I was now talking aloud. "I'll fix you!" I remembered that Roberto, the *Willy B.*'s cook, often used kerosene to start the oven. I looked in a cupboard near the stove and quickly found it in a coffee can.

I opened the fire-door. Another blast of smoke aimed for my face, but I ducked it. I looked inside — not spark, only black smoke. "Okay, you bastard, here!" I flung half a can of kerosene onto the smoking pile. "Take that!" With one movement I struck a match, threw it into the firebox, and slammed its door shut. Boom! The explosion hit me with a sheet of flame from the blown-open fire-door. I staggered backward, arms flailing, bread pans flying, lungs aching, the stench of burnt hair in my nose, and my eyes burning from the black smoke that drove me backward, backward, unable to see through the black air, until I banged into the dough trough. I turned my back to the oven, and as I wiped the tears from my burning eyes I saw *it!* I was paralyzed! I couldn't believe my eyes!

A monstrous mound of dough was rising out of the trough. It had pushed the hundred-pound lid open and was already creeping over the adjacent work tables, trapping many cups, ladles, towels, and pans in its sticky morass; but the main thrust of the monster blob was forward, over the front edge of the trough, threatening to engulf everything in its path, including me.

The alarm system in my brain flashed a fact forgotten since Biology Two: Yeast is a living thing. It has three trillion cells to the pound. I had put in twenty pounds! I grabbed the heavy trough lid and slammed it down with all my might, but the lid bounced back, helpless against the still-emerging mass.

"Get back! Get back!" I shouted as I whaled into the Thing with flying fists. "Get back in that box you sonofabitch!" I pounded away, coughing and crying from the smoke and from despair, but the monster engulfed my fists and held them in its grip. "You dirty bastard!" I yanked my hands free, and despite the smoke, the coughing, and the tears, I kept on punching and shouting, "Get back in that box, you sonofabitch! Get back in that box you sonofabitch! Get back in that . . ."

"Take it easy, Baker! Take it easy!" Somebody grabbed me from behind. It was one of the Texans. "Can I help?"

I looked at him, blankly. He held a handkerchief to his face and he was coughing.

"Can I help you, Baker?"

"How the hell can anybody help me?" I shouted.

"Well, for one thing, Baker, you forgot to open the flue!"

As the smoke cleared, I saw several men, handkerchiefs to their faces, staring through the galley's wire fence.

"Sit down, Baker." The Texan pushed me onto a stool. "Now tell me what happened."

I looked up at him. "It's impossible, buddy, not now." I mumbled, "Just take my word for it: there is a God, and he gave me what I deserve. I'm a wise guy," I continued mumbling. "I know nothing about baking — just got what I deserve."

"Maybe I can help you."

"How can you help a dead man?"

"I like to fool around in the kitchen, and I'm hungry. Maybe I could —"

"Say no more, brother." I got up and took off my apron. "I'll be back to clean up later, but right now, my friend, this fucking galley is all yours!" I flung my apron at the overflowing dough and slammed the galley door behind me.

16

I went to my cabin. Cisco and Woody were still down below with the Texans. I took a bottle of rum from Woody's locker, climbed into my bunk, and proceeded to drink myself senseless. Just as I lapsed into unconsciousness, I thought: it's the first time I'm not afraid of the U-boats.

Then the nightmare started — ovens on fire; me choking in black smoke and sinking in a swamp of dough; and through it all, the tantalizing, insistent, torturing smell of hot bread to remind me of what should have been. I sat up abruptly and shook my head, but the dream was so powerful that I could still smell the bread. I shook my head again, but the smell persisted. I was *not* dreaming. I was smelling hot bread! I jumped out of my bunk, raced to the galley, threw open the door, and saw eighty loaves of golden-brown bread covering the spotless work table! The Texan stood before the loaves, beaming. Two men were with him.

"How? — What?" I couldn't speak.

"And look over there." The Texan pointed across the now immaculate galley to where twenty pans of chocolate cake lined the work table.

"And there." He pointed to the stove. "Six kettles of pudding."

"It's impossible! It can't be! How did you — when did you — how did you know what I needed?"

"I asked the chief cook, Mister Johnson."

"Oh, my God, it's a miracle! It's a miracle!"

"No, it's no miracle."

"What do you mean it's no miracle? Look!" I pointed to the bread. "It's the miracle of the loaves! Who are you? Where did you come from?"

"I'm Frank Strahele. I'm a chef at the Ritz-Carlton Hotel, and these two men are my friends. They volunteered to help."

"A chef? The Ritz-Carlton? Oh, shit, I'm dreaming! It's only a dream!"

"It's no dream, but I'm not *the* chef of the Ritz-Carlton. I'm the roast chef."

"All right then, tell me; what's the roast chef of the Ritz-Carlton doing on this ship?"

"I'm on my way to the Persian Gulf to take over a mess for two thousand American oil workers. But what I really want to do is be a pastry chef."

"I'm dreaming! I know I'm dreaming!"

"It's true; I'm a frustrated pastry chef. The hotel's pastry chef is a jealous cat. He won't let me near his ovens. That's why I'd be very happy if for the rest of this trip you'll let me bake in your ovens."

"Bake in my ovens? Oh, Frank! Frank!" I threw my arms around him and kissed him on both cheeks, wetting him with my tears, until he broke away from me.

"Okay, now, that's enough! Here." He threw an apron to me. "It's almost breakfast time, and we still haven't made the croissants."

"Croissants? My God, I can't believe it! Who ever heard of croissants on a merchant ship?"

"Baker, if you're going to do a breakfast, you might as well do it right."

"Wait, Frank, wait! Hold still!" Just let me look at you for a minute!" He was tall, open-faced, chestnut haired. "Tell me about yourself. You're not a Texan. You have a slight German accent."

"I'm Viennese — that's why the pastry. I'm married, two kids, and I'll be forty-five next month if I get across this ocean alive."

"Don't worry, we'll make it. God would have to be a real sadist to spoil this miracle."

"Holy mother of God!" Cisco stood in the doorway sniffing the air.

"Sweet Jesus, Reb." Woody pointed to the bread. "How in the hell did you accomplish all that?"

I tied the apron around me. "Well, frankly, where there's a will, there's a way."

"You mean you did all this?" Cisco bent down to stare at the bread.

"Well, when I said 'frankly,' I meant it was Frank here who did it."

Over cups of good coffee, accompanied by thick slices of Frank's hot bread with sweet butter, I told my buddies the story of my salvation.

"I tell you, Jim," Cisco said, "I've got new respect for the Saint Michael's medal your mother gave you. Can I borrow it for my next poker session?"

"Lend it to me." Woody held out his hand. "Cisco's already won five hundred from the Texans. I lost fifty."

"Sorry, but I'm not parting with Saint Mike. Now you guys go get some sleep." I shooed them out the door. "We bakers have work to do."

Frank then proceeded to give me my first basic baking lesson: how to make golden-brown, butter-crisp, lighter-than-air, honest-to-God French croissants. "Remember, be generous with the butter, and the dough must rise three times — the oven very hot — and don't forget to baste them with boiling water. Right?"

"Right!" I pulled the croissant pan out of the oven, and there were sixty golden miracles. I picked one up. If I had thrown it into the air, it would have floated down, and when I bit into it, a thousand crispy particles of pastry melted on my tongue.

"With a little more practice, you'll be able to make them by yourself." Frank pulled out the second pan. "Two for each member of the crew — we'll do something nice for the Texans another time."

We still had an hour before breakfast. It was my job to feed breakfast to the crew — Mister Johnson and his helper would take care of the Texans. Frank showed me how to save time and feed well. Under his supervision I made a big pan of scrambled eggs, which he showed me how to keep warm and moist and delicious with the use of a double boiler. Alongside of that we made a pan of fried eggs for the not-too-fussy egg-eaters. Alongside of that I prepared a pot of boiling water for the boiled-egg orders and another pan of boiling water for the poached eggs. On another section of the big coal stove we fried a batch of bacon and, along-side of that, a batch of sausage and a batch of ham. In the oven we had several pans of toast, hot and ready to serve. Ten minutes before break-fast everything was ready — the bread was still warm and fragrant, and the galley was spotless.

"Oh, Santa Maria, Santa Maria!" The steward, quite drunk, was star-ing at the miracle. He pulled a whiskey flask from his back pocket, looked at it, put it back in his pocket, crossed himself, and shuffled out of the galley mumbling, "Santa Maria, Santa Maria."

Mister Johnson came in a minute later. He surveyed his galley without the slightest expression on his face. He took an apron from the locker, looked at me for a moment with an expression of utter contempt, shook his head, and left.

But the crew loved me.

"Hell, you're some baker, Baker!"

"Boy, that was some bread!"

"Baker, I never did see anything like them there crispy croi-, croi-, like them crispy rolls. Mmm! Mmm!"

The captain himself stuck his head inside the galley doorway. "Baker, I'm sure glad it wasn't appendicitis."

After breakfast Frank and I had a cup of coffee. "What am I going to do without you tonight?" I poured Frank more coffee.

"Oh, you're not losing me. I can't sleep at night with all the gambling going on. Working in the galley would be a pleasure. I can sleep during the day."

"But night after night — that's a lot of work."

"Don't worry; my two Texan friends are happy to help. They know their way around a kitchen, and they'll eat better. You'll help too. I'll teach you for two hours each night, and then you'll be free. Is that okay?"

"I'm not sure; let me see. I'll be getting my regular wages plus four hours overtime for two hours work a night? Hell, hour for hour I'll be making only as much as the president of the United States!"

"That's the deal."

"No good — I'll give *you* the overtime and half my wages."

"No thanks. Just put in your two hours' learning and then stay out of my way."

"Frank, you sure push a hard bargain." I tried to embrace him, but he escaped.

That night I watched Frank and his helpers make bread. It was a beautiful thing to see. I saw yeast in a different light and marveled at its magic power. It brought the dough to its first rise, warm and fragrant. Next the dough was kneaded for a good ten minutes — firmly, not roughly — and then given an hour's quiet rest, after which it was again kneaded gently; carefully shaped to fit into buttered pans; and placed into easily fired ovens, where it baked for forty-five minutes of increasing fragrance. The results cooled on the tables in golden-brown rows, a tribute to the ingenuity of man who, thousands of years ago, learned to blend flour with living yeast to give us the miracle of leavened bread.

"Two hours up. Out!" Frank pushed me toward the galley door. "Enough questions — we still gotta make the rice pudding, the cakes, and the corn muffins for breakfast. Out!"

It was only eleven. I went down below to see how Cisco and Woody were doing with the Texans. A roar of cursing, laughing voices came through the open safety door of the 'tween deck. Through a thick fog of smoke and whiskey, I saw crowded dice tables and card tables. Of the two hundred Texans, only thirty or forty slept. Traveler's checks served for chips, and the stakes were often in the hundreds.

In five minutes I lost all the money I'd earned that night from "working" in the galley. I spent the rest of the time just watching Cisco and Woody playing. An hour before breakfast, I went to the galley to check on my miracle worker.

The sight that greeted me was as beautiful as that of the night before: eighty loaves of golden-brown bread, twenty pans of almond cake, six kettles of cinnamon-rich, egg-creamy rice pudding, and the corn muffins! A cruel and inhuman punishment would be to give a man one of Frank's muffins and then tell him, "Sorry, there's no more." But Frank was no sadist; he made enough muffins to give each crew member two. I had never tasted anything like that corn muffin drenched in butter. Its waist was necessarily as narrow as the muffin tin, but the top billowed out, twice as far as the laws of physics allow. It made a mound of light-brown, buttery-gold, whole-grained cornmeal that melted in your mouth.

"Baker, you're the greatest!" a gun-crew kid called to me.

A fireman picked up a muffin. "That's the goddamnedest corn muffin I ever did see."

Day after day Frank topped himself — prize-winning cakes, rich puddings, addictive cookies, fluffy rolls, and God, what pies! No wonder people paid what they did to eat at the Ritz.

"If you can't count seven layers in the pie crust, throw it out." Frank counted the layers. "Okay, there's eight in this one."

And Danish pastry! Danish pastry, as I knew it, was what you got in a diner for ten cents, a soggy mass of dough with a cheap filling of yellowish cheese or stomach-searing prune mix. Calling such things Danish pastry was like calling both me and Django Reinhardt guitarists. Just to see one of Frank's plump Danish morsels, with its glazed come-eat-me look, was almost ecstasy enough. Next was the touch, the thrill of picking up the delight that was so light you could almost blow it away. Yet its rounded little body was firm enough to just yield to the touch. As you brought the pastry to you, the perfume of its honeyed butter lured you into open-ing your mouth and biting through the divine dough to the scented mysteries of its magic filling. Then it was the palate's turn to be regaled by the myrrhlike juices. And then the swallow, followed by the aftertaste, which seemed to say, "Well, what do you think of that?"

"Oh my, Frank! Do you think I'll ever be able to —"

"No, forget it. Some things you have to be born to, and you're not Viennese. Just keep on kneading that dough."

No doubt about it, the patron saint of ship's bakers was watching over me — we were only halfway across the Atlantic, and I had already learned to make bread. It wasn't great bread, but it was good enough. In addi-tion, we hadn't lost a single ship, and my beard was growing beautifully.

"Now," Frank said as he stirred a concoction he was cooking in a fry-ing pan, "it's time for you to learn another basic — crepes suzettes." Frank had wheedled a bottle of brandy from one of the Texans. That plus oranges, butter, and thin egg-dough crepes five inches in diameter were the ingredients of the famous dessert. "Gently, gently." Frank showed me how to fold the crepes. He gently, but briskly, pushed the folded crepes through the orangy buttered brandy heating in the pan. Then he struck a match to the perfumed fumes. The pan blazed like a fantasy fit for the court of a shah. "Okay, let's go!" Frank insisted that I carry the flaming marvel to the men. The crew's applause was deafening.

The chief steward, who had been watching the crepe making, was not a malicious man, but he could no longer contain the secret. He silenced the men and told them about my qualifications and about Frank's contri-bution to the ship's happiness. He ended his speech by raising Frank's hand and proclaiming the embarrassed man to be the ship's savior, as well as "the best all-around baking champion of the world, including Puerto Rico." No, it was not out of malice that the chief steward spoke — it was out of a strong sense of justice, fortified by an even stronger Puerto Rican rum.

The men glared at me. For a moment I thought they would do some-thing terrible in revenge for my exposing them to the disaster of ship-ping without a baker, but then they cheered Frank wildly and called for him to speak.

"Okay, okay." Frank raised his hand. "I promise you, before we get to Oran, Jim will be a good ship's baker." There was faint applause.

"He'd better be!" A deckhand called out. "But right now, Frank, how's about another batch of them there creepy suzettes!" The cheers were louder than before.

The crepes were easy to make, and Frank kept them coming, until one of the men, obviously surfeited, rolled one into a ball and flung it at my head, shouting, "You lucky son of a bitch!"

By the time we got to Gibraltar, we still hadn't lost a single ship, and I had learned to make edible muffins, rolls, biscuits, and scones. But there was still so much to learn, and Oran was only two and a half days away. Luckily we had to spend a week in Gibraltar, waiting for a new convoy that would take us through the Mediterranean. During the blessed week I learned to make passable rice pudding, chocolate pudding, and what Frank called "blanc mange." It was blanc mange when he made it, a heavenly thing. When I made it, it was plain vanilla pudding.

"But it's good enough, Frank, good enough, knock on wood. With what you've taught me, I can at least get back to the States without being tortured by the crew. You've saved me!" I lunged to embrace him.

"Cut that out!" He ducked away from me. "Cut that out!"

"All right, then; hold still, and let's bow our heads for a moment, in memory of all the graduates of the Cook and Baker School who were forced to ship out with no Frank Strahele to save them." Frank grumbled something and left me to contemplate the fate of my unfortunate fellow alumni. Undoubtedly the poor bastards must have prayed for their ships to be torpedoed, as I had prayed before Frank appeared. But now my prayer could be more patriotic, and I could go back to my simple dread of being torpedoed — we were sailing out of Gibraltar with the weakest protection we had yet seen.

There were twenty ships in our convoy, but two damaged British destroyers was all the protection we would have for the six-hundred-mile run through that submarine-infested sea. I could taste the fear in my throat as we moved away from the safety of the rock. The incredible beauty of the sea and the sunset made my fear all the more bitter. There was very little talk. Cisco played lonesome ballads on deck — alone — just for himself. Woody wrote endlessly, furiously, as though needing to finish his book before a torpedo got us, and I watched the horizon. The only communicating thing on that ship was the gun crew's portable phonograph. A young gunner kept playing the same two records, Glenn Miller's theme song and a sweet, rolling melody by the Three Suns, "Moon Light Saving Time." Nobody yelled at the gunner for playing the same records, even though the songs made us all the sadder and sicker for home.

The gray mood prevailed until the next day, when Frank announced he was going to make a birthday cake for one of the gun-crew kids.

His announcement broke the gloom, and everybody took part in the plot to give the kid a real surprise party. All the crew's tension was diverted into the happy project — decorations, a specially written song, gifts, and Frank's cake.

"What I need to make the cake," Frank said, clearing the work table, "is some batteries, a light socket, and a hundred-watt bulb."

"Frank, are you going to make a cake or open a hardware store?"

"Jimmy boy, you get what I said, and then you'll see."

And boy did I see! It was a great round creation — half cake, half baked Alaska, richly decorated with whipped cream and jellied rosettes proclaiming "Happy Birthday." The center of the cake had a hole in it into which Frank inserted the batteries with the light bulb. Frank constructed a hollowed-out tower of meringue over the hole and rising two feet above the cake, so that, when the lights were put out for the surprise and Frank presented the cake, the lighted bulb glowed through the meringue tower like an enchantment for a king. The birthday boy cried.

The boy soon recovered, the cake was sensational, the gifts were touching, and Woody's fiddle flew into hoedown after hoedown, accompanied by Cisco, me, and twenty shouting, clapping couples sashaying and do-si-doing between the tables and down the alleyways, way past midnight — indifferent to the U-boats — until somebody announced that we were within sight of Oran. Then we went to sleep, most of us probably dreaming happy dreams of Frank's goodness and of Hedy Lamarr. Oran's casbah was the place where Charles Boyer had made passionate love to her — well, maybe it was in the Algiers casbah that Hedy devastated Boyer, but it *could* have been in Oran.

We woke up at anchor in the harbor, several hundred yards from the docks. From that distance the city looked beautiful, and we were dying to get ashore. But the approaching launch was not for us. There was no word about shore leave. The launch was for our passengers, come to transfer them to a ship bound for Bahrain. The entire crew lined the rail to say good-bye to Frank.

While we waited for the launch to be tied up, Frank and I stood alone. "Remember, not too much vanilla in the blanc mange."

When his turn came to climb down the gangway ladder, we embraced, and he patted my back. He turned away, and as he started down, the whole crew began wailing, "Frank, Frank, come back, Frank! Please don't leave us at the mercy of that bum!" They pointed to me. "Please Frank, don't leave us to that bum!"

"Don't worry," Frank shouted as the launch roared away. "He'll be all right!" He waved to us, and we kept waving until we could no longer distinguish him.

17

That night I made my first solo flight as a ship's cook and baker. Mister Johnson came into the galley presumably to prepare a stew for the next day, but that was an excuse. He watched me surreptitiously as I prepared for my next day's menu. We were back to forty loaves a day, five pans of cake, and two kettles of pudding — a snap compared with what was needed to feed the Texans.

I prepared the bread dough without a wasted motion, keeping everything about me absolutely clean. Frank had taught me to clean up as I proceeded from step to step, so that the galley always looked spotless. I was intensely aware of Mister Johnson's silent presence, and when I finished the dough, I said, "Well, that's that," seemingly talking to myself but actually intending to evoke a response from Mister Johnson. Instead he just mumbled something, and when I turned to him, he looked away.

I then started the fire in the oven. I had it going in a minute, and in ten minutes it was well on its way to the 450 degrees needed for the bread.

"And that, too, is that," I said aloud.

Mister Johnson mumbled something and looked away.

After I put the bread in the oven, I lit a cigarette and offered one to him. He looked at the proffered cigarette and then turned away as though I hadn't said anything. "Listen, Mister Johnson, I've been fighting for the Negro people since I was sixteen! 'Jim Crow must go' are not just words to me."

Without turning around, he said, "You weren't fighting for my people. You were fighting for your own! Until my people are free, your people are going to pay plenty."

"You're right, Mister Johnson."

"You thought you were doing an act of charity?"

"Of course not. I did it because we're all brothers."

"Ha!" He banged a pot onto the stove.

"Don't you believe I mean it?"

"Do you believe you mean it?" He still wouldn't look at me.

"Of course we're all equal."

He turned to me, his great eyes glistening with anger. "Equal?" He stared at me for a moment. "If you think the black man is as smart as the white man, how come the black man is still living in the jungles?" His voice thundered against me as though I was a black man and he my white prosecutor.

"Well — the climate — the people don't need to work hard to get what they need for the good life."

"The African people are *starving*, you ignorant man! The white man lives twice as long, and jungle babies die twice as fast! Now try again." He glared at me. "Why are the Africans still living in jungles?" Without giving me a chance to answer, he pointed his finger at me. "And why don't black kids do as well as white kids in school? Why are there so many black criminals? Don't you think the black man is closer to the gorilla than the white man? Come on, man, can't you even answer the first question? Why is the black man still living in the jungles?" He glared at me as I stood before him, speechless. "Because they're not as smart as the white man? Isn't that what your smarter white brain is saying? Go on, Mister Charity — you got any other answer to my questions?" He looked at me for a moment and then turned away and strode out of the galley, leaving me to answer his ugly questions by myself.

A few minutes later Mister Johnson came back. "Made me forget my damned stew!" He went to the stove without looking at me. I said nothing while he fussed with his stew pot. I just continued making my corn muffin mix. "And that ain't no damned way to mix that stuff!" Mister Johnson grabbed the ladle out of my hand. "You stir it gently, from the bottom — like Mister Frank told you, you stupid man!"

He stayed with me while I did my baking. In his gruff, lordly way he took up my culinary education where Frank had left off, and as the night wore on, he told me of his life in Jamaica. He described the misery and the shame of the caste system, where even the blacks discriminated against each other according to the darkness of their skin. Our own captain, he said, could not abide black-skinned men and had hired Mister Johnson only because they were cousins. That threw a different light on the haughty, old British-sounding captain of the *Floy-Floy*.

Mister Johnson told me that Captain Brown owned three ships, that he had come out of retirement at seventy only to fight the Nazis, and that the "old bastard" was still the best seaman afloat. My baking finished,

Mister Johnson went to bed, leaving me to prepare for breakfast and to await the ship's verdict.

That morning there was no comment from the crew. They just ate every last corn muffin I had baked. There was no doubt about it; the *Floy-Floy* had a second cook and baker. The main problem now was shore leave.

Cisco, the ship's chairman, talked the problem over with the first mate, but nothing could be done until the captain received orders about dock space. The ship's mood again turned ugly and stayed ugly all day until Gali-Gali came aboard. In all probability there was nothing Oran could offer that would be half as memorable as Gali-Gali. Not its women or its whiskey could match one hair of that wizard's head.

Gali-Gali was the greatest magician we'd ever seen. He made his living visiting ships in Oran's harbor. He would convince tough captains to allow him onto their ships by the sheer beauty of his magic, despite all the rules for security. And how right the captains were in letting him come aboard — he made the men forget the frustration of having no shore leave.

Gali-Gali's magic was very simple: chicks, little baby chicks. He made chicks appear everywhere — out of the air, out of your nose, your ears, your inside pockets, even your closed fist, their master calling "Gali, gali, gali, gali!" At first it just seemed like a very good trick, but the chicks kept coming and coming — out of your wallet, from your trouser cuffs, from the inside of your shirt, and when Gali-Gali told you to open your fly and out fell four cute little chicks, the trick started to be something else.

Chicks came from everywhere, and in no time the space inside the big circle of sixty men was packed with the little feathery balls. Where they could have come from was impossible to guess. Gali-Gali was a small man dressed in shirt, trousers, and sandals. He carried no bag. Where could these dozens and dozens of chicks have come from? And when you thought it was impossible for Gali-Gali to produce any more, he would turn the faucet of your nose and out would come another dozen. His endless, ever-increasing number of chicks turned a chick into an awesome experience, a perfect example of the law of quantitative change producing a qualitative change. If Oran had anything else to equal him, it would indeed be a magical city. We'd soon find out; after dinner Cisco brought the news that shore leave was on as of the next morning.

Even though the captain had not yet received orders about dock space, the "old bastard" made arrangements for a launch to take us ashore.

Bosun gave us a short, sharp lecture about the army's MPs. "You guys watch your ass in Oran. Two N.M.U. men were shot dead by the fucking MPs — caught off-limits. There was a fight, and the bastards just let the seamen have it. They hate us because we're good union men. They hate us because they think we're making a fortune out of the war, and they hate us because in a couple of weeks, God fucking willing, we'll be back in the States. So just watch your ass."

Cisco confirmed the story about the two dead seamen and told us that Joe Curran, our union president, had come to Oran to investigate the case.

"It's a good thing we grew these." Woody pulled on his dark, full beard. "We can pass for Ayrabs and go anywhere we like."

"Having beards helps, and with a fez on our heads, it's even better." We had bought the fezzes from an Algerian bum boat.

With the fezzes, the beards, and our dark coloring, Woody and I looked like a couple of honest-to-God Arabs. But Cisco's fez did nothing for him — with his blond beard, his fair skin, and his blue eyes, he looked like a musical-comedy Arab. We tucked every strand of his blond hair under his fez, darkened his face and beard with butter mixed with cocoa, and told him to shut his blue eyes if the MPs caught us off-limits.

"What about the soap?" I asked Woody. On the first day after leaving the States, Woody had asked Cisco, the ship's chairman, to call a special meeting.

"What for?" Cisco had asked.

"Soap."

At the meeting Woody told the men that from the little he had seen of the Arab people on our last trip, he had come to the conclusion that they cherished cleanliness and that their dirt came from poverty. He asked the men to save soap. "Take your soap ration, but don't waste any, and by the time we get to Oran, we'll have enough to give some Ayrab mothers a little of the soap they've been hankerin' for so's their kids can walk around in cleaner clothes."

The men voted unanimously for his charitable proposal. Cisco proposed that Woody be given the job of distributing the soap and that even though Christmas was over, Woody should be given the title of ship's Sani-Clothes. That proposal was also unanimously accepted.

Our soap allotment was two medium-sized bars per week, more than enough for our needs, including laundry. Woody got the men to get by on one bar a week. "It's amazing how people waste soap!" He'd come out of the shower room with ten bars. "These poor little soap bars would have melted away if I hadn't rescued them." By the time we got to Oran, Woody had two hundred and forty-three bars of soap.

"We'll distribute the soap tomorrow — after I get the lay of the land."

"God willing." Cisco adjusted his fez at a rakish angle. Woody and I did the same, and we were off to retrace Hedy Lamarr's footsteps through Oran's glamorous casbah. Since neither Cisco nor Woody had seen Hedy's movie, I would act as their guide, which I was well qualified to do. I was, in fact, an authority on the subject, having seen Hedy's picture twice, as well as the original French version, *Pépé le Moko*.

The launch left us near the dock gate. There I reenacted the scene when Charles Boyer, clinging to the wire barrier that separated him from his departing love, shouted his unforgettable cry, "Hay-deee! Hay-deee! Come back, Hay-deeeee!" Then I confidently led the way up what the Americans called "Piss Falls" — a urine-smelling, steep stairway leading to the top of the cliff, on which lay Oran, with its Hedy Lamarr casbah. We were hot when we got to the top. Although it was February, the temperature was in the seventies.

The center of Oran was surprising; it was so French, with its sidewalk cafes, French restaurants, and chic French women. Another surprise was the main square, which was packed with tens of thousands of people come to hear Charles De Gaulle. We listened as he appealed to the people to rally behind the Cross of Lorraine, the symbol of the Free French. He spoke slowly, clearly, and with such intensity of expression that I, with my limited French, could easily understand him. It was thrilling to see the response he got when he assured the people that the Allied invasion of France was not far off.

"Well, we've witnessed a piece of history," Cisco said after the rally. "Now how about a piece of tail?"

"We're married men." Woody looked at me. "But we'll go along to see that you don't get in trouble. Right, Reb?"

"Of course." I led the way to the casbah, which the Algerians called "Old Oran." Big wall signs proclaimed, "Off-limits to U.S. personnel." Two MPs stood at the entrance to the casbah. The three of us started a heated argument in fake Arabic and walked past the MPs without their even looking at us.

A solid shock of living sound hit us as we passed into the casbah's narrow main street. A barrage of loudspeakers blared out Arabic singing at full blast. Each loudspeaker hung over a cafe entrance and competed with the others. The tables in front of the cafes were crowded with gamblers silently studying their dominoes, totally indifferent to the cacophony of loudspeakers; food vendors; mule drivers shouting at their braying beasts; storekeepers shouting at passersby; barefoot children begging, shouting "Backsheesh! Backsheesh!"; cross-legged money changers chanting and clinking stacks of gold coins; frenzied shouting from a crowded hovel where a belly dancer gyrated wildly; and street musicians blowing reed-pipe accompaniment to barefoot girls dancing and singing in courageous competition with the noise about them. The cafe gamblers silently studying their dominoes must have lost their hearing ages ago.

We made our way through the crowded "streets," which were just alleys only an armspread wide, or else they were just steps twisting and turning, criss-crossing with other steps and alleys in a crowded noisy maze of two-storied hovels with shuttered windows and beaded curtains at their open doorways. We caught glimpses of the poverty inside, but despite the poverty there was a vibrancy in the air, an aliveness, almost a happy air.

We surreptitiously watched veiled women surreptitiously staring at us from their open windows, and we exchanged greetings with passing men, "Salem Aleikum!"

"Aleikum Salem!" they replied and grinned, seeing through our disguises and pleased that we made an attempt to speak their language.

The clanging of cymbals and the gay sound of reed instruments accompanied a wedding party of twenty singing, clapping people. We whistled and cheered the bride and shouted "Salem Aleikum!" to the groom. Then we followed a man wheeling a brightly painted, yellow-and-red hand truck loaded with cases of Coca-Cola, until he disappeared behind a beaded curtain of what could have been a restaurant. A loudspeaker above its doorway blared the sensuous chant of a woman singer. The casbah was alive, and the good smell of frying mutton, saffron, and other cooking spices hung over everything, as did the yelling of the children, who followed us everywhere.

To escape the children, we entered the bazaar — "Souk" in Arabic — a maze of roofed-over alleyways jammed with hundreds of little shops, some of them only four feet wide. A dense crowd of veiled women and men in long robes moved slowly, carrying us along, past imploring shopkeepers whose steady flow of jabber was welcome relief from the deafening noise outside. But there was no rest for the eyes.

The bazaar was a feast of colors and a confusion of fascinating sights. There were gorgeous carpets in brightest reds, brilliant blues, the palest greens, and the softest golds — woven jewels. There were silks of every shade, some as transparent as air, and hundreds of bolts of colored cottons of every texture and imaginable design. And in front of the food stalls, golden corn meal in brown sacks, with neatly rolled-down tops, vied with other sacks of bright crimson paprika, dazzling white beans, sea-green dried peas, opalescent fat-grained rice, yellow-gold saffron, bright-red devil peppers, almonds, and jewellike dates. Filigreed silver lamps hung in front of the stalls where their makers welded them in front of our eyes, glass blowers twisted and blew brilliant balls of molten glass into splendid forms of every kind, cross-legged tailors stitched varicolored robes, and countless other craftsmen beat fiery iron, shaped fragrant leather, and planed wood just as they did in the days of Christ.

Nor was the nose excluded from the feast of Oran's bazaar: cinnamon, cloves, curry, coriander, nutmeg, and roasting coffee combined to produce a headiness, a sharpening of the senses, and the smell of roasting lamb and mutton chitterlings became irresistible.

"Man, we better quick get us some of that Araby-baraby food!" Woody pushed aside the beaded curtain of a restaurant, and we eagerly followed him. The place was crowded with men seated at bare tables. They ate with their headgear on — fezzes or skull caps. There was not a woman in sight. Boys served the food, and a cook carved the meat, which he took from a slow-turning spit.

"Remember, don't ask for beer or pork," I said to Woody, "and don't forget to eat with your right hand only." The left hand was reserved for bodily functions.

As each man came into the restaurant, he went to the sink against the far wall, where he washed his hands. Though there was no soap, they washed their hands thoroughly and then wiped them on a communal towel hanging by the sink. Several men stared at us until we got up and went to wash up too, but we used our handkerchiefs to dry our hands. After eating, each man went to the sink, cupped water into his hands, rinsed his mouth, and then used his right forefinger to brush his teeth. We had to do the same.

From the bazaar restaurant we wandered through the alleyways of Old Oran until we came to a house in front of which stood a line of twenty people. A brass plaque on the wall proclaimed it to be the office of a doctor with a French name. A middle-aged European man opened the door for the next patient. He looked at us. "Can I help you?" he asked in French.

"No, thank you." I was proud to be using my college French. "We're American seamen just strolling through your fascinating casbah."

The man was the doctor himself: French, charming, and delighted by the fact that an American was attempting to speak French. "Your French is very good!"

"Thank you, but I've got a long way to go to achieve my ambition."

"Which is?"

"To read Proust in French."

Proust was our instant passport to the doctor's house. "Enter, enter!" He insisted that we have tea with him in his house, which was adjacent to his office. He said it was time for his break anyway. He said something in Arabic to the waiting patients and led us inside. The house was small but as beautiful as a joyous Matisse painting, with Algerian tapestries on bright white walls and hundreds of gaily covered books. His wife, also French, was as warm and as charming as her husband. They had come to Oran twenty-five years before.

In English they both bombarded us with questions about life on the ships, about our being torpedoed, about New York, about the plight of the Okies (they had read *Grapes of Wrath*). When they allowed us to ask questions of them, they told us about their fascination with Arabic culture.

"No matter how poor they are," the doctor's wife said, "or how little their schooling, the Arabs have a love of beauty which shows itself in their relationship with each other, as well as in their art."

"I love their poetry." The doctor picked up a leather-bound book. "Their language has the richest vocabulary and a flexibility that permits the utmost delicacy and imagery of expression." The doctor's French accent added to the music of his words. "The language of the Koran, the poetry of al-Hariri and of Imru'-al-Qays, it is all as beautiful as anything in Western literature. We cannot judge these people by their present backwardness. Their present condition is due to the uneven economic development of the world."

"My husband is right; one can never judge a people by its present backwardness," the doctor's wife said as she poured tea. "There was a time when the African jungle culture was thousands of years ahead of the rest of the world." Not only did our new friends give us a charming tea, they also gave me an answer to at least one of Mister Johnson's taunting questions.

It was almost dark when we tried to find our way out of the casbah's maze of alleys. The deeper we went into Old Oran, the worse the poverty. Old Oran looked nothing like that glamorous casbah I had seen in Hedy's movie. More and more it began to look like a filthy, sinister place. The whores' quarter was the worst.

Instead of exuding the scent of perfume evoked by Hedy in the casbah movie, the whores' quarter had a distinct smell of urine and a faint smell of feces. As for the girls themselves, to say that they were hideous is an insult to the hideous. The slimmer ones were as fat as Oliver Hardy. The prettiest ones looked like him. Most of them were between forty and fifty years old. They stood in the dark doorways, yelling at us and fiercely gesticulating for us to enter. The older ones sat at the open windows, yelling and gesticulating just as fiercely. They all wore makeup. The more modest ones looked like jungle warriors going into battle, painted with bright reds, greens and blues, with white stripes around the eyes and nose and tattoos on their arms, on their chests, and even on their faces.

Woody shook his head. "I never dreamed that keeping my marriage vow could be so easy."

The one thing the Oran whores had in common, even the occasional teenager, was gold teeth. The darkening alleys flashed with gold teeth as the whores yelled and gesticulated commandingly.

"Where's Woody?" Cisco looked around anxiously.

"Where the hell could he have disappeared to?"

"That crazy son of a bitch." Cisco started to retrace our steps.

"Woody!" I shouted.

"Don't shout, for Christ's sake! The MPs'll spot us!" Cisco grabbed my arm.

Angry shouts came from one of the doorways, American voices shouting something about being robbed and dirty whores followed by a smashed bottle and women shouting in Arabic. Two Americans in civilian clothes were pitched into the alley by four Arabic Amazons, just as the shrill sound of the MPs' whistles reached us. In seconds we were surrounded by a squad of military police.

Cisco and I hid in the dark doorway while the MPs focused their attention on the two Americans, who were hurriedly buttoning their trousers. The MPs grabbed them and flung them into a jeep. Two of the MPs started to search the doorways near to us. Cisco and I ducked into the courtyard of our building, and there was Woody, surrounded by several children.

"What the hell are you doing here?" Cisco grabbed Woody by the back of his shirt collar.

"Negotiating."

"Negotiating what?"

"Negotiating to keep half my cigarettes. The little bastards already talked me out of half a pack. If you hadn't come along, I wouldn't have any left."

"How the hell did you wind up here?"

"The little one signaled to me."

"Guthrie, you are one hopeless nut." Cisco pulled him toward the exit.

The MPs were getting closer to our doorway. In perfect fake Arabic I let my buddies know that it was time for us to get the fuck out of there. The two MPs barely glanced at us, and we quickly turned into the next alley. Suddenly a military jeep blocked the far end of the alley. An officer jumped out and walked toward us. As calmly as we could, we ducked into a cafe. The place was half-filled with men playing dominoes. An empty table had a chess set on it ready for play. We sat down and ordered tea, and Woody and I started to play.

Before we could make three moves, the beaded entrance curtain parted, and there in the doorway stood a United States Army colonel, six feet three, blond, and altogether as Prussian looking as only West Point can make them. He clapped his steel-blue eyes on us, and we froze. Mother of God — six months in jail! We turned our eyes away and pretended to proceed with the chess game. Out of the corner of my eye I could see the colonel approaching. I bent my head closer to the board, my face in tortured concentration. None of us dared to look up at the Prussian-necked bastard who was now actually looking down on us. I picked up a chess piece at random and started to move it.

The colonel gripped my shoulder and snarled, "Oy vay, schmuck, dot's the wrong move!"

The three of us jumped up like one man at the sound of that heavy Jewish accent. "You're Jewish!" My voice rang with joy. "You're Jewish!"

"What then?"

"And you're *not* with the military police?"

"What, are you crazy? I'm a doctor. I came from Poland. I joined the U.S. Army and now I'm a colonel, not a policeman. I'm —" Before he could finish, the three of us were pumping his hand and pounding his back.

"Wait a minute! What's the matter with you guys? Wait a —"

"Doctor, Doctor!" I kept pumping his hand. "Are we glad you're a doctor!"

"Why? You caught the clap already?"

"Oy, God forbid, Doctor!" I punched my breast. "It's just that we thought you were an MP. You see, we're merchant seamen, and to tell you the truth, I think maybe we're a little bit off-limits," which in New York Jewish parlance was an admission of guilt with a plea for leniency.

"Of course, that's what I figured."

"That we're off-limits?"

"No, that you're American merchant seamen."

"You mean we don't look like Arabs?"

"Are you kidding? You look like a couple nice Talmudic students. Which reminds me, what is a nice couple Jewish boys doing in the casbah — and on the Sabbath night yet."

"Goyisha Kups!" Cisco put his finger to his head. "We're not Jewish, Colonel."

"Oh — well, that explains it." The colonel shook his head. "But I want you should know, the girls are full of diseases."

"Don't worry, Colonel." Cisco crossed his heart. "We were just looking."

"And what are you doing in the casbah, Rabbi Colonel?" I asked.

"I tell you the truth. I come as often as I can. That chess set belongs to the chess champion of Algeria. We play a lot. But since you shmendricks don't know nothing from chess, I better take you back to the town center, in case the MPs also mistake you for New York Talmudic students. Come on, my jeep is outside."

"I'll bet you miss New York," the colonel said as he stopped the jeep to let us off.

"Colonel," Woody answered, shaking his hand, "we miss New York so much that just listening to your accent brings tears to my eyes."

"Better than eating a pastrami sandwich." Cisco shook the colonel's hand.

"Shalom Aleikum!" I gripped his hand.

"Give mine regards to Broadway!" he called out as he pulled away.

18

It was only eight o'clock, too early to return to our ship, so we explored Oran's European section. In one of the smaller streets a store window said, "Maritime Union of France." The lights were on, so we went in to see how our French seamen brothers were doing.

Twelve men were seated around a big table in serious discussion. I took the liberty of bringing them greetings from the National Maritime Union. They all stood up and shook our hands warmly. Wine was poured and many toasts drunk to "our brave American comrade seamen." They also asked many questions about the American working class, particularly whether the American workers "would join in the postwar struggle to bring about the final defeat of capitalism." I answered no. I explained that even Earl Browder, the leader of the American Communist party, was for close postwar cooperation between the United States and the Soviet Union to work for a better world through peaceful competition.

The French seamen said that they had heard about Browder's blasphemy and hoped that we were not of the same mind. I said we were, whereupon there began a most passionate battle to decide the future of humankind. We were outnumbered, my French was poor, the wine flowed steadily, and our opponents were explosive. But, despite the odds, we began to make headway, and after two hours we created a split in their united front. After three hours half of them were on our side, and the rest were neutralized — all except one. Our victory might have been complete, but it was late, and I had trouble understanding the accent of the stubborn holdout.

The discussion broke up with serious hand shaking, much head shaking, and everybody's begrudging thanks for having been given a lot of food for thought — everybody's thanks except the holdout's. However, he did invite us to his house for a little late supper. We heartily agreed. We were hungry, and it would give us a last chance to convert him. Also, we were intrigued by how different he was from the others.

Jacques had been very calm throughout the fiery debate and had not drunk any wine. He was frail and only five feet tall. During the long argument he was exceedingly polite. The little smile that occasionally flickered across his sad face was never contemptuous or condescending. We were glad that he had asked us to his house, but we were sorry when we saw the miserable tenement where he lived.

We followed him up six flights of dark, foul-smelling stairs. His "house" was a small prison cell with one bare light bulb, a cot, a table, and one chair. The three of us looked at each other. How in hell were we to get out of there without offending our host?

"Jacques, we know how difficult it is for you to entertain us." I pulled some franc notes from my pocket. "But we have enough money to go someplace. Please let us be your hosts."

"Thank you, but we can manage here." He gave the chair to Woody and sat Cisco and me on the cot. He opened the satchel he wore over his shoulder and took out handful after handful of franc notes until the table was covered with hundreds of dollars' worth of francs. Then, from the same satchel, he took out two packages wrapped in newspaper. One package contained about a pound of raw chopped meat. The other contained some dry black cherries, and from the bottom of the satchel he fished out a piece of dark bread. He stuffed the francs back into the satchel, put a half-filled bottle of wine and one glass on the table, and pointed to the meat. "Alas," he said, "it is not beef, but it is good chevaline."

"Maurice Chevaline?" Woody bent over the meat.

"No, plain chevaline — horse meat," I answered.

"Oh." Woody straightened up, dead pan.

"Jacques, my friend, excuse me." I tried to put it in the politest French. "But why in God's name do you have to live like this when you have all that money?"

"Oh, but that's not my money. That belongs to the army."

"What army?"

"The Maquis, the resistance army of southern France. I was wounded. They arranged for me to come to Algeria to recuperate and to collect funds from our friends here. I am better now. I am going back tomorrow." Cisco and Woody were as moved as I was to be in the presence of one of the heroes who were pinning down several German divisions. Jacques was touched by our reaction, but he disclaimed any special credit.

"C'est normal," he said in his heavy accent.

"And that also explains why I have trouble understanding your accent. You're from the south of France."

"No, I'm a Polish Jew; my family name is Levy. I went to Paris in 1940 with my wife and two little girls, to escape the Nazis. I'm a tailor. I worked in Paris until we were caught by the Nazis. My wife and children have disappeared. I escaped from a train, and with the help of the resistance I got to Marseilles, where I joined the Maquis. And now I have a new trade: I am a dynamiter, a specialist in blowing up truck convoys."

"A little more dangerous than tailoring." I tried to be funny. There was nothing I could say about his wife and children.

"A little more dangerous." Jacques ran his fingers over his thin face and smiled wanly. "But the worst part, comrades, is the lack of food, especially when we're fighting. There is so little, so little. But there's food on our table now!" He rubbed his hands gleefully and then carefully proceeded to divide the food. "Bon appetit, comrades!" He gestured for us to start. The three of us ate every last morsel of Jacques Levy's feast — probably the most memorable Sabbath supper we would ever have.

When it was time to leave, Jacques said, "It was an honor to spend my last night in Algeria with you." Then, formally, with great dignity, he kissed each of us on both cheeks. "Adieu mes amis."

"So long, buddy, it's been good to know you." Woody asked me to translate.

Cisco said, "Tell him — when he gets to France — tell him to watch his ass."

"Guarde ton derrière, Jacques!"

"Okay, merci, okay." He waved as we descended the dark stairway and headed back to our ship.

■

The next morning Woody put his two hundred and forty-three bars of soap into three empty pillow cases. He slung a pillow case over one shoulder and his guitar over the other. We did the same and followed him off the ship. He led us straight to the building in the casbah where the children had talked him out of his cigarettes.

"Cigarettes! Cigarettes!" The children, about ten of them, recognized Woody at once. In French they referred to him as the "Cigarette man" and begged him for some more.

"No cigarettes!" Woody waved them away, but one of the little ones sneaked around him and smelled the pillow case.

"Soap!" the child cried out in French. "The cigarette man has soap!"

As the children closed in on him, Woody handed his guitar to Cisco and clutched the pillow case. "Line up! Line up!" he shouted as he fought off his besiegers. "Tell them to line up!" he called to me.

When the children realized that Woody was going to distribute the soap, one to a child, they began to shout for their brothers and sisters to come down from the surrounding houses. In a few minutes there were more children than bars of soap, and as soon as Woody began to distribute the bars, it was clear that the distribution wasn't going to work fairly — the bigger children stole from the little ones. "No more! No more! Tell them to call their mothers!" Woody pointed to the women watching us from the courtyard steps, from their terraces, and from their windows.

It was incredible to see how many people lived in those few buildings, more than seventy-five women lined up quietly in front of Woody. He gave each woman three bars of soap. One by one the women took the soap, looked at Woody strangely, bowed as they said something in Arabic, and passed on. The last women got one bar each, but they were just as grateful. The children, by then more than two hundred of them, stayed until the last bar was gone. Woody turned the pillow case inside out to show that it was empty, pressed the palms of his hand together, and bowed to the crowd.

The children cheered him with shouts and screams, again and again, forcing him to take more bows until he held up his hand for silence. When the children were quiet, he took his guitar from Cisco and motioned to them to sit down. Instantly every child obeyed and stared at him in absolute silence.

Woody struck a chord, threw back his head, and sang out, "There's a better world a'comin', wait and see, see, see! There's a better world a'comin', wait and see!" On the next verse Cisco and I joined in, and on the next one, Woody shouted to the children, "Now clap your hands!"

All the girls and the boys under six clapped their hands with great energy and perfect rhythm. The boys over six banged their shoe-shine boxes with their brushes — every Oran Arab boy over six had a shoe-shine box. The powerful beat of the boxes, together with the clapping, had an amazing effect; it turned the event into a demonstration, a driving, insistent, demanding demonstration. Somehow the children had caught the meaning of Woody's song; perhaps his distribution of the soap had broken through all language. They seemed to understand his every word, and the more Woody sang, the louder they banged the boxes and clapped their hands, inspiring him to invent new verse after new verse about hunger and child whores and freedom, until the boxes and the clapping, growing louder and louder, drowned out his voice, and the children themselves began chanting their own words. Suddenly a ten-year-old boy stood up, arms outstretched, brown, skinny body naked to the waist, and he began to dance. He began slowly, like a snake, at one-tenth the speed of the pounding rhythm. He moved with the self-assurance of a master, hypnotizing, slowly increasing his movements, his thin arms rippling, his waist barely moving, until little by little, responding to the beat of the boxes, the clapping, and the chanting, he began to twist and turn, every movement of his body expressing the power of that bizarre moment, twisting and turning faster and faster and faster. Suddenly he stopped, held his arm up in salute to Woody, and sat down. There was no applause, not for the dancer or for Woody. The children rose — the demonstration was over. Yet it continued in a different way; the entire audience surrounded Woody and followed him to the gates of the casbah. Not one child asked us for money or for cigarettes.

By the time we reached the gates, every child knew Woody's name.

"Woo-dee! Woo-dee! Woo-dee!" they shouted as we crossed over to the European side. Two MPs stopped us. "You guys Americans?" Just the sound of their southern accents was terrifying.

"Of course." Woody looked up at them.

"Did you come out of the casbah?"

"Hell, no — I'm an Oklahoma boy — wouldn't be caught dead in that there Ayrab casbah."

"Well, what the hell are them kids shouting at you for?"

"What kids?"

"Them Ayrab kids there!"

"Oh, they're not shouting at me. They're just shoutin' 'Woo-dee.'"

"What's that?"

"That's Ayrab for cotton candy."

That night we sailed for Arzew, a small Algerian port where our cargo would be unloaded.

"If you think the Arabs in Oran are poor, wait till you see the ones in Arzew!" Bosun said after he heard about our soap distribution.

19

At dawn of the next morning we were anchored off Arzew. There being no dock space available, we would be unloaded offshore. Two barges were already moving toward us, and as they approached, we could see that each carried about a hundred Arab longshoremen wearing dirty rags around their heads, their faces gaunt, and all of them staring at us without a wave of the hand or a shout of greeting. They just stared in absolute silence. The moment the barges touched our ship, however, there was an explosion of shouts and cries from the two hundred longshoremen as they swarmed aboard us, racing to beat each other to the pop-eyed American seamen lining the rails.

"Backsheesh! Backsheesh!" they shouted, crying for alms as they raced toward us. "Cigarette! Cigarette!" They surrounded us. "Allah! Allah!" They pulled at our shirt and trouser pockets.

The hungry longshoremen of Palermo were princes compared with these men, who were emaciated, barefoot, unshaven, and half-toothless, with rags wrapped around their heads and covering their bodies, sores on their foreheads, arms, and legs, and the sores covered with flies.

"Get out of here, you fucking rag-heads!" I heard somebody shout. I was shocked by the hatred in his voice. How could we hate these beggars? Disgusting as they were, they were our brothers and deserving of compassion.

"Backsheesh! Backsheesh!" Some hands were in my trouser pockets. I grabbed a man's wrist. He grinned at me as though it was just a game, but the grin didn't hide the look in his red-rimmed eyes, the look of grim determination to get something from me despite the risk of violence and the shame. I pulled other hands out of my pockets, but despite my pleas of "Take it easy, mates!" and "Just a minutes, fellas!" they tugged at me, invoking Allah all the time, following me as I backed into the alleyway and retreated toward my cabin, horrified that I might touch their pus-filled sores.

"Open up!" I pounded on the cabin door. "Open this goddamned door!"

Cisco opened it just enough to let me through, but before we could close it, three grinning beggars pushed their way in and were already attacking our lockers. I climbed up to my bunk, shouting, "Get out! Get the hell out!" I was disgusted by their open sores and frightened of the flies that had come into the room with them. The three of us kept shouting with no effect until I took off my shoe and flung it at the head of the one ransacking my locker. "Get out, you fucking rag-head!" I shouted with all the hatred I had heard in my shipmate's voice out on deck. The shoe caught the man in the back of the head. He turned to me without the slightest expression of surprise and left, followed quietly by the other two.

"Goddamn it!" I slammed the door with all my might, more disgusted with myself than with the beggars. So much for my brotherly compassion.

Barred from our cabins, cursed and repulsed by everybody, the begging longshoremen turned to the garbage cans. They jostled each other to dig into the garbage, salvaging what food they could, littering the deck with coffee grounds, fruit skins, and cigarette butts. One of the longshoremen begged me, in pidgin French, for an empty can so that he might scoop up some of the garbage for his family.

"Come with me." Woody led Cisco and me to the storeroom. We opened fifty one-pound cans of coffee and dumped the contents into a burlap bag. We distributed the empty cans to the longshoremen and explained, through their foreman, who spoke a little French and a little English, that we would try to find more cans for the rest of the two hundred men. The longshoremen were deeply moved and praised us to Allah for our kindness.

From then on we kept the garbage as clean as we could. Cisco called a meeting and got the crew to refrain from extinguishing cigarettes in leftover food and to avoid mixing the leftovers with dirt. Our uneaten food was placed in a clean garbage can, and although it looked terrible, it was food.

Each morning we got the longshoremen to line up in front of the garbage. We had managed to find enough empty fruit cans, tomato cans, and whatever else we could empty. Each man got a scoopful of garbage — that, plus their daily wages of a dollar a day, was supposed to keep their families alive and give them the strength to unload us. Their bosses charged the Allies regular stevedoring rates and made fortunes for themselves.

At the rate the poor longshoremen worked, it would take a month to unload our ship even though we had found dock space. A month in Arzew! The miserable town offered nothing, absolutely nothing. Aside from its small, dull European center of two or three streets, it consisted mostly of decrepit Arab mud-brick houses, dusty unpaved streets, open sewers, and hundreds of open-sored children covered with flies. Bosun was right about its poverty, and the few GIs stationed there said that if the world had to have an enema, the tube would be inserted in Arzew.

To keep from being bored to death, we would have to find our excitement aboard ship. Next to fly killing, the most interesting activity was watching the longshoremen at work. They were a mystery. Where did these emaciated, starving men get the strength to work? They started at sunup and stopped at noon, when they took a short break to eat flat bread and whatever they could salvage from our garbage. They would work till sunset. Perhaps their strength came from the song they chanted over and over again as they worked. At lunchtime I asked their foreman what it was they sang.

"Omar Khayyám."

"Omar Khayyám? Why?"

"Omar Khayyám say Allah is great and we will go to paradise when we die."

"But Omar Khayyám does not believe in life after we die." I spoke my French slowly and distinctly. "Omar Khayyám does not believe in God."

The foreman looked at me blankly, but I could tell that he had understood my words. Suddenly his eyes rolled upward. He threw his head back and raised his arms at the sky, shrieking a barrage of Arabic, evidently asking the heavens to bear witness to my blasphemy against Omar Khayyám, the poet of Allah, the eulogizer of his divine mercy and of the paradise to come after this miserable life on earth.

"Why the hell did you have to tell the poor bastard that?" Cisco shook his head as the man continued wailing, one arm waving at Allah and the other pointed at me.

"Because it's the truth." I turned away from Cisco and tried to quiet my accuser.

As soon as the Arab stopped to catch his breath, I attempted to explain that there was nothing personal in what I had said. It was just that the Omar Khayyám I knew said that our life on earth was the only paradise we'd ever know and that all talk of the hereafter was false. The poor man promptly threw up his hands again and continued shrieking to Allah.

"Why don't you leave him alone?" Cisco was becoming angry.

"But it's for his own good."

The foreman's cries to Allah brought all his longshoremen running, and when they heard his accusation against me, they too ranted and rolled their eyes and waved their arms to heaven. Some of them spit on the deck in front of me.

"You lie about Khayyám!" the foreman shouted at me in English.

"No, I do not lie to you! Let the men sing Khayyám, and you translate for my two friends and me. But you translate honest — okay?"

The foreman angrily accepted, and the two hundred ragged, sore-covered longshoremen lifted their heads in defiant chant. There was not one atheistic word in the first ten verses, nothing but praise for Allah and the paradise to come.

"All right?" the foreman glared at me triumphantly as the longshoremen shouted and jeered at my defeat.

"Something's wrong!" I shouted. "Tell them your rulers have changed Khayyám's words! Your rulers want you to dream of paradise while they keep you working in this hell on earth! Now translate that!" I knew that his translation was correct because of the explosion of fury from the longshoremen. Some of the nearest actually moved toward me, shaking clenched fists.

"You are betraying your proud Arabic heritage!" I shouted.

"You lie!" the foreman shouted. "Khayyám's words have not been changed!"

I turned to the longshoreman who had spoken to me in broken French and asked him to translate for me. I did not trust the foreman. "Ask your brother longshoremen why they cannot at least discuss the question."

There was a profound silence as the longshoreman translated my words. Then one of the Arabs nearest me, the first man to whom I had given an empty can and who had blessed me in Allah's name, raised the can above his head and hurled it at my feet. For a second there was such silence we could hear the can rattling along the steel deck. I still hear the rattle of that can; I still feel the chill of his sacrifice. No other word was spoken between us. The work bell rang, and they went back to work.

Nor did Cisco or Woody say a word to me until we got back to our cabin. "Now what the hell did you accomplish!" Cisco threw himself on his bunk. "Why did you have to disillusion them?"

Woody said nothing, but it was clear that he was just as annoyed as Cisco was.

"And what happened to your ideas about the mysteries of life after death and Einstein's many dimensions?" Cisco raised himself on one elbow. "You jumped on me for criticizing Klotski's religion, and now you're stomping on those poor Arabs for believing like Klotski!"

"It's one thing to defend faith in the abstract, but when faith keeps people living like slaves, it has to be attacked!"

"I know that better than you, you dumb bastard, but it's a question of how to attack it. When Woody and I were organizing the fruit pickers, they would have stoned us out of their camps if we had blasted away at their Jesus. Blasting Jesus wasn't our goal. Our goal was how to get an extra ten cents a bushel. Same thing with the Arabs; when we cleaned up our garbage and gave them tin cans, they became our friends. In a month, nice and slow, we could have taught them something about getting better wages — maybe even something about Omar Khayyám — but when you got up on your soapbox and blasted their most fundamental beliefs, you turned them into our enemies, and they stoned you with the cans we gave them."

There was nothing I could say.

"You dumb, big-mouth Wop." Cisco tried to save me from my embarrassed silence.

That evening, after the longshoremen had quit working, there was a light knock on our cabin door. Six Arab longshoremen were standing in the alleyway. In pidgin French one of them very quietly asked if I would tell him and his companions more about Omar Khayyám.

The three of us took the men to the afterdeck, and there we began our first lesson: The Meaning of Omar Khayyám and Its Relationship to the Working-class Movement.

"Well, at least we've got six seeds to plant, right?" The pride in my voice turned to embarrassment before I finished my sentence, because I knew what the answer would be.

"Could have been two hundred." Cisco and Woody answered simultaneously.

The first problem with our students was communication. Only three of them spoke Pidgin French, so that everything had to be kept simple. Pantomime, mimicry, and Cisco's Indian sign language helped a great deal.

Our second problem was security. The rest of the Arab longshoremen would make life very difficult for our six students if they found them fraternizing with us. We instructed our students to tell the others that they were taking it on themselves to convert us to the ways of Allah. It worked. Our students were treated as heroes, and we were free to teach them while their fellow Arabs smiled on us from a discreet distance.

The third problem was how to solve the problem of a social class acting against its own self-interest, that is, how to get the longshoremen to take back their tin cans. We instructed our students to tell the others that our giving of the tin cans was an act of charity, and charity being close Allah's heart, their rejection of the cans would be an offense to Allah. The cans quickly came back into use. We then took up a more formal curriculum.

We began with geography. We had each man draw a map of the world. They all drew more or less the same thing: three-quarters of the page was Algeria, one-quarter of the page was France, a dot in the left corner represented the United States, and another dot in the right corner stood for the Soviet Union. There was so much to teach and so little time.

We taught for an hour every night, the three of us competing in developing teaching techniques. Woody was the champ. The students understood his Okie a lot better than my French, and his songs about the unions and about black slavery were what they wanted to hear more than anything else.

By the time we were unloaded, a month later, our students had a rudimentary theoretical knowledge of trade unionism, and on the practical side, they had some simple truths drummed into them: limit your efforts to easily achievable goals and never get too far ahead of the others. We had planted six seeds, but Cisco and Woody were right: we could have planted two hundred.

Just before the ship was ready to sail, our students came to bid us goodbye. Since our cabin was too small, we led them to the afterdeck. There, with great solemnity, Ibrahim, one of the French-speaking ones, said that henceforth my Arabic name was Khalil ben Khayyám; *Khalil* meant "friend," *ben* meant "son of," and *Khayyám* was for the great poet who brought us together.

I opened my arms and embraced each student in turn. They did the same for Woody and Cisco, calling them "Woody ben Khayyám" and "Cisco ben Khayyám."

Then they presented each of us with an empty glass — a plain ten-cent water tumbler. They offered it as the precious thing it was to them, and Ibrahim said, "May your lives be as rich and full as these glasses are poor and empty."

We accompanied them to the gangway and watched them descend. As our ship moved away, Ibrahim and his friends waved to us and shouted "Salem Aleikum!"

"Aleikum Salem!" We waved back. "Peace be with you too!"

And so we said farewell to Algeria, the land of Hedy Lamarr dreams.

■

We steamed westerly, with five other freighters and one destroyer escort for protection, and after a couple of days we put in at Gibraltar. The rumor was that we might be sent to the Far East. Two days later word came through: we were to be part of a big convoy, and our destination was Newport News, Virginia, home port of the *Floy-Floy*.

"Leave it to Cap'n Brown — somehow the old bastard always gets his way." Mister Johnson pulled some money from his pocket. "I'll wager two to one his wife will be standing on the dock waiting to greet him."

Just as we were getting ready to sail, we had an accident with a hawser that became entangled in the ship's propeller. After an hour's work, the rope was still stuck fast.

"You watch the old man." Mister Johnson pointed to Captain Brown standing on the poop deck and taking off his trousers. The old captain looked ludicrous in his skinny, milk-white, old-boned nakedness, and even more so when he clamped a long knife between his teeth and dove off the stern. A minute later he still hadn't surfaced, but then up he shot, smiling, knife held high, and ten minutes later we were ready to join the convoy assembling outside Gibraltar. But this time Captain Brown did not get his way. The *Floy-Floy* was assigned to coffin corner, portside aft.

Spain was still being used as a haven for German submarines, and the very first night, just after midnight — DRRRINNNGGG! We were jolted out of our bunks by the general-alarm bell. A red rocket was seen in the sky; it seemed to come from the ship in coffin corner starboard aft. The moon made the convoy a well-lit target. Our naval escort furiously dashed up and down our flanks, desperately dropping depth charges. Suddenly our engine stopped dead.

Captain Brown signaled the commodore ship, saying he would try to catch up with the convoy as soon as the engine was fixed. We watched the silhouetted convoy disappear, leaving us at the mercy of the wolf pack. An hour later our engine was working, and although we were alone on that moonlit ocean, Captain Brown called off the general alarm and ordered us to get some sleep.

"Go on, do as he says." Mister Johnson shooed me out of the galley. "You got enough bread and stuff for tomorrow. Get some sleep and don't worry."

We woke up to find that we were back in the safety of the convoy, although we were still in our coffin-corner position.

That night, just after sunset — DRRRINNNGGG! Another general alarm. Even before we got to our gun stations we could tell that our engine was slowing down, and in a few minutes the convoy was moving away from us, signaling us good luck but leaving us once more to the mercy of the wolves. Again, after the convoy was well out of sight, our engine recovered, and although we were all alone, the captain called off the alarm.

I worked all night, and at dawn, when I went out on deck, there we were, back in our convoy position. The *Floy-Floy* might have a lousy chief engineer, but she sure had a great navigator in Captain Brown.

On the third night the U-boats were still with us and shortly after dark — DRRRINNNGGG! This time when the ship's engine went dead, the fury of the men broke out in catcalls, boos, and vicious curses for the black gang and their idiotic chief. For the moment the terror for the U-boats was overcome by our anger. Everybody shouted and cursed — everybody except Mister Johnson, who held his sides while he doubled up with laughter.

"Lord, Lord," he gasped, stamping his foot and wiping his eyes, "can't you see that the captain is doing it on purpose? By dropping back we got a damn sight better chance of staying alive than if we stayed in coffin corner all night! Lord, Lord, you whities are all so dumb." He wiped the laugh tears from his eyes. "Cap'n thinks the subs are too busy to chase a straggler, and he's got the guts to bet on it. Does it every time we're in coffin corner, God bless his black Jamaican ass!" Luckily we had no other occasion to prove the wisdom of Captain Brown's theory: there were no more U-boat attacks. The danger came as we approached Newport News.

We were at the tail end of a single file of twenty ships, steaming slowly into port. First ships in would have a better chance of getting dock space. Captain Brown obviously wanted dock space. At full speed he began overtaking the ships ahead of him. Despite the danger of collision in such a busy port, our crazy old captain wove in and out of the line of ships like a teenage hot-rodder, leaving the overtaken ships aghast and scaring the hell out of all of us on deck watching his mad maneuvering with pop-eyed horror until, having overtaken the first ship, he slammed his engine into reverse and skidded to a halt nicely just a few yards from an open dock.

In minutes we were tied up alongside, and the old bastard was gone. Some said they saw him go off arm and arm with his wife, an old lady in black, umbrella in hand, come to fetch him home.

It was late the next night that our train pulled into Penn Station, where the three of us parted, agreeing to meet soon to make plans for our next trip. It wasn't until three in the morning that I got a chance to embrace *my* wife. I slipped into bed and rubbed my new beard against her back.

"Hello, darling," she murmured in her sleep.

"Hello, darling?" I turned on the light. "How the hell did you know who it was? What's going on around here? What bearded rabbi's been sleeping in my bed?"

Gabrielle put her arms around me and assured me that there was no rabbi to worry about. Thus ended my trip as the *Floy-Floy*'s second cook and baker. Would that my next trip end as happily.

The SEA PUSSY

20

My thirty-day shore leave was over. I hated the thought of shipping out again as a second cook and baker. I had learned only enough to get me past the crew's minimum standards of criticism. Any increase of standards by the next crew could be dangerous. I wasn't going to risk my neck again if I could help it. I remembered Courtroom Kelly's brilliant improvisation about a flour allergy and presented myself to the Maritime Hospital.

"Sir, you must save me!" I pleaded with the doctor. "I'm a ship's baker and I love my job — I love it! Unless you find a cure for my allergy, I won't be able to ship out as a baker. I'll be forced to ship out as a lowly messman! So, please sir, please find me a cure!" I sneezed three times as loudly as I could and gasped for air. "You see, sir, just thinking about flour makes me sneeze!"

"I'm sorry, son, but there's nothing we can do for you. We could give you some medicine that might help you, but if you got a severe attack at sea, you might die. We can't take the responsibility for that. I'm sorry, son, but you'll have to ship out as a messman." The doctor put his arm around me.

"That's all right, sir. Don't worry about me. I understand. I accept my fate. Just change my papers from second cook and baker to messman, or else the union will force me to ship out as a baker."

"Of course." The doctor made the change. "I'm sorry for you, son. Maybe someday you'll get over your flour allergy." I immediately telephoned Cisco and Woody, and we agreed to meet the next day at the hiring hall.

■

Cisco and I got to the hall ahead of Woody and had our eyes on three messman jobs advertised on the big blackboard. "Hope he gets here before those jobs go," I said, looking toward the door.

"Relax, there'll be others. There's no telling when Woody'll show up. Anything could happen to that guy on his way from Coney Island to —"

"Oh, my God!" I interrupted him. "Here he comes!"

"You guys starin' at me as though you hadn't seen me in twenty years." Woody lifted his face to Cisco and me. "It's only been three weeks."

"No man could get so dirty looking in three weeks!" Cisco looked at him closer.

"And I thought we agreed to shave off our beards." I added. "What happened?"

"Had a good run of writin'. No time for prettyin' up," said Woodrow Wilson Guthrie, at that moment undoubtedly the dirtiest-looking seaman in the United States Merchant Marine. A frayed woolen cap clung to his overgrown dark, curly hair; his face was covered with a beard in which were enmeshed bread crumbs and a bit of white string. His faded shirt was what Cisco called "chicken-shit brown"; a piece of rope held up his trousers, which looked as though they hadn't been changed since his first trip; he wore a beat-up pair of open-toed sandals without socks; and he was half-buried under his usual load of musical instruments, sea bag, books, and three bottles of rum.

"I'll say this for your appearance." I pushed his cap back from his eyes. "If it's your intention to scare the enemy to death, you look great."

Woody's answer was drowned out by the dispatcher's microphone. "All right. I've got three messman jobs on this lovely ship!" he shouted to the crowd milling about the hall. "She's a beauty!" the microphone squawked. "In fact she's a luxury liner, a regular cruise ship. Who's gonna be the lucky guys! Step right up now, step right up. The jobs are going, going —"

"Cut the crap, Joe." Cisco shoved our cards under the dispatcher's grill. "We'll take the jobs."

"Gone to these lucky dogs."

"What do you know about her, Joe?"

"Nothin' Cisco, but I can tell you she's got a big crew — about fifty, not counting the officers, plus twenty-four navy gun crew, so she's probably a converted troop carrier."

"Holy shit, give us something else!" Cisco threw the job slips back at the dispatcher.

"Too late, buddy. I stamped them already." The dispatcher turned back to his microphone. "All right, I've got another beauty here needs a couple of ..."

"Fucked." Cisco handed each of us our slips. "Let's go." We strapped our guitars to our backs and went to see what kind of ship fate had dealt us.

■

"Well, at least she's a beauty." I tried to reassure Cisco, who was squinting at our new ship. I wasn't kidding him; she was a new C-3, one of the best freighters ever built, eighteen thousand tons and more than two city blocks long. Her name was the *Sea Porpoise*.

"Is she welded or riveted?" Cisco asked.

"Riveted, thank God."

The plates of the C-3 were lavishly riveted, giving the ship strength and flexibility. "She's got more stitches to the square inch than a high-priced Oriental carpet," Woody said as he led the way up her gangway, insisting on carrying his load of instruments by himself. If ships have souls, that beautiful ship must have shuddered at the first touch of Woody's beat-up sandal on her polished deck.

"Seen the chief steward?" Cisco asked a deckhand.

"He's wanderin' around someplace."

The *Sea Porpoise* had the smell of a good-feeding ship — fresh-baked bread, spices, and cleanliness. Her galley was walled with aluminum, not the rusting metal of the Liberties, and instead of the usual coal-burning oven, hers was electric and made of gleaming stainless steel. Her galley's crowning jewels were the electric potato peeler and the electric dishwasher, undreamed of on ordinary ships. But above all, the most beautiful thing about her was her spotlessness. Everything on the *Sea Porpoise* gleamed, even her engine room.

We had accidentally opened a door leading to the engine room's ladder, and standing on the top landing, we looked down through the three-story maze of intertwining tubes, boilers, ladders, gear wheels, and vents. There wasn't a spot of grease to be seen. I was sure that even at sea, with the noise of her engine blasting your ears, the smell of oil everywhere, and the great shaft of tempered steel pounding and thrusting along its lubricated track — even then there still wouldn't be a spot of grease to be seen.

We went up to the boat deck. Everything was spotless and gleaming. "The *Sea Porpoise* shore is a beauty," said Woody, and he promptly re-named her the *Sea Pussy*.

"Hey! You with the beard!" somebody barked from the bridge. It was an officer in a dazzling white uniform with a lot of stripes.

Woody tilted his head up toward the vision in white, closed one eye, and lifted the eyebrow of the other one. "Yes, sir! Yes siree sir, sir!"

"What did you say?" the officer barked again.

Woody tilted his head a little further back and lifted his eyebrow a little higher. "I said, 'Yes, sir! Yes siree sir, sir!'"

"You crazy bastard!" I muttered to Woody as the officer stormed to-ward us. "That was the captain!" From his glistening blond hair to his spotless white shoes, he was the gleaming reflection of his immaculate ship. His dazzling white uniform deepened the blue of his eyes and gave them a sharp look. In fact everything about the thirty-five-year-old cap-tain was sharp: his nose, the straight line of his mouth, the crease of his trousers, and his astringent expression that made him look as though he were sucking a lemon. He wore white gloves. That a seaman as scruffy looking as Woody should come aboard his pristine ship — well, I could understand his point of view.

"What the hell are you doing on my ship?"

"Well, sir, somewhere in one of my pockets I have a job slip for this here ship." Woody slowly began piling his load onto the deck — violin case, mandolin case, books, brown paper bag of rum bottles, and his guitar.

The captain stared at the words boldly written across the face of the guitar, "THIS MACHINE KILLS FASCISTS." Then the captain stared at Woody, who was fishing for something in his pockets. Out came a kazoo, which Woody carefully placed on top of the guitar; two harmon-icas, which he placed next to the kazoo; and a Jew's harp, which he stud-ied for a moment before placing it carefully next to the others. Then from a back pocket he pulled out a soiled piece of paper, which he officiously unfolded and held at extreme arm's length. "It says here that I am a mess — man."

"You? A messman?" The captain's eyes bulged.

"That's what it says, sir: a waiter — I beg your pardon, sir: a messman." The captain gulped. "Have you signed the ship's articles yet?"

"Yep!"

The captain flushed. He pointed to Woody's trousers. His voice rising, he said, "How long have you been wearing those?"

Woody looked down at his trousers. "Cap'n, I was torpedoed and saved in these pants. If I change them, my luck might change for the worse, and somethin' terrible might happen to this pretty little ship."

The captain flushed deeper, pressed his lips, and in a very controlled voice said, "Report to my cabin at eight bells."

"Eight bells — that's uh . . ." Woody cocked his head toward Cisco.

"Four o'clock," said Cisco quickly.

"Yes, sir," said Woody, "eight bells."

The captain turned and hurriedly climbed the ladder back to the bridge, Woody staring all the while at the captain's dazzling white behind.

Cisco shook his head. "You're in for it now."

"Us too!" I said. "Guilt by association! We're all in for it!"

"Had to happen." Woody picked up his instruments. "Anybody wears a uniform that white is gotta be a fink." He led the way back to the crew's messroom to look for the chief steward.

"Hallo, keed." The chief steward greeted me in a rich Puerto Rican accent. "I hear you when you make speech in the union meeting in Manhattan Center. If you work as good as you talk, we get along okay. What job you want?"

"The crew's mess for me and Cisco." Two messmen were needed to serve the C-3's larger crew. "And the gun-crew mess for him." I pointed to Woody, who had dumped his load onto a mess table and was busily tuning his guitar.

"Holy geez!" The chief steward backed away. "I know we losin' lot of guys in the Merchan' Marine, but the union got no right to send me somebody look like that!"

"Hey, you beeg bums!" The joyous shout came from Roberto, the cook of the *Willy B*. "Chief, you gonna have a first-class band on dees ship!" He hugged Cisco and me. "An' dees little guy, he's better dan Xavier Cugat!" He gave Woody a big hug.

"I doan need no goddamn musician!" The chief glared at Woody. "I need a messman, an' he's too goddamn dirty!"

"No, chief, he's no dirty. He oney look dirty, but hees clean like a baby's ass."

"I go by what he look like!" The chief glared at me. "An' by what he look like, he gonna work nights washin' pots and moppin' the fuckin' decks!"

Woody resumed tuning the guitar.

"Chief, I swear we'll take care of him." I raised my right hand. "He'll be all right in the gun-crew's —"

"Pots! Pots! Anybody look like that, he's no good for nuttin' but pots and moppin' decks!" He turned and made for the door.

Woody struck a guitar chord. "La cookey racha, la cookey racha!" he sang out in his Okie accent. "El no puede caminar!"

The chief stopped in the doorway, listened for a moment, and then turned to Woody. "Doan try to get around me with that shit, buddy. Your Spanish ain't that good. I said pots an' moppin' the decks!"

Woody, eyes shut, went on singing. Cisco and I swung our guitars around and quickly joined him in a very good three-part harmony, Mexican style. Roberto began to drum on the table, and in no time guys were dancing all over the place with at least half a dozen mixed couples, engineers dancing with deckhands and stewards dancing with gunners. Roberto, shaking his behind to Woody's rhumba rhythm, opened his arms to the chief steward. The chief hesitated for a moment; then, without smiling, he began to dance, sensuously led by Roberto.

When the music stopped, the chief looked at me sternly. "Okay, he can have the gun-crew messroom, but doan you forget — you responsible!" He walked out.

Cisco put his guitar down. "Wait here, Woody."

I put down my guitar. "And don't go wandering."

Cisco and I scouted the big ship for good quarters. If we were lucky, we might get a big cabin just for the three of us. The best bet was the Glory Hole. It was a spacious cabin with two portholes about six feet above the waterline and four sets of double bunks. Four crewmen were already in possession of the best bunks and putting sheets on them.

"Hi guys. Is there room in here?" I asked.

"Sure." one of them pointed to the empty bunks.

Cisco lay down on one of the lower bunks, gave me a surreptitious wink, and began to moan.

"What's the matter with him?" another seaman asked.

"Nothing." I looked at Cisco pityingly.

"Whattaya mean, nuthin'? Is he sick or somethin'?"

"No," I whispered, my back to Cisco, "just seasick." I mimicked a man vomiting violently.

Cisco jumped out of the bunk and lurched toward the sink. I blocked his way.

"Quick, where's the head?" I asked the man.

"Two doors aft on the right!"

Cisco turned and dashed out.

"He's not so bad in the daytime. You see he didn't do it in the sink."

"The goddamned ship ain't even movin'." One of the men slammed the door in anger.

"Yeah, I know."

"What the hell is he doin' in the Merchant Marine?" the second man growled.

"He's scared shitless of the army."

"Boy, it must be some fun bunkin' with him." The third man shook his head.

"Whatta you gonna do? The guy's my buddy." I shrugged sadly.

"Well, I'm sorry for him, but we don't have to put up with it. There's plenty of room on this ship. I'm leaving."

Two of the others left with him.

The fourth man, older than the other three, kept right on making his bed until Cisco returned.

"Oh, boy," Cisco moaned.

The man looked at Cisco and said, "Okay, you can stop acting now. Courtroom Kelly pulled that one on me a long time ago." He stuck out his hand. "My name's George."

"Hi, George." Cisco shook with him. "This is Jim."

"Sorry about the act." I shook George's hand.

"Don't be sorry," said George. "We got the whole Glory Hole for the three of us."

"Four of us," I said.

"Four? Who's the other guy?"

"He's in the messroom, watching our guitars," said Cisco.

"You mean the little guy with all them instruments?"

"Yeah."

"Hell, I like music, but I gotta have my peace an' quiet. I sleep in the afternoon."

"No hard feelings," said Cisco, "but we practice a lot."

"That's okay," said George. "Music on a ship is good. I'll find another bunk."

"George," I said, "we weren't being bastards when we put this act on. It would be worse if you guys got stuck in here with all the noise we make and then found out you couldn't move to another bunk."

"I said it's all right — but you guys better play good." He closed the door behind him.

"We'd better level with the other three guys before we vote for ship's chairman," I said as I tested one of the bunks. "We can't afford to lose three votes."

"We'll do it later. Right now, keep an eye on this cabin — I'll go get Woody."

"You'd better. It's almost four o'clock, and if he keeps that captain waiting one second, we're all dead."

Before Cisco reached the door, the sound of hundreds of men singing at top voice came to us through the porthole. "And when the Yanks — go marchin' in — when the Yanks go marching in — Boys I want to be in that number — when the Yanks march through Berlin!"

Cisco and I rushed up to the messroom. Woody was gone. We went out on deck. The singing was louder now. Several seamen were at the rail, looking down at the dock.

"Roberto!" I called. "Did you see Woody?"

"Cugat? He's dere on the dock!"

I looked over the rail. Several hundred soldiers massed alongside our ship were singing Woody's song, while more hundreds poured through the dock gate. Woody, perched on a ten-foot-high crate, was wanging away on his guitar and shouting, "When our tanks roll through Berlin . . ." The soldiers entering the dock picked up his words, "When our tanks roll through Berlin . . . ," and soon a couple of thousand voices were singing, "Boys I want to be in that number, when the Yanks go marching in!"

"What the hell is going on?" Cisco shouted above the noise.

"We taking on three thousan' soldiers," Roberto shouted, "an' Cugat is pipin' them on board!"

"He's got no pass to be on that dock!" Cisco turned to me. "The sonofabitch is AWOL, and the trip hasn't even started!"

"And he's late for the captain!"

"Woody! Woody!" We tried to yell above the singing, but it was no use; three thousand soldiers were now singing, and the boarding had started. As each man passed the crate, he looked up at Woody and saluted him sharply. When the last soldier climbed the gangway ladder, Woody followed him.

"Which way to the captain's office?" He asked Cisco and me.

The three thousand tough-looking, hard-trained southern GIs hit the

Sea Pussy like a tidal wave. They were supposed to stay confined to their quarters in the ship's five holds, six hundred men to a hold in bunks stacked five high and only twenty-four inches apart. But the GIs struggle to escape topside started almost immediately. By bribing, cajoling, and threatening the MPs, a couple of hundred soldiers gained their way to the main deck — their objective, the messrooms.

Three soldiers tried to talk Cisco into giving them a loaf of bread.

"I can't. There wouldn't be enough for the crew."

"We'll give you a dollar for that loaf of bread."

"Come on, your chow can't be that bad," I added.

"Well, let's put is this way: we'll give you two dollars for that loaf of bread."

"We don't sell food, brother." Cisco cut off half the loaf. "Here, split this between you, and leave us alone now. We've got work to do, and we're late."

We were late because we had been searching for Woody. We hadn't seen him since he went to report to the captain. We had searched the ship from top to bottom, but there was no sign of him.

"You start setting up here," Cisco said. "I'll go set up for Woody."

A few seconds later Cisco was back. "They've got a new messman in place of Woody."

"That fucking captain." I stormed into the gunners' messroom. There was a clean-cut young man writing on the blackboard. Soldiers and gun-crew kids were quietly watching him. "Excuse me, mate." I tapped him on the shoulder. "Do you know what happened to —"

The young man turned to me. "Can't you see I'm busy?" It was Woody, decorating the menu. Cisco, with his bad eyesight, hadn't recognized him, and no wonder. Woody was clean-shaven; his hair was cut short; he was freshly showered; and he wore a new ship's stores shirt, new trousers, new shoes, and socks.

"What happened?" I said when I recovered from my shock.

"What happened what?"

"What happened to your beard, your hair, your shirt, your bare feet?"

"Oh, the captain and I exchanged a few ideas." Woody turned to the blackboard and continued with his decoration.

■

After dinner the tables were cleared and the deck swept as quickly as possible in preparation for the crew's union meeting.

There were about forty men present. The other men on duty would be relieved for a few minutes so that they might vote on important issues. The entire steward department was present. Most of the steward gang was Spanish speaking, from Puerto Rico, the Philippines, and Cuba. The rest of the crew was from all over the United States.

Cisco took the floor. "Before we get around to electing a ship's chairman, I just want to point out that with three thousand soldiers on board, we need a chairman who can keep this ship from becoming a clip joint. There's gotta be no selling food to the soldiers and no crooked crap games. Anybody caught selling or gambling with the soldiers is gotta have his union book taken away from him, and there's —"

"*Who do the hell you think you are?*" somebody shouted from the back of the room.

The speaker rose; he was dark skinned, short, and powerful, with a battered face. It was Jojo. That was all we needed on this trip. Jojo, a forty-year-old New York–born Puerto Rican, was the boss of a tough gang that ran crooked crap games on troopships. I knew him from the union meetings ashore.

"This is a union meeting," he yelled, "not a church meeting! Stick to union business!"

The son of a bitch was as clever as he was dangerous. He earned big money, and he permitted no interference with his racket. Rival gang members or interfering union do-gooders got their legs broken when they were caught ashore. There were also rumors of suspicious disappearances at sea.

"Sit down, Jojo!" Chips, the ship's carpenter, was on his feet. "All you're thinking about is your crooked crap game."

Jojo studied Chips for a moment. "My crap game ain't none of your business, my friend, and if anybody —"

"I move we appoint Bosun as temporary chairman, all those in favor say aye!" I said it all in one breath.

There was an immediate chorus of ayes.

Jojo shouted, "Just a minute! Wait a —"

The bosun banged the table. "Order! Order! Brother Cisco has the floor."

"All I was trying to say," Cisco said as he looked around the room, "is that keeping our union name clean is as much union business as any porkchop issue." He sat down.

The loud applause was broken by Jojo shouting, "Brother Chairman! Brother Chairman!"

"The chair recognizes Brother Jojo."

"Brother Chairman, nobody's got no right to tell no union brother what to do an' what not to do with his wife or with his friends or with any soldier who wants to shoot crap with him!" Jojo's three stooges applauded loudly.

The bosun waited for the applause to stop, and then in a quiet voice he said, "Brother Jojo, according to union rules, a brother is free to screw his wife any time he wants to, but he ain't free to screw a soldier on an N.M.U. ship. The chair recognizes Brother Roberto."

"Point of order! Point of order!" shouted Jojo.

"What is it?" asked the chair.

"According to the rules of McKesson an' Robbins, you ain't supposed to —"

The chairman banged the table. "Brother Jojo, McKesson an' Robbins is a pharmaceutical company. The meetings of the National Maritime Union are run by the Robert's Rules of Order, according to which, sit down!"

Everybody laughed except Jojo.

"Point of order!" Jojo flushed.

"All right, what's your point of order?"

"Brother Chairman." Jojo looked carefully around the room.

"Yes, Brother Jojo?"

"Brother Chairman, you and your Robert's Rules can go an' fuck yourself."

"An' the same to you, Brother Jojo. Brother Roberto has the floor."

Roberto rose. "I gonna nominate Brother Cisco for ship's chairman. He's a good man an' I know him."

"Second the motion," somebody called.

"Thanks." Cisco rose. "But this ship is going to have plenty of problems, and anyway, I was chairman on my last ship." He turned to me. "I nominate Brother Jim Longhi!"

I was thoroughly surprised, annoyed, and pleased. I was surprised because it was tacitly understood among the three of us that Cisco was the natural leader and that he would always be our candidate for ship's chairman. I was annoyed because the job would be tough enough with three thousand soldiers on board, but with rats like Jojo ready to pounce on them, it would be like being a sheriff in the Wild West. I was pleased because Woody and Cisco had obviously caucused and decided to put their faith in me.

"Second the motion," called Woody, "not because he's my buddy, but because he's got as good an antifascist head on him as I've ever seen."

"You mean he's a Red?" called Jojo.

Bosun banged the table. "Any other nominations?"

"What's the use?" another voice from the rear called. "The commonists got it all sewed up."

Bosun banged the table. "If you got any beefs, Brother, stand up and identify yourself."

"Mah name is officer's messman Shackleton." He stood, over six feet tall, his shirtsleeves carefully rolled up to show his powerful muscles. Shackleton! What a trip this was going to be. Shackleton gave karate demonstrations at the union hall, and although he always used strong lavender toilet water, dressed immaculately, and wore his hair in a high pompadour, nobody dared to tease him. Some said he was queer, and some said he was queer but didn't know it. In any case, latent or patent, that was one homosexual I wouldn't want to buck.

"*Buster* Shackleton!" He put both hands on his hips. "An' ah say the commonists got the N.M.U. all sewed up!"

Bosun banged the table. "Brother Shackleton, all I'm worried about is this ship and electing a ship's chairman in a democratic way. Sit down!" He banged the table. "Any more nominations?"

"I nominate Brother Hudson from the deck gang," called Chips. Hudson was a friend of ours and would be a good chairman.

The motion was seconded, and there being no other nominations, the vote was held. I won by a few votes. There was light applause as Bosun shook my hand. I took his chair. I looked at the men, not for effect, but because I couldn't think of anything to say. Then the words came. "I feel like a captain just given his first command. I'll do everything I can to help you make this ship worthy of our union's name. We're carrying a precious cargo, and we're going to treat those soldiers like our brothers!" Then I got carried away by my own voice and added, "There's no room on this ship for hustlers and crooked gamblers!" There was total silence except for the pounding of the ship's engine — we had not been aware that the ship was under way. All eyes shifted to Jojo and then back to me.

I realized the danger of the situation, but my fear pushed me further. "To help us keep things under control, I propose that we make it illegal for anybody to gamble with the soldiers." Nearly all hands were raised in favor of my proposal, some men boldly staring at Jojo, but most of the men raised their hands warily, carefully avoiding Jojo's eyes. Jojo muttered something in Spanish, and some of the Spanish-speaking brothers lowered their hands.

"The ayes carry!" I called out.

"You ain't the captain of this ship." Jojo was on his feet. "How you gonna enforce your Red dictatorship?"

The men waited for my answer.

"I'll think about it, Brother Jojo."

He and I looked at each other for a moment, and then I turned my eyes away and called, "Unless there's any other business, this meeting is adjourned till next Thursday night."

After the meeting I picked my way through the soldiers blocking the alleyway and got to the deck door. I pushed aside the safety curtain, entered the small area between the curtain and the door, and pulled the curtain behind me. A soldier coming from the deck opened the door.

"Got a cigarette, buddy?" My voice shook a little. I was ashamed for my weakness. The first bit of tension, and I was smoking again.

"Sure." The soldier pulled out a pack. I closed the door to keep any light from escaping. In the dark the soldier struck a match. My hands shook a little too as I sucked in my first smoke in ten days.

I cupped the cigarette in my hand and stepped out onto the deck. It was drizzling, but I made for the stern. As I went past the hatches, I heard the sound of the soldiers, even though the hatch covers were tightly sealed. The hatches had to be sealed. Any escaping light, even a cigarette, was a beacon to the U-boats waiting for us just off Fire Island.

I stood alone on the poop deck, watched the dimmed-out skyscrapers slowly receding, and thought of Gabrielle. A loud burst of sound from the soldiers in number-five hatch brought me out of my reverie. I brought my cupped hand to my lips and sucked in a deep draught. The dim lights of Governor's Island slipped by. We passed Buttermilk Channel, then Red Hook. I tried to make out the spire of St. Stephen's Church, where Pete Panto had held the great rank-and-file longshoreman's meetings. Pete didn't give in to his killers. He wasn't afraid of them. But I was afraid of Jojo, even though Jojo was a cockroach compared to Pete's killers, a cockroach. I squashed my cigarette against the rail.

It was too dark to see the spire, but I knew it was there. I headed back to the messroom.

Woody was singing a new version of his old song "This Train."

Most of the men had stayed on after the meeting. Some soldiers and gun-crew kids filled out the audience to standing room only. Woody sang:

> This ship don't carry no gamblers, this trip!
> This ship don't carry no hustlers, this trip!"

Woody stopped, took a pencil from behind his ear, and scribbled his words on a piece of paper. Cisco signaled to me, pointing to the guitar he had brought up for me. I picked up the drift of the new song as Woody continued:

> This ship don't carry no con men, two bit pimps, and crooked
>   crap games.
> This ship is bound for glory, this trip!

After playing the song a couple of times, everybody in the messroom joined in. They shouted when they came to the words "crooked crap games!"

Before Woody finished the song, the alleyway was packed with soldiers trying to get into the messroom. Woody stood near the doorway and went on to sing Dust Bowl blues, talking union blues, and work songs, as well as some of his own, such as "East Texas Red." After the singing came the dancing, Woody's fiddle flying in a wild hoedown and Cisco and I racing to keep up with him, accompanied by a couple of hundred whoops and hollers and stamping feet.

"What an opening night!" I gripped Woody's shoulder.

We were into another encore when Chips squeezed his way through to me and whispered into my ear. After the encore ended, I quietly said to Cisco and Woody, "Jojo's got a big crap game going in number-three hatch." We put our instruments away and made our way below.

The shouting of gamblers hit us before we reached the 'tween deck. We were too late. The game had reached a frenzy, an irreversible momentum. Hundreds of soldiers were hanging from their five-high bunks, shouting encouragement to the fifty-odd crapshooters packed in a tight ring around the small open space in the center of the hold. The players barked their bets, jostling each other trying to get their money down. The deck was covered with hundreds of dollars. The men in the bunks made bets among themselves. Every roll of the dice brought shouts down from the bunks.

Jojo, sweating like a prizefighter, with stacks of tens, twenties, and fifties stuck between his fingers, shouted louder and moved faster than all the others. His face was ugly with anger. He cursed the dice on every roll, and every losing throw was a body blow to him. "Oh, you rotten bastard!" he howled to the shooter. "A hundred says you're wrong! A hundred says you're wrong!" Dozens of players took Jojo's advice and made the same bet in tens, twenties, and fifties. The dice rolled.

"Ooooh, you rotten mother bastards!" Jojo pulled his hair as the winner raked in the money.

"What's happening?" asked Cisco above the yelling.

"Looks like Jojo's losin'," answered Woody.

"Yeah," I added, "but to whom?"

I stood on my toes to get a better view of the con men at work. Jojo's assistants were acting as though they were total strangers to each other, and Jojo was acting as though each of his assistants was his personal enemy.

"You bastards!" Jojo yelled, "I'm losin' over a grand! Just try to quit now an' see what happens!" He threw four fifty-dollar bills in front of one of the stooges. "Two hundred says you're wrong! Now throw them fuckin' dice, buddy!" For the benefit of the soldiers, he added, "He can't win all the time."

A dozen players took his advice, rushing in to lay down their bets, Jojo spurring them on like a traitor general leading his men into a trap. The dice rolled.

"Oh, no!" he cried out as his stooges scraped up practically all the money on the deck.

I had grown up with masters of the art of crooked crap shooting. Once I had even been privileged to watch Johnny New Orleans, but Jojo was a master in his own right. A good operator's success turns on five things; a big bankroll, a computer brain, a mastery of gambling psychology, some assistants, and several pair of loaded dice. The loaded dice were rarely used; one roll in twenty was enough to give Jojo the edge that would take every dollar on board, given enough time.

When the loaded dice were brought into action, it was always done by one of Jojo's assistants, never by Jojo himself. The rolls with the most money riding on them were therefore won by one or the other of the assistants, accompanied by Jojo's curses and threats to do them violence if they quit while he was "losing." The real losers joined him in his "anger," their sharpsightedness diminishing as the emotion and the pace of the playing increased. When the loaded dice were used, it was one throw and out, with the dice disappearing as quickly as they appeared, thus making it almost impossible to catch the thieves in the act.

The con men were winning over a thousand. Jojo would stop playing soon — a good operator never steals too much at one time. But Jojo caught my eye, and despite the risk, he gleefully went on playing to show me what a true virtuoso could do with a pair of bones. My face flushed. It was my first test as chairman, and I was helpless.

I didn't feel like talking, but I explained to Woody and Cisco the fine points of Jojo's performance, and after a few more rolls I said to them, "Let's go — it stinks down here." Some of the soldiers were already seasick, and the smell of dirty socks and sweaty clothes fouled the air. I led the way topside, through the narrow spaces between the bunks.

Woody stopped at the galley to pick up an empty cardboard box, which he carried to our cabin. Neither he nor Cisco said anything to me about Jojo. We made up our bunks in silence. I had an upper bunk. Cisco had the one beneath me. Woody's was the lower bunk next to Cisco. His bunk done, Woody picked up the cardboard box and cut it into five even pieces. I climbed into my bunk, turned out my bed light, and lit a cigarette.

After a few puffs I looked down at Woody. He was decorating the cardboard with a piece of crayon. Cisco was sitting on his own bunk, softly singing a lament about a young cowboy who walked the streets of Laredo and his appointment with death.

Woody finished the cardboard with a flourish and a heavy dot. He studied it for a moment, said, "Mmmm," turned out his light, and as usual, immediately began snoring. Cisco continued singing softly. Eventually Cisco put out his light and said, "Try to get some sleep."

But I lay awake for hours, thinking about Jojo. When I did fall asleep, I dreamed my recurring nightmare — Albert the Assassin, standing before me, grinning, while I punched at him with all my might; but my arms moved in slow motion, my fists were soft as pillows, and Pete's killer never stopped grinning.

21

We were awakened at six. The ship was pitching steadily. The steel covers of the cabin's portholes were locked. "One of the deckhands must have closed them while we were asleep." Cisco grabbed his bunk rail to steady himself. "Pity those poor GIs below."

I dressed hurriedly, skipping my usual shower and shave. "I'm going up to the boat deck to have a look around. You better wake Woody."

A strong headwind whistled through the rigging. The sun barely shone through the low, gray sky. I stared at the convoy around me. After a few minutes, Cisco, shaved and showered, joined me. "What do you see?"

"Mamma mia!"

"What is it?" Cisco strained to see.

"At least a hundred ships, ten across and ten down. Fast ones — we must be doing fifteen knots."

"What's our position?"

"Coffin corner again."

"Dead smack in the corner?"

"No, third row in — next to last from the bottom."

"Count your blessings. Who's on our portside?"

"A C-3. She's got Sherman tanks lashed to her decks."

"What's on the outside line?"

"Freighters and tankers."

"Thank your mother's Saint Michael medal for the soldiers we're carrying. If it weren't for them, we might be on the outside line."

"Jesus, with three thousand of them on board, why the hell didn't they put us in the center!"

"Because the center is probably filled up with other troop carriers."

"Then we must be an invasion fleet."

"What kind of protection have we got?" Cisco squinted toward the horizon.

"I can spot six destroyer escorts — that's just on our side of the convoy."

"What else?"

"Two destroyers, a heavy cruiser, and — an airplane!"

"An airplane? Are you kidding?"

"No, right there!" I pointed to the center of the convoy, where a spotter plane had just taken off from the deck of a freighter that had been converted to a miniature aircraft carrier.

"It's an invasion fleet all right. Which way are we headed?"

"East-northeast."

"North Atlantic." Cisco's head shook a little more noticeably. "We're probably going into northern France."

"Jee-sus!"

The French cliffs facing England were honeycombed with Nazi concrete bunkers from Dunkerque to the Atlantic. Hundreds of thousands of Germans waited behind thousands of cannon and machine guns. The men we were carrying down below would have to face a solid wall of fire. But before they could reach that wall, they would have to cross a thousand yards of open water, in small boats, from the troop carriers to the beach, and then cross the beach, every yard of which was barbwired and mined. The first troops would have to make a path for their comrades while the Germans poured down cannon and machine-gun fire point blank. If the soldiers we were carrying were to be among the first, half of them could already be counted as dead men.

"Hey, mates!" the GI who had wheedled the bread from Cisco called out. He and some other soldiers had managed to sleep on the boat deck. "We're hungry, mates, hongree. How's about a little more of that good bread?"

"We'll see, we'll see," I answered. The soldiers followed us below.

The messroom was already half-filled with irritable crewmen, hungry not so much for breakfast as for news about the convoy.

"What's going on?" one of them asked a deckhand who had just come from the bridge.

"How the fuck would I know?"

"Thanks."

"Don't get so damn huffy. I got two minutes to drink this coffee. Whatta ya want, a briefing? All I know is what you see — a hundred ships packed together like sardines, no moon, no stars. Go ahead an' steer her without hittin' anything! We nearly rammed the ship ahead of us last night, and the goddamned mate tried to pin it on me!"

Another deckhand came in. "What's up, Bill?"

"Who knows? The blinkers were goin' all night."

"Well, what were they sayin'? Where we goin'?"

"All I could make out is we're stoppin' off in Newfoundland to pick up two hundred blonde nurses."

"Come on, cut the crap. Where do you think we're goin'?"

"Seriously?"

"Yeah."

"Up shit creek." He downed his coffee and rushed out.

One of the soldiers who followed us down from the boat deck stood in the doorway. "Sailor," he said, "you give us some of that there hot braid, and I'll tell you wheah we're goin'."

"Okay, where are we all going?" I tried to be funny, but I couldn't help thinking that two of the four soldiers standing before me were dead men.

"Well, the You-nited States Army has trained us for one solid year to hit the beaches. Since we already hit the beach at Casablanca, Sicily, and Anzio, the general staff of mah platoon reckons the only beach left for us to hit is Paris, France, an' gimmee that braid!"

I gave them the whole loaf.

"Get your ass moving, you sentimental Wop." Cisco nudged me toward the tables. "It's almost chow time."

After Cisco and I set up the tables, I went to see how Woody was doing. Not a table was set up. Woody was busily decorating his cardboards. Some gun-crew kids were watching him.

"For Chrise sake," I hollered, "you know what time it is?"

Woody lifted his wrist, studied an imaginary watch, and said, "I make it about six and a half minutes after seven bells, but don't worry. I'll be ready."

As soon as breakfast was over, Cisco and I made our messroom spic and span, ready for the crew to use as a social room. Then we went to look in on Woody.

His tables were cluttered with dirty dishes, and the floors had not been swept, let alone mopped. Only one table was cleared off. Woody sat at it, surrounded by half a dozen gun-crew kids watching him decorating the cardboards.

"What are you waiting to clear up for?" I threw a broom halfway across the room.

"That can wait," said Woody without looking up. "This cain't." On each cardboard he had drawn a shark with a soldier in its mouth, and under the picture he had written a legal-looking document, beginning with

HEAR YE! HEAR YE!

This is to inform each and every member of the armed forces of the United States of America who are fortunate enough to be travelling as passengers aboard the Sea Pussy, that in addition to passengers and general cargo, the aforesaid good ship Sea Pussy is also carrying sharks of which the said members of the armed forces of the United States of America are hereby warned to be aware of.

These sharks are identifiable by the fact that they do not wear uniforms of the said armed forces of the United States of America, and also by the fact that they eat soldiers — not with their teeth, but with loaded dice.

Your civilian brothers of the National Maritime Union are 99 and 9/10 percent honest, but to avoid being eaten, don't risk playing with anybody not in uniform because the said sharks are extremely tricky.

Then he went on to briefly explain the cheating techniques he had learned the night before and signed the document,

The world's most famous gambler —
Woodrow Wilson Guthrie
The only man who ever broke the bank
At Okemah, Oklahoma.

Woody continued putting the finishing touches to the decoration. "When I get done with these, we'll hang one in every hold." He passed a blank cardboard to one of the gun-crew kids, who began to copy the text from Woody's original. Some of the other kids did the same. Woody did the drawings of the shark with the soldier in its mouth. Cisco and I cleaned up Woody's messroom. By the time the messroom was finished, the five posters were copied and decorated.

"We'll start with number-one hold." Woody rolled up the posters and led the way. "Wait a minute." He went into the galley, said something to the cook, and came out carrying a large steel kettle and a big ladle. "Now let's go get the geetars."

Woody had his hands full — guitar, kettle, ladle, and the posters, which he insisted on carrying. But despite the heavy pitching of the ship, he managed to keep his footing. We stopped at the entrance to the hold. The stench was terrible. One out of every three soldiers moaned and rolled in his bunk, seasick. The bad cases lay still and white. Those who weren't sick also lay in their bunks, most of them propped up on their elbows, chattering to each other. The only soldiers on their feet were the crap shooters and the army cooks. The cooks stirred powdered eggs and powdered potatoes in great steaming cauldrons under the combing on one side of the hold. The smell of that concoction combined with the smell of the seasickness was almost invincible. If we were to do anything, we would have to do it fast.

Woody hurried to the middle of the hatch and hooked a poster onto a bunk. Before any of the soldiers had a chance to read the text, he picked up the kettle and started to beat it with all his might. Even the deathly sick soldiers sat up dazed, bewildered, frightened.

"What's the matter!"

"What is it!"

"What happened!"

Woody continued banging until he had everybody's attention. The soldiers packed the center space, they hung from the bunks, and they crawled over each other from the outer rows to the inner ones so they could look down on Woody. They jammed the narrow aisles. Even the perpetual crap game came to a halt.

All of a sudden Woody stopped banging, pointed the ladle at me, and called out, "This here is the ship's chairman!" The surprise introduction and the sudden silence of the soldiers paralyzed me for a moment. I could hear the pounding of the ship's engine and the pounding of my heart. Then I held up my head and started to speak. I was amazed at how easily my voice carried through the hold. The six hundred soldiers were listening intently. I explained the facts and ended with, "But the best way to explain the situation is to read from one of the greatest proclamations I've ever seen." I turned to Woody's poster and read it off as proudly as I could.

A roar of cheers, whistles, and yahoos broke out as I finished, and it kept up until Woody's voice sang out, like a call to battle, "This ship don't carry no gamblers this trip." He put down his kettle and brought his guitar in front of him. Cisco and I did the same, and the three guitars hit the first chord together as Woody sang out the song he had composed in Jojo's honor: "This Ship Is Bound for Glory." Cisco and I joined him in singing the words the second time around, and every able-bodied soldier in the hold, including most of the seasick, joined us in the final chorus.

"More! More!" they shouted.

"Cain't," said Woody when he quieted them. "We've got four more holds to do." We left with the soldiers still cheering.

The reception we got from number-two hatch was even greater, and by the time we finished with number-three hatch, our performance was so perfected that we had to push our way through the mob of soldiers shouting for encores. "Cain't," Woody shouted to the soldiers. "We're late for work."

"The little fucker can be a genius when he wants to," I said to Cisco as we hurriedly set up our messroom. "But he sure can be a fuck-up when he wants to. Listen. He's playing the guitar now instead of setting up. I'd better go goose him."

Woody was playing "Red River Valley" to a couple of gun-crew kids quietly listening to him. The messroom was completely set up to the last detail, with everything is its proper place and the floors freshly mopped.

"Who helped you?"

Woody looked up at me without interrupting his playing. "Nobody." He looked down at the guitar, and then, after a couple of bars, he looked up again and said, "Why?"

I shook my head and went back to my messroom. "What are you shaking your head for?" asked Cisco.

"Go take a look. When the little fucker wants to, he can work faster than any machine."

Cisco came back shaking his head. "I never know how he does it."

Because of the worsening weather a couple of hundred GIs sneaked out of their stinking quarters in search of some breathing space. The rain and cold kept them off the decks, so they milled around in the alleyways and sat all over the ladder steps. Each time I went down to the storeroom for supplies, I had to fight my way through a double line of soldiers. They tried to grab whatever I was carrying. It was all in good humor, but they grabbed anything — salt, mustard, toothpicks. I managed to set the last table just before the chow gong sounded.

After lunch we took Woody's proclamation to the last two hatches and had the same success we had in the other three. But we had to cut short our performance because of gun drill.

The three of us were told to report to the navy lieutenant on the poop deck. Cisco and I were assigned to the five-inch cannon as loaders. Woody was made a loader on the twenty millimeter machine gun, which he loved. By the time we finished gun practice, it was time for the dinner chores.

The crew's mess was crowded with soldiers huddled around the radio. General Eisenhower had just announced that the Allies had landed in Normandy — D day — and that the German resistance was fierce. The soldiers listened quietly. It seemed certain that we would head straight for the Normandy beaches.

After dinner Woody said, "Well, the Allies are taking care of Hitler. Let's go see if we can take care of Jojo." On our way below we stopped to pick up our guitars.

We found Jojo in number-one hatch. He had just gotten there. The game was already running at the steady, low pitch typical of round-the-clock games. Jojo and his men took their stations around the ring of players, and they began their attack. When it was time for one of Jojo's stooges to roll the dice, Jojo yelled, "All right, you bastard! I'm gonna get you tonight! Fade this!" He threw fifty dollars down. "Fifty says you're wrong!"

"Big deal!" The stooge promptly covered the bet.

"Fifty more says he's wrong." Jojo looked around at the soldiers, but there were no takers. "Come on," goaded Jojo, "who'll take fifty more?" Still no takers.

"I'll cover that bet." The second stooge put down fifty dollars.

"Good for you, buddy," said the first stooge, with the conviction of a fine actor. "I'm gonna take that sonofabitch! I feel it in my bones — I'm gonna take him." He rubbed the dice in his hands, warming them while Jojo tried to get a bet out of the soldiers.

"You guys chicken? Fifty more says he's wrong! Nobody? Okay, shoot!" ordered Jojo. The dice rolled. "Seven!" The two stooges picked up their "winnings."

"All right, another hundred says he's wrong! A hundred says he's wrong! Who'll take part of it? Who'll take part of it?"

No bets.

The third stooge joined the act. "I'll take fifty of that."

"Good for you, buddy," called the first stooge. "I'm hot, I'm hot!"

"All right, who'll take the rest, who'll take the rest?" Jojo was getting redder and redder. He looked around at the ring of silent soldiers.

"Whatsa matter, ain't any of you guys bettin'?" He glared around the ring.

"Sure," said a rough-looking sergeant, "fade this!" He flung Woody's poster onto the deck in front of Jojo.

Jojo picked it up. Nobody moved as he read it. When he finished, Jojo looked around. He saw the three of us, guitars in hand. Woody nodded in answer to Jojo's stare and then threw his head back and called out, "This ship don't carry no gamblers this trip!"

Our three guitars hit the opening chord together, and though we sang with all our might, we could not hear ourselves above the accompaniment of six hundred soldiers singing and shouting the words they had learned from Woody that morning. We finished in a roar of cheers followed by a storm of boos and catcalls for Jojo. But Jojo and his men had disappeared.

Woody held up his hand and got immediate silence. "We got to go now," he called out. "We got a little exterminating to do in the other hatches."

"The other hatches," the rough-looking sergeant called out, "will take care of those finks." The scowl on his face deepened as he turned to the men around him and shouted, "We want more Woody, don't we?"

"More! More! More! More!" The six hundred voices began to shout in terrifying unison. Woody raised both hands to stop them, but the roar-chant got louder and louder, pounding and reverberating against the steel walls until the very deck seemed to heave in time with their insistent frenzy. "*More! More! More! More!*" Their arms were raised, and their fists beat the air.

I looked at the shouting faces packed in front of me and around me, and those hanging from the high-stacked bunks, like screaming gorillas. I shouted into Woody's ear, "They're madder at us than they are at Jojo!"

Woody put his mouth to my ear. "You'd be just as mad if you had to put up with pitchin' an' vomitin' and the guy in the bunk above you breaking wind six inches away from your face!"

We stayed with the soldiers. We played and sang and the soldiers sang with us until we almost forgot the stink and the pitching of the ship and the rolling that had begun since the singing started.

During the next hour the weather got steadily worse. The bad rolls, the ones with their own built-in thunder, were now coming every two or three minutes. The casualty list began to mount. Every roll was like a barrage of mortar fire steadily taking its toll of trapped soldiers.

As for us, we were not only losing our audience — we could barely keep our footing. We had nothing to hold on to. Both of our hands were busy playing our guitars. We spread our legs and tried to keep our balance as the deck seesawed under our feet. Each bad roll drowned our voices. The waves pounded the side of our ship like she was a giant steel drum. They lifted one side of her and pushed the other side down so deep that everything not lashed down smashed and banged together — steam-pots, dishes, loose stores, footlockers. The ship groaned as an extra heavy wave hit her and sent her into the heaviest roll yet.

"Hey! Hey! Hey!" the more frightened of the men shouted to disguise their fear.

BOOOOOM! went the backlash of the roll as eighteen thousand tons of steel were released by the giant wave's deadly grip. All these sounds combined into a terrifying din, but Woody's voice rang out between the din of each roll, leading the survivors into yet another song, inspiring each of them to sing louder as the ranks got thinner. The cheer at the end of "Rock Island Line" was the biggest we'd heard yet.

"All right now, that's enough! It's too rough!" I swung my guitar around to my back. Woody just looked at me with that Woody Guthrie "you must be some shit-ass" look of scorn, until I slowly brought my guitar in front of me in shamed surrender. The next roll sent Woody charging downhill, guitar held straight out in front of him, when the reverse roll suddenly changed his descent into a steep climb. The roll brought Woody back to the center of the hold, feet flailing backward, guitar held up like a flag.

"This here rollin' may rob me of my balance, but I'll be damned if I'm gonna let it rob me of my audience!" Despite the heavy losses, at least four hundred voices roared their pledge to sing on.

Woody shouted, "I ain't gonna be treated this way!" and led us into his song "Going down the Road."

And how we sang! Yet each roll took its toll of our audience. Cisco and I managed to go on playing by bracing each other, back to back, knees bent, swaying with the shifting deck, looking like a couple of Martha Graham dancers doing an African ritual dance. Woody struggled alone like a forlorn general, determined to stand and sing until his last soldier dropped — his guitar was his weapon; his songs and humor were his ammunition. Keep 'em singing! Keep 'em laughing! It was Woody Guthrie against the sea. "That there pitchin' an' rollin' at the same time is what we laughingly call the 'corkscrew effect.' Pay it no mind. But if you don't feel like laughing, let's sing 'Birmingham Jail.'"

By the end of the song, the ranks were thinner by half again. "We're just goin' through a bad patch," Woody reassured the survivors. "We'll soon be through it. In the meantime keep your minds off these rolls. Think of other kinds of rolls. This 'Ocean Roll Blues' ain't the only kind of roll blues! There's the 'Jelly Roll Blues'! There's the 'We Stopped the Crooked Dice from Rollin' Blues'! There's the 'Buy Your Own Damn

Cigarettes or Go Roll Your Own Blues'! There's the 'Wish I Had a Hot Roll and Sweet Butter Blues'! And then for those of you who are constipated, there's the 'Bolls Rolls Laxative Is Better Than X-Lax Blues'! And if you're scared shitless, there's the 'Toilet Roll Blues'! And if you're feeling poor, there's the 'Money Roll Blues'! And the 'Rolls Royce Blues'! And for those of you lucky enough to feel horny, there's the 'Roll Over Momma, I've Got a Surprise for You Blues'! And if you're through with the blues, let's sing 'When Our Tanks Roll through Berlin'!"

The hundred-odd survivors sang with more bravery than they'd ever again be called on to show, and the greater my terror, the louder I sang. But the last roll was the worst one yet. I thought the ship would never roll back. If you held a broomstick straight out at arm's length, you could almost touch the inclined deck. The old anxiety in my head began flashing, "Capsize! Capsize! Capsize!" Considering my normal anxiety about the ship's turning over, I thought I had taken the ten-degree rolls with exemplary calm. At fifteen degrees my hands were sweating. At twenty degrees all the sweat glands in my body were turned on and I was soaking. At thirty degrees red lights in my head started flashing and all other fears were nothing by comparison. U-boats, torpedoes smashing into the engine room, our ship sinking in two minutes — they were quick-death pleasures compared with being trapped upside down in the bottom of this ship with three thousand soldiers. At thirty-five degrees I was paralyzed, because I knew that at forty degrees the ship would indeed capsize.

"Let's go, for Chrise sakes!" I barked at Woody.

"All right!" Woody looked straight at the remaining fifty survivors. "Now let's sing 'Gypsy Davy.'"

"Fuck 'Gypsy Davy'!" I yelled. "Let's get out of here!"

"What's your hurry?" Woody looked at me disdainfully. Cisco reached out just in time to save Woody from being flung across the deck again. "Come on," Cisco said quietly. "I think we've all had enough." He put a hand under Woody's armpit; I put a hand under his other armpit, and as we carried him toward the lurching ladder, Woody turned his head for a last look at his soldiers. No general ever made a more touching farewell address to his troops. "Keep your peckers dry!" he called out. And no more loving cheer was ever heard as Cisco and I pushed Woody up the bucking steps.

22

When we reached our cabin, I was so tired I could barely climb into my bunk. Cisco lay stretched out, as still as a dead man. Woody sat on the edge of his own bunk, heedless of the storm, plunking away at his guitar and singing:

> Fishing worm danced the fishing reel;
> Lobster danced on the peacock's tail.
> Baboon danced with the rising moon,
> Jig along, jig along, jig along home.

I let my head hang down from the bunk. "Haven't you done enough singing for one night?"

"You guys tired?" Woody kept right on plucking.

Cisco, without opening his eyes, said, "If Lana Turner walked in now stark naked and said, 'Come an' get it,' I wouldn't have the strength to open one eye, let alone my fly."

Woody kept plucking. "Just goes to show you how class will tell." Plunk — plunk — plunk. "You guys got no sta-min-ah." Plunk, plunk, plunk. "Guys got no phil-ah-so-fee." Plunk — plunk — plunk. "Guys got soft squash for peckers." Plunk — plunk — plunk. "I haven't felt so good since we sang at the California's Lettuce-Pickers Strike Fund Picnic." Plunk — plunk — plunk. "Chased the growers' goon-finks clear across the county line." Plunk — plunk — plunk.

"Yeah," drawled Cisco sleepily, "but they came back the next day and beat the shit out of us."

Woody put his guitar down.

I propped myself up on one elbow. "Jojo's an animal. There's no telling what he's gonna do now."

"I know what *I'm* gonna do." Woody got up, went to his locker, and fished around in his duffel bag. "Been savin' this bottle of rum for somethin' important, and I think we've earned it tonight."

Cisco jumped out of his bunk. I climbed down from mine. Woody held the bottle up and suddenly swayed, although at that moment the ship was not rolling. Cisco grabbed the bottle, and Woody grabbed the bunk rail. He lowered himself into a seating position.

"What's the matter?" I turned his face up to me.

"Nothin'!"

"You sure it wasn't all that singing and rolling?" Cisco bent down to look into Woody's face. Woody took the bottle from him.

"No, it's not the rollin' and it's not the singin'. It's just the old Oke-mah Mamma Blues, and when it comes, there's nothin' like a good bottle of rum to chase it away." Woody took a long pull at the rum, shook his head, and passed the bottle.

We drank without much talking. We just listened to the noise of the storm and rolled with the waves. When the bottle was empty, we fell asleep.

"Six o'clock!" the wake-up man's call was like a cannon shot in my brain, and the blazing overhead light forced me to open my eyes.

"Put that goddamned light out!" I shouted.

"Put it out yourself!" The wake-up man slammed the door.

"What's that!" Cisco jumped out of his bunk as though the ship had been torpedoed.

"Six o'clock." I slowly brought my legs out from under the bedclothes and let them hang over the edge of my bunk. "It's no use; Italians can't drink."

"Get your stinkin' Wop feet outa my face!"

"Don't holler! Don't holler!" I slapped my foot on top of Cisco's head.

"You Guinea bastard!" Cisco got up, his pillow held high in the air, about to strike, when the ship gave a lurch that catapulted me into Cisco's arms, knocking both of us down onto the deck. The back of my head hit the raised steel threshold of the cabin's door, but it was miraculously cushioned by Cisco's pillow.

I felt the pillow with my hands; turned to look at it; looked up at Cisco now standing above me, and said, "Now ain't that a miracle to make you think? That wave hit at the precise second when I was perched on my bunk with nothing to hold onto, and if I hadn't stuck my feet in your Anglo-Saxon face, you wouldn't have called them 'stinkin' Wop feet,' and I wouldn't have slapped you on the head, and you wouldn't have tried to hit me with this pillow, and I would have hit my head against this god-damned threshold and maybe died."

"So what are you gonna do now, go back to being a Catholic?"

"No, but I'll never again get mad at anybody who calls me a dirty Wop."

Cisco extended his hand. I clutched it and pulled myself up.

"Hey, Woody, wake up! You want to hear a miracle?"

Cisco stopped me just as I was about to shake Woody, who lay doubled up, knees under his chin, his blanket on the deck.

"Don't touch him!"

"Why not? It's time."

"You don't know what he's like when he's sleeping in that position after a night's drinking. If you touch him before he's ready to wake up, he'll blow your head off."

"Stop babying him. I'm not going to do his work again. Hey, Woody —"

"I'm warning you, don't —" Cisco tried to grab my hand, but I touched Woody. The explosion staggered me; he broke wind just as I bent over him. I stumbled backward.

"I warned you!" Cisco shouted as he dashed into the alleyway, stark naked, colliding with a man in oilskins.

"What the hell are you doing running around this ship like that?" It was one of the mates, an arrogant ninety-day wonder just out of the Merchant Marine Academy.

"I'm sorry. I didn't realize, sir. I tried to get out —"

"Is that your cabin?"

"Yes, sir."

"Well, get back in there!"

"Is that an order, sir?"

"Yes, that's an order! What the hell is going on in there?"

"Human mine, sir."

"What are you, some kind of comedian?" The mate pushed the door open and entered the cabin. "What's going on here?" he yelled at me. "Is that man supposed to be up?"

"Ye-yes, sir. I was just trying to wake him."

"Trying to? I'll wake the lazy —"

Just as the mate's hand touched him, Woody broke wind with a roar that sent the mate staggering backward into the alleyway where Cisco was still standing.

"You . . . you tell that man . . . you tell that man . . ." The red-faced mate turned and rushed down the alleyway through the deck door into the relative calm of the storm.

Cisco eventually came back into the cabin, picked up his guitar, and, still naked, began to croon, "Come on, Woody — time to get up. Come on, Woody baby, it's time to get up."

Woody stirred, opened his eyes, and said, "I just had the most realistic dream. If I didn't *know* I was dreamin', I'd swear that I just farted in a ninety-day wonder's face."

"You son of a bitch!!" I pointed my finger at him. "You crazy son of a bitch!"

Cisco put down his guitar. "One of these days, Guthrie, you're going to get us put in irons."

We stared at Woody as he quickly put on his trousers, slipped into his sandals, and pulled his shirt over his head. He emerged wearing an angelic smile. "Why are you guys standing around bare-assed when you're supposed to be at work?" We continued staring at him as he went toward the door. "Don't you know there's a war goin' on?" he said as he closed the door behind him.

Woody out of sight, my fear of capsizing came rushing back as a roll flung me against the door. "How long do you think this is going to go on?"

"Stop worrying." Cisco struggled to get a sock on. "C-3s don't capsize so easily — they're bigger."

"What about the *Queen Mary* — fifteen thousand troops aboard — didn't she come within two degrees of turning over?"

"Are you going to start that whole neurotic routine again?"

"Well, didn't she?"

"You chicken-livered Wop, who told you to join the Merchant Marine?"

"You did, you bastard!" The roll nearly threw me through the door.

"Come on now, all kidding aside, relax. We're all in the same boat. Why should you be so neurotic? Try to dig into your head to find out why you —"

"Save the bullshit." The reverse roll flung me back to the bunks.

"All right, then," Cisco said, bracing himself for the next roll. "If you won't dig into your head, the only other thing I can think of is practice standing on your head. That way if we do turn upside down, you'll feel at home."

The roll threw me toward the door. I opened it violently. "Up yours!" I shouted as I slammed the door and started for the boat deck to find out what the hell was going on.

The wind-driven rain forced my eyes shut, but one look was enough. We were surrounded by four-story waves playing seesaw with the convoy. The ships were scattered in total disorder, and three-quarters of them were nowhere in sight. A wave picked us up and held us teetering on its crest. I watched hypnotized as the ship crashed against the bottom of the trough and started her climb up the other side of the wave. Count your blessings, I thought to myself; imagine the soldiers down below. I thought of the Chinese workers in Joseph Conrad's *Typhoon*, trapped below deck, a ball of two hundred humans rolling uncontrollably from one side of the hold to the other. Count your blessings and keep your mind off this goddamned storm. I turned my back to the wind and started for the messroom.

A deckman in oilskins lurched down the alleyway. As we came abreast of each other, a roll threw us together. We swayed in front of each other for a moment, and then I grabbed his outstretched arm. "Shall we dance?"

"I promised this one to the third engineer," he growled as he broke away and staggered toward the deck door.

A crash of pots came from the galley. "Sonofebeeeeech," somebody in the galley screamed, "I burn my fuhkin' hand!" I hurried toward the commotion. Miguel, the Puerto Rican second cook, was running around the galley, shaking his head, shouting "Dee butter! Dee butter!" while his frightened potboy — a middle-aged compatriot — was doing a kind of Irish jig in open-toed sandals. A steel kettle was rolling and banging across the deck, the big, hot stove was hissing and steaming from spilled liquid, and boiling water was sloshing from one side of the deck to the other.

"Dee butter! Where's dee fuhkin' butter!"

"No sé! No sé!" The tiny potboy had stopped jigging and was hysterically trying to lift himself backward onto the worktable, but he kept slipping off. "No sé!"

I spotted the butter can sliding along the table. In one swoop I picked up the potboy, sat him on the table, grabbed the can, and quickly spread butter over the cook's hand. "That's a pretty bad burn, Miguel."

"Yeah, but he be worse if you doan find dee butter so fast. If I wait for heem" — he pointed accusingly at the potboy — "I boil to death!"

"Dee water boil my feet!" The potboy appealed to me, whereupon the cook let loose a torrent of boiling Spanish. A furious look of indignation came over the middle-aged potboy's face as he hurled back a Spanish curse and picked up a large steel ladle, which he was about to hurl at the cook.

"Hey! Hold it, old man!" I stepped between them, hands raised. "The captain'll put you in irons if you hit a shipmate, and furthermore, this cook here is your superior!"

"Dat sonofabeech is no my shipmate — he my *shit*mate! An' dat sonof-abeech no my shuperio — ees my *son!* You get out of dee way an' I break hees fuhkin' head, he talk to hees poppa like dat!"

I grabbed the ladle. "I'm the ship's chairman! There'll be no fights on my ship, not even family ones." The ship rolled, and the cook dove for the stove just in time to save another large kettle from sliding off. "Nice stop, Cookie. Now you better go see the purser about that hand."

"I go later." The cook looked contemptuously at his father. "Dee boys got to eat breakfas' now."

Breakfast! I was late! I hurried to the messroom, which was empty; not a thing had been done to get it ready. I looked at the clock; it was only six-thirty! Time tricks again — I could have sworn it was half an hour since I had left the cabin to go to the boat deck, when in fact it was only three minutes.

"What are you shaking your head about?" Cisco stood in the door-way.

"Nothing." The ship pitched me into him, and clutching each other, we nearly fell onto a table.

"Grab the ketchup!" Cisco tried to stop the sliding bottle, but it es-caped and smashed against the bulkhead.

"Wha' hoppen?" Pedro the dishwasher, carrying a stack of dishes through the pantry entrance, tried to keep his footing. I grabbed the dishes from him just as he lost his balance. Cisco caught Pedro. "Ees too rough. You no can set up."

"Don't worry, Pedro. It takes more than this to keep an N.M.U. ship from feeding."

"You make all the nice speech you wanna Brother Chairman, but I betcha we no feed."

"He's right." Cisco sat down.

"Get off your lazy ass and do a day's work." I set down the sugar bowl.

"My God, Brother Chairman, you sound like a newly ordained priest. Take it easy."

I continued to lay out the condiments, and just as I placed the last one, the roll caught me. I braced myself against the bulkhead and stared at the bottles and bowls as they slid and banged into the raised ridges sur-rounding the tables. Every last one of them flipped over the ridge in perfect formation, back-somersaulting onto the deck with one crash.

"I tole you." Pedro grinned.

Cisco swore and glared at the littered deck. I stormed out and went to the officers' messroom. The officers' tables were covered with tablecloths. The tables hadn't been set up yet, but I knew that Shackleton the messman was around somewhere. I could smell the stink of his lavender toilet water. I stripped the tables as fast as I could. Officers shouldn't be the only ones to get tablecloths. I took away my load of tablecloths with a clean conscience. I carried the tablecloths into the pantry and dumped them into Pedro's sink.

"Ey hombre, dis ain' no fuhkin' laundry."

"Pedro," I said as I fished out a wet tablecloth, "help me to ring these out, and I'll show you how we're going to set up, okay?"

Cisco was trying to sweep up the broken glass that kept sliding all over the deck. "What the hell are you doing with that pile of wet laundry?"

"You'll see." I covered the first table with a cloth and laid out the unbroken bottles and bowls. The next roll was heavy enough to pin us against the bulkhead, but the wet tablecloth kept the articles from sliding. "Awright, wiseguys?"

"Meester Sheep's Chairman, dats preetee smart." Pedro grinned.

"Not bad for a dumb Guinea." Cisco started to lay out the next table. In a few minutes we had everything set up: cups, cutlery, condiments, milk jugs, water jugs, water glasses, butter plates, napkins, and toothpicks. Everything was perfect, including a sprig of celery in place of flowers at every table.

"What the hell are you doing with my tablecloths?" Shackleton's voice screeched behind me.

I had smelled his toilet water before I had heard his voice. I decided to keep my voice nice and civil — as becomes a ship's chairman. "Take it easy, Brother Shackleton, I'm just borrowing them until the storm's over."

"Don't you Brother Shackleton me!" he yelled. "You goddamn commonists think you can take anything from anybody?" His hand was already gripping one end of the tablecloth.

"Take your fucking hand off that tablecloth!" I shouted, loudly enough to scare myself.

Shackleton stared at me, and his face turned fiery red. His hand still gripped the tablecloth. My challenge hung in the air, and there was no way I could take it back. If he pulled the tablecloth, I would have to hit him. How could I be such a schmuck? One karate chop, and he could break me in two — in addition to which, the captain would punish me for hitting first. A captain like ours might jump at the chance to put the ship's chairman in the brig for the rest of the trip, but my main fear was the karate chop. Shackleton tightened his grip on the tablecloth, his eyes fixed on mine. He knew he had me. He pushed his grip forward, ready to jerk back the tablecloth.

"All right, Shackleton," Cisco said quietly, "let go that tablecloth."

"Stay out of this, Cisco." My mind raced for a way out.

The karate bastard, it wasn't fair. I could just see him, knees bent, arm stretched out, the yell before the lunge. He'd kill me! And before I knew what I was doing, a demon seized me. I bent my knees, stuck out my arm, and released all of my fear and fury in one sudden soul-piercing shriek: "FINK," I hurled at him.

The shriek stunned Shackleton, and before he could recover, I launched into a tirade. "It's finks like you we've had to fight to win whatever we've got!" I desperately thought ahead for things to say, at the same time backing away for fear that he might grab my still-outstretched arm and fling me over his shoulder, but I tried to make it look as though I was backing away for theatrical effect, to get a better view of my audience. Since only Cisco and Pedro were present, it was not illogical for me to back out of the doorway and into the alleyway, appealing to whichever of my shipmates might happen to be there, without breaking my tirade. "It's finks like you we had to fight to get rid of the two-pot system. It's finks like you we had to fight to get sheets for our bunks, and after this war's over, we'll fight to get tablecloths for the crew even if we have to strike until —"

A tremendous roll hit us. Crash! The giant steel kettle flew off the galley stove. The cook and his father screamed at each other, and before I could get back to my speech, the chief steward stumbled toward me.

"No feedin' today," he called out, "just sangwiches an' coffee. Clear your tables."

"Okay, Chief." I entered the messroom, and to Shackleton, who was still watching me speechlessly, I said, "You can have your fink tablecloths. You heard the steward — we don't need them!"

Cisco and I cleared the tables hurriedly and gathered together the wet tablecloths. Cisco picked up the bundle and offered it to Shackleton. "You see, man — no need to get excited."

Shackleton took the wet bundle and stared at me. "You better stay out of mah goddamned messroom!" He wheeled to go through the doorway and collided with Woody.

The bundle fell to the deck. Woody picked it up promptly and handed it to Shackleton with a big grin. "Drop your laundry, Mother Shackleton?"

"Goddamned commonists!" The karate champ stormed toward the officer's messroom. "No good goddamned commonists!"

Saved by the storm!

The old-timers said it was one of the worst they'd ever seen. One out of every four of the regular crew was sick. Two out of four of the gun crew were sick, and as for the soldiers trapped below, I couldn't think about them. All I could think about was what to do if the ship capsized. Where would the deck be? Where would the overhead be? Where would the door be? Would I remember to climb downstairs instead of up? The terror was too much for me, and after dinner I took to my bunk. Cisco turned in too, but not Woody. Woody found a way to beat the ship's rolling.

There was a pipe running through our cabin, just below the overhead. Woody jumped up, grabbed the pipe, and just hung from it with his eyes closed. The ship rolled from side to side, but his body hardly moved. Sometimes the roll was so bad that his feet seemed to touch the bulkhead, but in fact it was the ship that moved, not Woody.

"You see," he said, "all you have to do is hang in there."

I didn't fall asleep until after midnight. When we were awakened at six, the ship was steady. I went up to the boat deck. A brilliant sun was coming out of the sea, and the convoy was reformed in perfect order. I marveled again at the skill with which the ships regrouped — as easy as saying, "If we lose each other, we'll meet at 42d Street and Fifth Avenue."

In the messroom the crew made happy sounds. Wrong orders, undercooked eggs, mistakes that ordinarily caused angry complaints, were now greeted with good-natured speculation as to whether the messman's mind was going soft from lack of sex or whether he was actually born dumb. Normally unexpressive men pummeled their neighbors playfully, and jokes that would have been hissed at any other time now brought the house down.

"Hey Mister Ship's Chairman!" It was one of Jojo's stooges — the older and toughest looking one — standing in the doorway.

"Oh, it's you. I didn't see you guys at breakfast. What's the matter, too sick to eat?"

"No, we ate something in the galley." He smiled.

"Oh, good. You see I was worried about you."

"That's funny, because Jojo, he's worried about you too. He wants to see you."

"He knows where to find me."

"No, he wants to see you in the butcher shop."

"Jojo's the ship's butcher?"

"Well, that's what he signed up as."

"Who does his work — you?"

"No." He grinned. "Luis does his work. Anyway he wants to see you down there."

Cisco clutched my shoulder.

"No, Cisco, it's okay. Jojo's not stupid enough to try anything, not after this open invitation. I'll be back in a few minutes. Let's go, muchacho."

"My name is Panama."

23

I followed the stooge below. He held the huge chill-box door open for me. Jojo was seated on a crate. Luis was sawing away at a carcass. He stopped sawing and left without a word, through the door still held open by the other stooge. The door slammed, and I was alone with Jojo. After a slight pause Jojo said, "I doan unnerstan' why you gotta fight me about this thing."

"Nothing personal, Jojo."

"Right — business is business. Right?"

"Right. I got a job to do, and you —"

"Yeah, but there's no point beatin' each other's brains out." He pulled a wad of bills from his shirt and spread it out on the butcher's block, tens and twenties. "There's a grand for you. Okay?"

"Look, Jojo, I told you, no hard feelings, but it's no good."

"Now wait a minute. I can't go higher than that. You guys already did enough damage. I'm gonna have to start all over again. We gonna have to go easy, easy, an' the trip may only be for ten or twelve days. Two grand is the most I can do." He pulled out another wad and placed it on the block.

"You don't understand, Jojo. We can't make a deal. I can't do it. I'm sorry. No hard —"

"Whatta you crazy?" His voice rose sharply. "What the fuckin' business is it of yours if I take a few bucks from the monkeys? They gonna blow it on whores anyway!"

"They won't have a chance. I hear we're going straight into France."

"Then most of them are gonners anyway, an' what good is it gonna do them when they're lyin' dead in the sand?"

"It's no use Jojo. There's nothing' you can say to —"

"Listen, you motherfucker!" He scooped up the money without taking his eyes from me. "You think I'm gonna let you rob me of my livin'?"

"Now wait a minute. No use getting hot." I eyed the door.

"You know how much I could make on this trip?" he growled.

"A lot, I guess."

"You know how much?" His face was getting red.

"Five grand?"

"Twenty-five!" he shouted. "An' you think I'm gonna let you fuck me outta twenty-five gees?" He shook the wad of money under my nose. "Take it, you dumb bastard."

"I can't, Jojo."

Without taking his eyes from mine, he slowly put the money into his shirt. "You know what happens to guys like you?" He started to take off his jacket.

"Don't be stupid, Jojo. You try any rough stuff, you know the penalty for starting a fight."

His eyes went to the door and then back to me. "You gotta have witnesses, buddy."

I was too scared to make a move for the door; instead, in the coolest possible voice, I asked, "Are you from 116th Street?"

Jojo was slightly taken aback. "So what?"

"I'm one of Marcantonio's boys!"

"That don't cut no ice with me." He slipped out of his jacket.

Quickly I added, "After all we did for your people?" My voice started to rise.

"What's that got to do with you tryin' to fuck me outta twenty-five gees?" His arm reached toward the wooden meat pounder on the butcher's block.

"Jojo," I said, with all the fervor I could command, "when the Italians rioted against the Puerto Ricans, breaking heads right and left, I was side by side with Marc, and we made them stop."

"That ain't gonna help you." He picked up the meat pounder.

In a flash I was inspired to use the same technique I had used so successfully against Shackleton. *"You ought to be ashamed of yourself!"* I shouted at the top of my lungs as I backed toward the door.

Like Shackleton, Jojo was stunned.

"You're a disgrace to your people!" I kept shouting until I reached the door and made my escape, leaving Jojo with the stunned expression still on his face.

After I told Cisco and Woody about the butcher-shop incident, they wouldn't let me out of their sight. I made believe I wasn't scared and protested against their constant bodyguarding. I could understand their following me when I went out on deck that night for a breath of air, but Woody carried it too far when he insisted on accompanying me to the head. It was embarrassing — the cubicles had no doors. I made a note to fight for toilet doors as well as tablecloths.

That night we should have started our regular poker game, but we didn't. Cisco said he didn't feel like it and lay in his bunk reading. Woody said he wanted to finish writing a song that was running around in his head.

"Look, no more goddamned bodyguards, all right?" I jumped down from my bunk. Cisco didn't say anything, and Woody kept plucking away at his guitar, making believe he hadn't heard me. I went to the sink to wash my face. My towel was dirty. "Shit!" I had forgotten to get the linen. I flung the towel across the cabin.

"Don't worry about it; you'll get it tomorrow." Cisco didn't take his eyes from his book.

"Look, it was my turn to get the linen, and I fucked up. I'll try to get it now." I angrily picked up the dirty towel.

"It's too late," Woody said, still plucking his guitar.

"I'll try to find the laundry steward." I opened the door.

Cisco snapped shut his book. "Will you stop being a pain in the ass and stay here?" I slammed the door behind me.

The laundry room was usually closed at this time, but now it was open. I heard voices and went in. Jojo's three stooges were playing cards. "Ah, amigo." Juan, the oldest of the three, threw down his cards. The youngest one went past me, straight for the door. I was about to say something when I was hit square on the left jaw. I never saw the punch. As I spun around, I could see the young stooge trying to close the door, but the door kept bouncing back at him. I thought I was hallucinating, but it was Cisco and Woody trying to get in.

The door burst open. Cisco took the young stooge in his usual style, tying him up with one hand, the other hand pounding away at the stooge's ribs like a sledgehammer. Woody was not so efficient, but much more dramatic. He rushed toward the other two stooges, his head down, his arms flailing away so fast you couldn't see his fists.

I let out a karate shriek. "*Hold it!*" Again the technique worked — everybody stopped fighting and looked at me as though I had gone crazy. To Cisco and Woody I calmly said, "If we get caught fighting, we'll be confined to quarters, which is just what Jojo wants, so that he can operate again."

"You fuckin' bum," the oldest stooge shot at me as he tried to stop the nosebleed Woody had given him. "We gonna fix your wagon."

The middle stooge said nothing. He just kept spitting blood and glaring at me. The youngest one broke away from Cisco and held his ribs. "This trip ain't over yet," he said to me.

"Good thing I didn't hurt my hands," Woody said to his two victims. "Otherwise next time I'd be obliged to go after you with a meat-ax."

"Let's go." Cisco grabbed Woody by the belt and pulled him toward the door.

I led the way back to our cabin, too embarrassed to say anything. They had rescued me once again. Woody's poster had saved my honor, and now the two of them had saved my ass. When we got back to the cabin, all I could say was, "Thanks."

"Don't be silly." Woody picked up his guitar, flexed his fingers ostentatiously, and started to play.

"Hurt your hands?" I asked.

"Nope."

"What about you, Cisco — you all right?"

"Yeah, but next time they're really going to do a job on you!"

Woody stopped playing. "Let's call a special union meeting."

"Wouldn't do any good," Cisco said. "Jojo would deny everything. When he does do something, there won't be any witnesses. So what can the crew do for Jim? Give him a couple of bodyguards?" Cisco stretched out on his bunk. "He's already got two."

"I'll be goddamned if I'm going to be nursemaided for the rest of this trip." I climbed into my bunk. "I can't even take a shit without Grandma Guthrie sitting next to me!"

"Well, then, if you go around alone," Cisco replied, "the best that can happen is Jojo'll kick the hell out of you, and the worst that can happen is that you'll go over the side some night without any witnesses to say good-bye to you."

"I don't care — no more nursemaids!"

"What are you trying to prove, that you're a born hero?"

"Ain't no such thing," Woody drawled. "Any Italian grocery man'll tell you that heroes are made, not born."

I snapped my bunk light shut.

A little later Cisco turned off his light. Woody went on playing for a while. When he turned off his light, I lay there in the dark, thinking of Pete Panto and his assassin. I was ashamed of my fear of Jojo. Even though I was busting to pee, I didn't have the courage to go to the head by myself.

When I couldn't stand it anymore, I climbed down from my bunk as quietly as I could and peed in the sink. Then I rinsed it as noiselessly as I could, thoroughly disgusted with myself. If either of my mates heard me, they didn't say anything. I climbed back into my bunk and lay there sleepless. A little later Woody began snoring. The little sonofabitch — he *was* funny — "ask any Italian grocery man . . ." And then I got my brainstorm. I climbed down from my bunk without making a sound, felt for my trousers, slipped into my shoes, and quietly opened the door just enough for me to slip through. I closed the door softly behind me. I looked up and down the alleyway. Nobody in sight. I went down to the nearest hold.

"Hey, you one of the guys that was singin' to us. What are you doin' in this hellhole in the middle of the night?" a GI asked me.

"I'm looking for some Wops."

"Some what?"

"Wops — Guinzos — Italians like me."

"What for — you homesick?"

"No, it's something personal."

"You mean something religious, like the Jew boys always getting together?"

"No, I'm not looking for altar boys."

"Well, we got about ten Eyetalians, and ah can tell you, they ain't altar boys. That's their leader over there, fadin' all those bets. Sonofabitch never sleeps. Hey, Mando."

"Yeah, Slim." Mando looked up as he gathered in his winnings.

"Ah got a new recruit for your Wop Mafia."

"No kiddin'?" Mando rose, stuffing money into his pockets "You a paisan?"

I stuck my hand out. "Yep, born and bred in Little Italy, New York City." I wondered why this skinny, little, fine-featured kid should be the leader. He looked no more than twenty-one, and with a white mantle around his shoulders, he'd have easily passed for an altar boy.

"Well, ah sure am glad to meet you, paisan." He pumped my hand and kept slapping me on the shoulder.

"Hey," I said, "hanging around this outfit, you picked up a southern accent. Where you from?"

"Born an' bred in Little Italy, Atlanta, Georgia."

"Stop pulling my leg."

"Ah ain't kiddin' you. Ah admit there ain't many of us south of the Dixie line, but we make up in noise what we lack in numbers. Hey, Boom Boom! Hey, Meatball! Come here!"

The two men came quickly, leaving their fellow players to watch their bets. One of them looked like the heavyweight fighter Maxie Baer. The short one looked like a real bear. Both of them seemed much older than their leader.

"You all shake hands with — what's your name, paisan?"

"Jim."

"Shake hands with Jimmeh. He's a paisan from New York." He put his arm around me. He put his other arm around the short one. "This is Meatball, from New Orleans."

"Hi, paisan!" Meatball grinned as he pumped my hand in his powerful grip.

"And this banana here is Boom Boom, from Birmingham, Alabama."

"Ah am pleased to meet you." Boom Boom squeezed my hand in his big fist.

"It's so funny to hear paisans talking with a southern accent. It reminds me of the old rabbi who got on a Texas bus and absentmindedly walked past the driver without putting his fare into the box. The driver glared at the old rabbi and called out, 'This bus ain't movin' until that dirty Jew puts a dime in this box!' A little old lady sitting next to the rabbi says to him, in a frightened voice, 'Excuse me, suh, but did you hear what the driver said?' The old rabbi turned to the old lady and said, 'Ah heard him Ma'am — fuck him'!"

The soldiers roared.

"Well, ah'm glad you found your Wop friends," Slim said, "and ah hope they can take care of your problem."

"What problem?" Mando asked.

"Well — is there some place where we can talk?"

"You mean just you an' me?"

"Maybe that'll be better." I smiled apologetically to the others.

"Let's go this way." Mando led me away from the crap game. "You want a beer or whiskey or something? Ah can get you whatever you want, except girls."

"No thanks, I don't want anything."

We sat on a crate near the army cooks' section.

"Well, what's up?"

"You remember," I began, clearing my throat, "you remember the phony crapshooters we chased out of the hold?"

"Yeah, that's where ah know you from! What about 'em?"

"They're after me." I told Mando the facts.

"Cisco's right," Mando said. "Jojo would deny everything, and when he'd get around to dumping you, there wouldn't be any witnesses. We run across that problem all the time in mah business." Mando's voice was deeper now, and he seemed older.

"What business is that?"

"Well, let's say that mah family has a couple of things going for them in Atlanta."

"Oh." My eyebrows went up far enough to make Mando smile.

"And what kind of business are you in, or don't you want to answer that?" Mando grinned.

"Come on, man, not every Italian is involved — at least 10 percent of us are legit."

"Right, right," he chuckled.

"I'm a law student, Mando, and I'm not connected."

Mando took a long puff on his cigarette. "That's okay; we'll take care of the bum for you." The look in his eyes augured badly for Jojo.

"Now wait a minute. I don't want to get you into trouble. What I have in mind doesn't call for any risk."

"Risk?" Mando smiled. "Ah'v been in Africa, Sicily, Anzio. We were twenty-two paisans in mah old outfit when we started; when they sent me home, there were only nine of us left, and now we're going to hit the beaches in France, so what the hell have ah got to risk, man?"

I looked at the ribbons on Mando's chest. "What's that one for?" I pointed to the only one I didn't recognize.

"You won't laugh?"

"No, I swear."

"The Silver Star."

The Silver Star, the second highest decoration a soldier can get! "And they're sending you back in again?"

"That's all right. Ah had it good for six months. They had me selling war bonds while my leg healed. Now ah'm a 100 percent, so you just leave Jojo to me, okay?"

"No, Mando, that's not what I've got in mind."

"Okay, what've you got in mind?"

"Something very simple. You and a half-dozen paisans walk in on Jojo and tell him plain, if something happens to me, he gets his."

"Ah like that. It's very simple, and ah'm glad you didn't go to the other GIs. This thing is our affair."

"Thanks. I understand what you mean, but the reason why I came to you is because Jojo would be more scared of Italians; he's from East Harlem, and the guys who run East Harlem are all paisans."

"No kiddin'?" he said, slightly sarcastic. "Anyway, consider it done."

"Thanks. Of course, if anything should happen to me, I don't really expect you to get him, but the chances are that he'll lay off me if he sees a half-dozen crazy Wops like you."

"Six is too many. In this kind of thing, the fewer guys involved, the better. It'll just be Boom Boom and me, together with you."

"But six would be —"

"You don't understand. It can't be more than two, because if anything should ever happen to you, there ain't no way that bum would get off this ship alive."

I stared at him, trying to think of something to say, but he stood up as though the meeting was over. "When do you want us, Jimmeh?"

"After breakfast, the crew's messroom."

"See you there." He smiled.

"Okay, boss." I said as I walked away.

"An' Jimmeh," he called after me, "of the twenty-two paisans we started with, twenty-one were legit!"

I climbed into my bunk without waking anybody. Woody mumbled something about my not leaving the cabin without him, but he wasn't really awake.

I lay in bed with my nerves twitching. I'd had no more than a couple of hours sleep. I thought of the contradictions of life: me turning to Mando, a connection guy, for help. And didn't Mando have contradictions? The Silver Star! With all his pull, he certainly could have stayed out of the army, and what made the whole thing even crazier was that sure as hell after the war, he'd go right back into his family's business. Not that Mando would ever hurt an innocent person, not in a million years — unless it were absolutely necessary. But what charm! The bigger they are, the bigger the charm — and ice-cold guts. Death is nothing to them, people are nothing; the Church, one's country — nothing. The only thing that counts is the family and power. That's what makes them what they are. Their behavior and their philosophy are all of one piece, not like mine — too often my behavior contradicts what I believe. But then, Mando's got his contradictions too, and he also must have his doubts about his belief. How else could he have won the Silver Star, and why did he swear to avenge me? Contradictions — I fell asleep thinking that Mando and I had more in common than just being Italian.

Next morning Cisco had a mean scowl on his face.

"What's eating you this morning?" I said as I set up the tables.

"Lack of sleep." He stopped what he was doing and looked at me, his head shaking just a little. "What the hell were you doing in number-three hold in the middle of the night?"

"How do you know?"

"I followed you, but then I lost you. When you got back to the cabin, I didn't say anything because I didn't want to wake Woody. What the hell were you doing with the soldiers?"

"Well, maybe we won't have to worry about Jojo any more."

"Why?"

"I'll tell you later. It's a long story. I'll see what Woody's doing."

Woody's messroom was beautifully set up, and Woody himself was the image of efficiency. He placed each spoon precisely next to each knife and each ketchup bottle precisely in the center of each table, and after placing each item, his hand would make a self-satisfied little flip. The scene was doubly funny because of the life jacket that Woody was wearing, tightly laced and immobilizing his chin, like a neck brace, making each movement grotesquely difficult. He looked like Frankenstein's monster delicately planting little flowers.

"What are you doing with the life jacket?"

"There's gonna be a general-alarm drill."

"How do you know?"

The loudspeaker crackled. "Attention, attention. General-alarm drill will be held at ten o'clock. All hands are required to wear life jackets. All army personnel are required to wear life jackets."

"How the hell did you know there was gong to be a drill?"

Woody pointed to the open porthole. "Any experienced torpedoed seaman can tell you that's perfect submarine weather." I picked up the wet sponge and threw it at him, but he ducked and it went out the port-hole. "You owe me a wet table sponge, Rabbi Longhi."

Breakfast didn't go very well. The men were edgy — a smooth sea was good for U-boats, but bad for the appetite. I tried to get through the meal as fast as I could, which added to the general tension. I started to clean up before the last men were served.

"Mornin' Jimmeh!" Mando was standing outside the door. Boom Boom, grinning, stood next to him.

"Come in, come in. Cisco, these are my friends, Mando and Boom Boom. This is my buddy Cisco."

They shook hands. Cisco offered them chairs. "You guys want something to eat?"

"Sure thing." Boom Boom started to sit down.

"No thanks." Mando put his hand on Boom Boom's shoulder. "Maybe later, Jimmeh. Let's get this thing over with."

"Okay. Cisco, would you mind finishing up?"

"Get what over with?"

"I told you it's a long story. I'll explain it later, okay?"

"All right, I'll finish up."

I led Mando and Boom Boom to the butcher shop below.

"What do you want me to do, Mando?"

"Just be your natural self, Jimmeh, just be your sweet natural self. Go in there an' ask to parlay with him — alone. We'll wait under the stairs here."

There was no one in the chill-box except the young stooge Cisco had roughed up.

"Where's Jojo?" I asked.

"What for?" He was very surprised to see me.

"Go tell him I'm ready to talk with him — alone."

"Oh — okay!" The stooge smiled. "I'll get him right away." He opened the door and left.

I went out to where Mando and Boom Boom were waiting.

"He'll be right here."

"Okay, just go back in there and wait for him."

I sat on a box, looking at the slabs of frozen meat. Jojo opened the door with a big grin. "I hear you're ready to do business." He pushed the door behind him, but before it could close, it burst back on him, and Mando and Boom Boom were in the room. Boom Boom slammed the heavy door shut. Jojo grabbed a butcher's knife and lunged for the door. Mando did something fast, and with a twist of his body he took the knife from the older man and propelled him toward Boom Boom. Boom Boom's arm was around Jojo's throat and Jojo's eyes were already popping. Mando signaled, and Boom Boom immediately released Jojo. Mando offered the butcher's knife to Jojo.

"Take it easy, suh. We only came to have a little talk. We meant no disrespect." He proffered the knife a little closer. Jojo slowly took it, walked over to the butcher's block, dropped the knife, and rubbed his neck.

"Now, suh, may we all sit down an' reason for a little while?"

Jojo glared at me and then at Boom Boom; then, without looking at Mando, he sat down.

Mando pulled up another box and sat down facing Jojo. "Mister Jojo, ah know you are a busy man, so ah'll make it short and sweet." His southern accent got thicker and honeyer with every word. "Now ah appreciate that you've got to make a livin', but sometimes we've got to make compromises, and ah'm sorry to tell you that you just gotta accept the fact that you may not carry on your trade on this ship."

Jojo now looked up at Mando.

"I offered him two grand."

"Fair enough." Mando nodded.

"I'll cut you in for five."

"Mister Jojo, if we were goin' to allow your kind of business on this ship, we would be the ones who would be runnin' the game. Do you understand?"

"This is a free country," Jojo growled. "You can't tell me what to do!"

"Mister Jojo, ah haven't got the time to argue the point. Ah'm just here to give you a life-insurance policy."

"A what?"

"An insurance policy" — Mando pointed to me — "on Jimmeh's life, an' you, Mister Jojo, are the beneficiary. If somethin', God forbid, should happen to Jimmeh, our company will pay you off. An' don't you be worried about our keepin' our word, because we've been in business for a long time. An' as for the risk, we have nothin' to lose — we've done so much business in Africa, Sicily, Anzio" — Jojo's eyes went to the ribbons on Mando's chest — "that one policy more or less just don't make that much difference."

Jojo looked from Mando to Boom Boom and then back to Mando.

"An' after we leave this ship, the policy continues in force; in fact the expiration date is left open. Ah have written a letter to that effect to our partners back home — you may know some of them. Jimmeh here tells me you're from East Harlem, therefore ah presume you know Mister Michael Lucchese?"

Jojo looked up at Mando.

"Ah say, you know Mister Lucchese?"

"So what?" Jojo growled and lowered his head.

"Well, next time you see him, you tell him that Mando, son of Nardo from Atlanta, Georgia, sends his love — an' that ah asked you to kiss his hand for me."

Jojo slowly looked up at Mando.

"Will you do that for me?" Mando smiled gently.

Jojo looked at Mando steadily and calmly. "Okay."

"Good — now shake hands the two of you."

Jojo embarrassedly offered his hand. I shook it.

"No hard feelings," I managed to say.

"Okay, okay," Jojo mumbled, avoiding my eyes. Then he turned away, and just as he shook Mando's proffered hand, DRRRINNNGGG! the general-alarm bell jolted us all and went on ringing deafeningly.

Mando said something in Jojo's ear. I couldn't see if there was any expression on Jojo's face, because his back was to me. Boom Boom opened the heavy door, allowing Jojo to go out first. We followed Jojo out. Men were already dashing through the alleyways.

"See you!" Mando called out as Jojo walked away. Without turning around, Jojo raised his hand weakly and disappeared around the corner.

"Mando!" I grabbed his arm and shouted above the alarm bell. "I don't know how to thank you! And you, Boom Boom!"

Mando put his arm around my shoulder. "What for?" he hollered. "We ought to thank you for protectin' our boys from that scumbag!"

"No, no, I've got to thank you properly — but this goddamned drill. I've only got a minute to get to my station. I'll see you later!!" I broke away and ran to my cabin.

24

"Get a move on!" Cisco grabbed a life jacket from under his bunk. "The fucking captain called the alarm early. He'll log us if we're a minute late."

Woody was the only one who had outsmarted the captain — he was already jacketed and calmly waiting for us at the gun station. "Thought the war'd be over before you'd get here."

The gun crew had already stripped a twenty-millimeter machine gun. As usual there was nothing for us to do except stand around looking at each other strapped into our grotesque life jackets and make the usual "Mae West" jokes, but as soon as the seamen on the boat deck stripped the lifeboats of their protective canvas, the talk stopped. All eyes were on the lifeboats as they were swung outward in ready position to be lowered.

"What a waste of time," the youngest gun-crew kid said as he stared at the lifeboats.

"The truth from mouths of boobs!" Woody slapped the young gunner a little too hard on the back of his life jacket. "We don't need to be reminded. We can all count the lifeboats as well as you can."

"With three thousand soldiers on board," a machine gunner moaned, "what the hell are we gonna do with only six lifeboats?"

"Worst kind of mystics," Woody answered, "are the pess-ee-mystics. You forgot to count the six life rafts."

"For Crise sake, stop jokin', Woody!" the machine gunner snapped. "The boats and the rafts can't hold more'n forty men apiece. That's only room for — how many men?"

"Four hundred and eighty," Cisco answered without turning around.

"There." The machine gunner continued his lament. "With three thousand soldiers fightin' for four hundred an' eighty places, what chance in hell would anybody have to survive?"

"Son," Woody drawled, "if you'd ever ridden in the New York subway, you'd be more optee-mystic about survivin'. The last time I rode the subway, it was so crowded you couldn't even fall down. I changed stations twice, and both times I came out with a different pair of shoes."

The laughter was cut short by the sharp, angry blasts of a mouth ·istle. Several MPs were trying to push back the GIs who were climb- ₋f their hold onto the poop deck below us. But the force of the massed GIs in the holds pushing to get out made it impossible for the first GIs to push back. An MP lieutenant furiously blew on his whistle, and several other MPs came running. The GIs kept pushing onto the deck. The lieutenant gave one long blast on the whistle and then two short ones. Immediately the MPs drew their pistols and aimed at the men. The front GIs turned, shouted to their comrades behind them, and fought their way back into the hold.

"It's the only way." The navy lieutenant stood next to us watching the commotion below. "Otherwise it would be chaos. If we were under attack, with those three thousand GIs swarming all over the place, it would be chaos." The lieutenant went to another turret.

"If we were hit," said the youngest gunner, "nothin' could hold those guys back, an' I wouldn't blame them. T'ain't fair the way they're bein' treated."

"The lieutenant's right," Cisco said to the young gunner quietly. "There's no other way to move an army across this ocean."

"Well, they oughta at least provide enough lifeboats." The young gunner's voice cracked.

"Where they gonna put them, Bainbridge?" another gunner called out. "Tighten your life jacket and pray to God you get picked up before you freeze your balls off."

"When the *Russell* went down," another young gunner observed to nobody in particular, "the men only lasted three minutes."

"Hell," Woody explained, "that was in February; this is May. In May a man could last at least three an' a half minutes!"

That shut everybody up. We stared down at the cold water — it had to be cold water, because the air was cool enough to chill us through.

"Why the hell doesn't the old man call off the drill?" The machine gunner moved his arms about. "Everybody's long since present and accounted for."

"Maybe it's a general-convoy drill." Cisco squinted toward what he thought was the center of the convoy. In fact there was a lot of activity in the convoy. Signal lights were blinking on every ship — radio silence, of course, being maintained at all times. Two destroyers were racing up and down the exposed side of the convoy.

"There goes the airplane from the carrier!" someone called out. The airplane turned and came straight at our corner of the convoy.

Whoom! Whoom! Whoom! While we were watching the plane, three destroyers off our port flank were dropping depth charges. "Hey!" A gunner's high-pitched voice carried all over the gun deck. "This ain't no practice! This is for real!"

"Get that cannon ready!" the lieutenant shouted. "Load that god-damned machine gun!"

Everybody around me burst into action, but I stood paralyzed, waiting for the torpedo that I was sure would hit us.

"Move it!" Cisco dropped a cannon shell into my arms.

"Okay, okay." I passed the shell to the next man.

The circle of depth charges narrowed. If they did hit a submarine, we couldn't tell. Gradually the circle widened and narrowed again further up along the line. There was no way of telling what was happening on the other side of the convoy, but the general alarm continued all day. The only hands allowed to return to their regular watches were the black gang, the helmsman, the second cook, and his father. The rest of us had to stand by our stations except to make quick sorties to the galley, where Miguel and his father supplied us with coffee, hard-boiled eggs, and assorted sandwiches.

Some of the men, exhausted from the tension, tried to catnap on the corrugated steel decks of the gun turrets, using each other for pillows because their life jackets made it impossible for them to lie down. Whenever a depth charge exploded near us, the sleepers would all jump up like one man.

Around nine o'clock the loudspeakers crackled. "The general alarm continues until further notice, and life jackets must be worn at all times, but all personnel are to return to normal routine."

"'Bout time." Woody stretched, did a couple of knee bends, and tried to touch his toes.

I grabbed the back of his life jacket. "Well, you were right about it being submarine weather."

"If I'd have been the least little bit more righter, the fishes in these waters would have had themselves a nice Italian dinner and an Oklahoma rooster for dessert."

"What about me?" Cisco asked.

"Fishes wouldn't touch you — too tough — bust their poor little teeth."

"Listen, talk about tough . . ." I went on to tell them about Mando.

When we got back to the messroom, we found a big bowl of hard-boiled eggs and piles of sandwiches on each table. The men, all in life jackets, sat around eating and going over the day's events.

"Mando! Boom Boom!" I spotted them in the alleyway and dragged them into the messroom. "These are the guys I told you about." I introduced them.

Woody pumped their hands. "Speakin' of hard-boiled eggs, these are soft-boiled compared with you two." He picked up a bowl and offered it to them. Both refused.

"You guys must have lost your appetite down in that hold today," Cisco said.

"You might say that, 'cause to tell the truth, we were a little nervous," Mando said. "Boy, when you guys hold a drill, you sure make it sound real."

"In fact," added Boom Boom, "if I didn't *know* it was a drill, I'd swear that some sonofabitch out there was tryin' to blow my fuckin' head off."

"You guys kidding?" I said. "Didn't you know that —"

"Yeah, we're kidding." Mando stopped smiling.

"Awright, you guys!" a tough-looking sergeant, both hands on his hips, yelled. "Get back in that hold!"

Mando looked at the sergeant for a moment and then broke into a grin. "Sure, Sarge, sure. Come on Boom Boom. See you guys." He waved to us.

A depth charge boomed against the side of the ship.

"Let's go," said Woody.

"Where to?" asked Cisco.

"Get the geetars."

"Not me, I'm beat," Cisco said.

"Me too." I followed them.

Just as we got to the cabin, another depth charge boomed, but the sound of it was much more frightening than it had been topside. Cisco took off his life jacket. "I'm hitting the sack."

"Me too, but not down here." I stripped my bed.

Woody took his guitar from under his bunk, his violin and mandolin from his locker, and his harmonica and Jew's harp from a shirt pocket and went toward the door.

"Where are you going?" I asked him.

"I think the soldiers could use a little music." A depth charge boomed.

"Are you crazy? If we get hit while we're down below with three thousand guys, we haven't got a chance! We've got to play the odds — find the highest spot — sleep in the crow's nest."

"I'll be in number-three hold." Woody closed the door behind him.

I opened the door and shouted, "Come back, you crazy bastard!" but Woody was gone. I slammed the door as hard as I could. "That sonofabitch, what chance would we have?"

Cisco lay on his back, without answering.

"He's too damned stupid to be scared!"

Cisco didn't answer.

"He's crazy! He lives in another world!"

No answer.

"He has no feelings! He's an iceberg!"

Another depth charge boomed. I picked up my bedding. "Are you coming topside?"

Cisco swung his legs to the deck. "He sure is one crazy sonofabitch." He picked up his guitar and went toward the door.

"Wait a minute! What good would it do? If we stayed topside we might have a chance!"

"You're right, you're right, but what are you gonna do?"

"What am I gonna do? You can both drop dead, that's what I'm gonna do!"

Cisco opened the door and said, "See you."

I picked up my guitar and followed him, cursing Oklahoma and every motherfucking sonofabitch that was ever born there.

As we approached the hold, a depth charge boomed, followed immediately by a strange sound of how-how-how-how coming from the hold. Just as we entered the hold, another depth charge boomed, but like nothing I had heard before; the force of the underwater explosion hit the steel plates of the cavernous hold, making it a gigantic drum. The explosion was immediately followed by the how-how-how-how, which was the sound of the frightened comment and questioning of six hundred trapped men.

"How close was it?"

"How can the ship's plates take it?"

"How long can it go on?"

"How are we gonna get outta here if we're hit?"

"How-how-how-how-how?"

And the sound of prayers — "Holy Mother pray for us . . . ," "The Lord is my shepherd, I shall not . . ."

Boom, boom!

Woody stood in the center of the hold, quietly tuning his guitar, his other instruments at his feet. All six hundred men in the hold, those who could see him and those who couldn't, waited silently for him to begin. Without looking at Cisco or at me, Woody plucked his E string so that we could tune to him. "A little higher," he said to me as he winced with his eyes shut tightly. Then he turned to the soldiers. "Like to start off with a little song I helped write which I think is appropriate to the occasion — it's called 'The Sinking of the *Reuben James*.'"

"Holy Mother." Cisco looked at me.

"Just what we need!" I said, but Woody ignored me.

"It's about a U.S. destroyer protecting a convoy like ours" — Woody's voice rang through the hold — "and how the Nazi U-boats torpedoed it and sent it to the bottom of the sea. It's a cheerful little tune that goes rippling along nice and easy." A roar of laughter came from the soldiers. "You guys join in the chorus, which goes, 'Tell me, what were their names? Tell me, what were their names? Did you have a friend on the good *Reuben James*?' And remember to sing loud, because our scientists have discovered that loud singing sends out sound waves that confuse the Nazi U-boats and causes them to shoot crooked. So to save your asses and in memory of the men who went down on the *Reuben James*, let's hear it loud and clear."

Whang! We hit the first chord just as a depth charge boomed, and Woody sang the first verse. When we got to the chorus, the soldiers sang it so loudly they barely heard the boom of the next depth charge. But I heard it, and I mentally crossed myself — for my mother's sake, of course.

Verse after verse, depth charge after depth charge, Woody sang out the whole song, which I had never heard him do before. We got to know the men on the *Reuben James*, and when Woody came to the last verse, he sang it very slowly. The six hundred soldiers, as though they had been rehearsed, sang the last chorus softly and lovingly,

Tell me, what were their names? Tell me, what were their names?
Did you have a friend on the good *Reuben James*?
Tell me, what were their names? Tell me, what were their names?
Did you have a friend on the good *Reuben James*?

When they finished, there was dead silence followed by an explosion of cheering. "Sing, Woody, sing!"

And how he sang. He soon had the hold jumping with hillbilly hoedowns, Woody Guthrie war songs, and anything else of a spirited nature that could possibly be sung. And we weren't the sole performers. Half a dozen country musicians came forward out of that mass of wild southerners. One grabbed Woody's fiddle, and another picked up the mandolin. All the instruments went, the harmonica, the Jew's harp, everything. One of the soldiers even produced a washboard as a substitute guitar, and when it came to the hoedowns, everybody danced in the narrow aisles and in the bunks, jumping, shaking, and hollering to the sound of the goddamnedest country band I'd ever heard. Woody called the turns as the depth charges boomed:

> Grab your partner by the hand
> Dance to the *Sea Pussy*'s country band.
> Don't let those U-boats get you down
> And we'll dance all over Hitler's town.

After an hour and a half of Woody Guthrie against Hitler, we stopped for a smoke. Suddenly we heard the sound of a glorious Negro chorus.

25

"Now where could that heavenly singing be coming from?" Woody pointed like a hound dog. He followed the sound, and we trotted to keep up with him. Closer and closer, the voices rang out, "On Judgment Day — Lord — Lord — on that Judgment Day!"

Woody stopped in front of an open door; we were staring into a soldier's toilet room that was packed with at least fifty singing black soldiers, some standing on the toilet seats, some sitting on the crossbars over the cubicles, and most of them standing in the middle of the aisle, crowded around their leader. He was pure black; he had a voice like Paul Robeson's, and he was singing with the fire of the vengeful Lord himself.

"And the bolts of lightin' will strike him daid!"

"Yes, Lord! Yes, Lord!" Every man responded in perfect harmony, in perfect time.

"And the wolf will burn in that fiery hell."

"Yes, Lord! Yes, Lord!" They responded, with increasing fervor.

"I said the wolf will burn!"

"Burn! Burn!"

"And the chains will burn!"

"Burn! Burn!" Their voices soared toward a climax.

"And the lamb set free!"

"Free! Free!"

"An' the goose set free!"

"Free! Free!"

Then, without a signal, there was total silence. The leader held out his arms full length, stared down, and boomed louder than the depth charge, "Goose set free!"

"Amen!" The chorus roared.

"*On that* — on that — on — that —" The leader's voice diminished until, with his eyes shut tight, he whispered, "On — that — Judg — ment — Day."

When the men nearest the door opened their eyes, they noticed Woody standing inside the toilet room. Laden as he was with his instruments, they stared and made way for him as he approached their leader. We followed Woody. The leader was a staff sergeant.

Woody looked up at him. "That's about the best darn singin' I ever heard."

"Thank you. Comin' from you, that is something." The black sergeant spoke with a heavy southern accent.

"Why, 'coming from me'?"

"Because according to all them instruments you're carryin', you must be the music man everybody's talkin' about. Only we didn't ever expect that you would come to us."

"Why not?"

"Because our bunks is scattered in different little corners of the ship, and you only been singing to the soldiers in the holds."

"Well, I'd rather listen to your singing, but if you want to hear my buddies an' me, come with us to number-three hold."

"That is kind of you." The sergeant's majesterial voice rose as he looked around at his black brothers. "But we can't do that."

"Why not?"

The leader studied Woody for a moment to see whether he was joking or whether he was truly innocent, and then he answered quietly, "Because we're colored."

Woody looked at Cisco and me and then said to the leader, "Where is your section of the ship — where do you get together?"

"We cooks in a little place back there, but it's too small for us to get together. This here is the best place."

Woody put his instruments down onto the tiled toilet deck. "Well then, this here is where we give our next concert."

"That's very kind of you, but you can't do that."

"Why not?"

"This here is the colored toilet."

"So what?"

The leader looked at the amazed men around him and then back to Woody. "It's against the rules."

"There's one rule that's bigger than all the other rules — the Golden Rule — an' we're goin' to do for you what you did for us. We're goin' to sing for you."

"But —"

"Anyway, the acoustics in here is better than in the holds." Whang! Woody struck a chord on his guitar, threw his head back, and let out a wild cry: "John Henry-y-y-y-y —" He held the note, like a call to action, until his voice broke; then he sang out the story of the black baby who grew up to be the best steel-driving man in the land.

The soldiers listened in dead silence as the little white man and his two buddies sang the first verse; throughout the second verse they stared at each other in disbelief; by the third verse they were grinning broadly, despite the boom of the depth charge against the side of the ship; at the end of the fourth verse they shouted the last line, "Death of me! This hammer be the death of me!" And from then on they sang out the rest of the song like a black national anthem. When we finished, there was no applause, just "Yes — yes — yes — yes."

"Where did you learn all them words?" the leader asked.

"Lots of white folks know lots of your songs," Woody answered. The leader looked at him, at a loss for words.

"Where you all from?" Woody asked.

"Georgia — we're all from Georgia."

"Okay, now it's your turn. Let's hear some good old Georgia music." Woody shoved his guitar into the leader's arms.

The leader held the guitar in front of him and read softly, "This machine kills fascists." Then, with both hands, he raised the guitar above his head for all to see and said, "Brothers, it says on this here guitar, 'This machine kills fascists.'" His voice rose. "An' let this be our scripture for this meeting. We know what a fascist is, don't we?"

"Yes, Daniel! We know!" they chorused.

"A fascist is the same as a Nazi!" he called out, still holding the guitar over his head. "And we know what a Nazi is, don't we?"

"Yes! Yes!" The men chorused back.

"Make slaves of everybody, they say!"

"Slaves! That's right! Slaves!" The men's anger began to rise.

"An' we know what slaves is, don't we!" His voice was now a preacher's voice, invoking, exciting. "We've *seen* the boss slavers, *haven't* we?"

"Yes, Lord! You know we have, Lord!"

"An' we know that Nazis is the *kings* of the boss slavers, don't we?"

"We know that, Lord! We know that!"

"An' we know that after we win this war, when the king of slavery is dead" — his voice swelled with hypnotic conviction — "when the king of slavery is dead, things is gonna *change* for the people of Israel!"

"Change! Change!" The men cried out.

"And for *everybody*, Lord!" His face was distorted with pain. "For *everybody!*"

"Everybody, Lord! Everybody!" they shouted.

The guitar still held above his head, like a weapon, he cried out, "An' the walls will come tumblin' down!"

"Amen, Lord! Amen!" The men seemed ready to explode.

"Let's sing it then for these brothers who are fightin' 'gainst the same devil!"

"Lead us, Daniel! Lead us!"

"An' may the ever-lovin' light of God's freedom always shine on them!"

"Amen, Lord! Amen!"

The leader closed his eyes tightly and sang out, "Josh fit the battle of Jericho! Jericho! Jericho! Josh fit the battle of Jericho! An' the walls came tumblin' down!" The men's anger poured into the song. Verse after verse the leader's passion increased until it carried him into a semitrance, and the men with him, until the final victorious chord.

The leader then handed the guitar to Woody. "Now it's your turn, Brother."

Woody closed his eyes and wailed out, "Take this ham-*mer!* Carry it to the captain! *Huh!* Take this ham-mer! Carry it to the captain! *Huh!* Take this ham-*mer!* Huh! Carry it to the cap-tayn! An' tell him I'm gone, boys! Jus' tell him I'm gone!"

"Yes, yes, yes !" The black soldiers grinned and joined Woody, Cisco, and me in singing the work song about a black prisoner who escaped from a chain gang. The next verses ran fast with happiness.

"An' if he ask you, was I laughin'?"

"If he ask you, was I laughin'?"

"If he ask you, was I laugh-innnn?"

"Jus' tell him I was cryin'! Just tell him I was cryin'!"

As the song went on, the men jigged where they stood and swayed where they sat.

This time the leader cradled the guitar in his arms and struck his first chord not as we do, from top string to bottom, but upside down, from bottom string up — whang — whang, whang — whang, whang — eerie — bluer than blue. Then he began squeezing out single notes, torturing the strings out of their lines, holding them down hard, shaking them, forcing them to give out the tortured note he was looking for until there emerged the melody of a blues about work and love and yearnings, which he sang.

Between songs we learned that most of the black soldiers were sharecroppers and that their leader was Daniel Rutledge, a lay-preacher sharecropper. They were an all-black company in a white battalion of engineers, a battalion specializing in demolition of enemy beach defenses — the first of the first ashore.

After Woody's next song, one of them put his hand on Woody's shoulder and said, "Brother Woody, there's some soldiers outside wanna talk to you and your friends."

"Hold this, Reverend." Woody handed the guitar to the leader. "We'll be right back."

There was a crowd of twenty soldiers and a staff sergeant waiting for us outside the door. Woody looked up at the sergeant. "How long you been here?"

"Long enough! Now come back to our hold. The guys are hollering for you to come back." A depth charge boomed.

Woody pointed to the toilet. "Let's go inside and talk this over."

"You all know damn well why we cain't come in!" His face began to redden. The crowd behind murmured their support.

"Right, right," said Woody, "it is a bit crowded in there."

"Crowd's got nothin' to do with it, an' you know damn well you ain't supposed to be in that toilet either!"

"But we love singing' in toilets — good acoustics."

"Goddamn, man, you *know* that's a Nigra toilet!"

"What's the difference? A toilet's a toilet."

"You got no goddamned right to be in there, so what the hell are you in there for?"

"You got no right to ask me that, no more'n I have the right to ask you why you're all standing out here. Why *are* you standin' out here?"

The sergeant looked at Woody as though he were about to punch him in the mouth and barked, "Because we love your goddamned music!"

"That's right, that's right," the men around him grumbled.

"Tell you what we do," said Woody to Daniel Rutledge, who was now standing outside the toilet, surrounded by his men. "Why don't we all continue our singin' in their hold?"

"Daniel," the white sergeant yelled to the black sergeant as he rolled his eyes heavenward, "will you tell this maniac the score?"

"I told him, Brother Billy," the black sergeant said with an expressionless face.

The white sergeant looked at Woody, studied the black sergeant's face, and said, "Okay, it's okay with me if it's okay with you, Daniel."

The dead silence that followed was broken by grumbles of disapproval from the black soldiers. "We can't do that without permission, Brother Billy," said the black sergeant to the white sergeant, his face still expressionless.

"Then we'll get the goddamned permission! Come on men, let's go!" The white soldiers followed their leader as another depth charge hit us.

The rest of us went back into the toilet, and the Reverend Daniel began to sing "Noah," with its hypnotic "didn't it rain, rain, rain." The fifty black soldiers sang more joyously than ever until there was some movement near the door, and the Reverend Daniel suddenly barked, "'Tention!"

An army captain entered, followed by the white staff sergeant and some other soldiers. The men sitting on the crossbeams jumped down, and everybody stood at attention. "Ah'm Captain Taylor." The captain looked straight at Woody. "Please try to understand that there are rules and that I had nothing to do with making them."

"I understand." Woody looked at him steadily. "Only thing then is to find the guy who made the rule."

"But that's —"

"Only way."

"Okay." The captain sighed and said, "I'll try." He walked out with his entourage, and we all went back to singing "Noah" and "didn't it rain, rain, rain."

Five verses later somebody at the door shouted, "'Tention!" It was Captain Taylor again, followed by a major.

"Ah'm the battalion commander." The major stared at Woody. "And goddamnit, Sergeant Rutledge here knows his boys are mah boys just like everybody else! But there are certain rules that ah have nothing to do with! Now goddamnit, number-three hold is filled with six hundred screaming GIs hollering for you to come back."

Another depth charge reverberated against the ship.

Woody looked up at the officer. "Major, with all due respect to you, maybe your superior officer would change the rules."

"Jesus Christ!" the major bellowed and made a hurried retreat, followed by Captain Taylor and the other white soldiers.

The rest of us went back to "Noah," and three verses later someone near the door called out, "At ease, men!" The black soldiers made way for a tall, blond colonel. "At ease, men." The colonel smiled genially in every direction. He wore steel-rimmed glasses and a lot of ribbons on his chest. "I'm Colonel Stevens, commanding officer of all military personnel on this ship. You three men are civilians. I can't order you — and I can't decorate you. I'm here to thank you personally for entertaining army personnel under fire, and I am asking you to please continue to do so within the rules that apply — rules, I might add, that none of us here had anything to do with the making of."

Woody stared at the colonel's ribbons and then looked up at him. "Seems like the rules nobody made are the hardest ones to break."

Before the silence could become more embarrassing, I interjected, "Colonel, may I make a suggestion?"

The colonel looked at me, and Woody quickly added, "That's all right. Jim is the lawyer in our group; whatever he says is okay with me."

"I think it would be better if we talked this over outside," I said.

"Sure, let's go." The colonel led the way.

"Keep 'em singing," I muttered to Woody and Cisco, and as soon as we were outside the door, "Noah" recommenced with all its force.

"Colonel," I said, "We both want the same thing, and I understand about the rules. We can't break them, but maybe we can bend them a little."

"What have you got in mind?"

"Where you from, sir?"

"Ohio."

"Are you a fan of Benny Goodman?"

"Of course."

"You know how his quartet came into being?"

"No."

"Teddy Wilson and Lionel Hampton are a very important part of the Goodman Big Band. Without their arrangements — without their spirit — there just wouldn't be that magic. But because Wilson and Hampton are Negroes, they're not allowed to play with the band — the unwritten law against mixed dance bands. So what does Goodman do? He creates the quartet — Wilson, Hampton, Gene Krupa, and Goodman — and then it was okay for them to perform from the same stage, because their music was not for dancing; it was for listening. They played between the big-band dance numbers, and so, without breaking the rules, they made great music and a little bit of history. Now, you hear that singing inside? Woody wouldn't be half as great without that Negro chorus, so why can't we perform together — not for dancing, just for listening? The chorus'll be part of our group, not part of the audience, and I'll guarantee, your boys'll enjoy it twice as much."

"Brother, you're one hell of a lawyer." He shook his head and turned away.

"Wait a minute, Colonel. What's your hurry?"

"Gonna save me a front seat in number-three hold. Come on boys, let's go."

I entered the toilet and interrupted the singing. "Okay, men," I called out, "the colonel has invited everybody to number-three hold!" My announcement caused great excitement. Some of the black soldiers cheered, some just grinned, and many were dead serious.

"What the hell did you say to him?" Woody and Cisco looked at me dumbfounded.

"Nothing," I said, "just a little lawyer talk." I was tempted to keep my formula a secret, but on the way to number-three hold I explained things to Woody, Cisco, and Brother Daniel.

The GIs in number-three hold cheered us wildly when they saw us come back. The colonel and his officers, who were seated on boxes in front of the "stage," rose and applauded as we took our places. Of course there was no room on the little "stage" for the fifty black soldiers, so Woody seated them around us, and thus they became part of the audience. The black soldiers sat straight-backed, unsmiling, dignified.

"Folks!" Woody raised his hands for silence. "Tonight we have a double treat: the Benny Goodman Guthrie Trio" — he pointed to Cisco and me — "plus the hotdamndest American soldier chorus you guys ever heard!" He pointed to the black soldiers around him. The cheering was so loud nobody but I seemed to hear the depth charge. Then, when the singing started and the black chorus was augmented by six hundred white soldiers, the depth charges sounded no louder than little thumps. The soldiers cheered song after song — black songs, white songs, hillbilly songs — and when Woody's fiddle screeched out the first bars of a hoedown, the place went wild.

> Grab your partner from his bunk,
> Spin him 'round and show some spunk.
> Forget the depth charge, just be brave,
> And we'll dance round Hitler's grave!

In no time the jitterbugging started, a regular New Year's Eve party, wilder and wilder. Even some of the black soldiers began to relax. Boom! A very close depth charge exploded, but no one seemed to hear. The jitterbugging got so frenzied that the black soldiers began to dance with each other. They danced so great that some of the white soldiers began dancing with them, and then everybody was dancing with everybody.

"I thought you said no dancing!" the colonel shouted to me. I shrugged my shoulders. He turned away, clapping his hands to Benny Goodman Guthrie's swinging hoedown, and then suddenly he jumped up and began jitterbugging with the best-dancing black soldier.

When we got back to the cabin, Woody threw himself onto his bunk and lay there with his eyes wide open. Cisco sat on the edge of his bunk, quietly picking his guitar. It was after three. I should have been dead — I hadn't had a full night's sleep since we left port — but I was all charged up.

"What the hell made you go down there?" I asked Woody.

"Logic." Woody did not look at me. "We joined this Merchant Marine to kill fascists. This machine" — he reached down and patted his guitar — "kills fascists, but it won't do it unless somebody plays it. What made *you* do it?"

"Stupidity!"

"And you, Cisco?"

"Constipation." Cisco kept playing. "Goin' down there was a sure cure. If there's any action tomorrow night, we'll go to number-four hold — four's my lucky number."

"No, we don't," I said. "We're going to number-one hold. Number four is right next to the engine room!"

"You Philadelphia lawyers figure out all the percentages," said Woody.

"You got to! If the engine room gets hit and we're in number-four hold, we're dead. But if we're in number one, we've got a couple of seconds before —"

"Will you lie down?" Cisco stopped playing. "Go on, lie down. I'll sing you to sleep."

I climbed into my bunk without undressing. Cisco plucked away, softly, playing his favorite combination of sweet, lonesome chords. They mixed soothingly with the steady pulsing of the *Sea Pussy*'s engine.

"Tell me a story while you're playing."

For a while he didn't answer me. Then he said, "About the time my best friend's wife sneaked into my bed? Or the pickle factory? Or about the mountains?"

"About the mountains."

And as he played, he talked about the snow-capped mountains only two hours outside of Los Angeles. "I've got a bunk up there, nobody knows about — abandoned cabin — the fireplace works — the pines — the clear water — the quiet — and the stars. Once I took my girl. God's country — God's country." He kept playing the sweet, lonesome chords.

I swore I'd write to Gaby the next day, but what could I tell her? How could I describe things? If only there were wires from my head into hers so she could know what I was thinking, so I could know what she was thinking.

"And someday," Cisco said as he continued playing, "I'm going back."

26 ———————————————

The next two nights we entertained in number-one and number-five holds. The three of us hadn't averaged more than four hours sleep a night. The seaman who woke us in the morning of the ninth day had to shake us. "Land's End, England!" he shouted. "We made it!" The cry went through the ship, and the joy of the soldiers was unbounded.

"Good-bye, vomit heaven! Hello, France!"

I rushed to the boat deck. Way off in the distance, a cloud hung over Land's End, England's most western point. Out of the clouds a group of English bombers came to escort us through our final lap to the Normandy beaches. But instead of turning to starboard for Normandy, our part of the convoy turned to port, and by sunset we were anchored off Liverpool.

The main question in everybody's mind was shore leave. Normandy was for another day, tonight it was Liverpool! I stopped the first mate as he came down from the bridge. "What's happening? Why are we here? How long are we staying?"

"Slow down, Mess. All I know is we're leaving tomorrow morning. We may go straight into Normandy."

"Then — uh — there's no shore leave?"

The mate stared at me for a moment and then turned and walked away, mumbling, "Must be out of his head, out of his head."

I slunk back to the cabin, but instead of going in, I went to the gangway on the main deck. The gangway had already been lowered, and a British navy motor launch was tied up at the bottom of it. Several English officers, seamen, and civilians were beginning to board our ship. There were loving greetings all round.

"You limey bastards, good to see you!"

"Bloody Yanks! Thought you'd never get here!"

I grabbed one of the seaman and pulled him aside. "Come to my messroom — I got half a roast chicken for you." And there began my seduction not only of an English seaman but worse, of my conscience.

"Blimey, Yank, if you're pullin' my leg, I'll knock your bloody block off!"

"Come on, come on."

"Tim," he called to one of his mates, "I'll be with this bloke in the crew's mess if you need me." The Englishman finished the chicken in three minutes flat. "Now what's all this for?" He pushed his plate away, and I told him.

A few minutes later, I found Woody and Cisco in the cabin. They were in their bunks. "Okay," I said, "let's go! Let's go!"

"Where?" Cisco sat up.

"Ashore!"

"You're crazy!" Woody put his book down.

"No, I'm not. I've talked to the first mate. We're here until morning, and after that it's probably Normandy, so what the hell, come on, it could be our last chance. The launch'll take us ashore and back for a carton of cigarettes each, and Pat's on the gangway."

"Fine fucking example for the ship's chairman to set." Cisco got up from his bunk. "If you get caught, you could lose your wages. You could even lose your seaman papers."

"Count me out." Woody went back to reading.

"Okay, then, I'm going alone."

"No, you're not." Cisco put on a jacket. "I'll have to go along to keep you out of trouble."

"Have fun." Woody put out his bunk light.

The launch roared through the pitch black around us without smashing into the dozens of blacked-out ships lying between the shore and us. Then suddenly the motor cut out and we were easing up to a quay.

"Jump!" my hungry pilot shouted. "And don't forget, a quarter to twelve — sharp!" He roared off a split second after we leaped onto England's soil.

"We're here!" I jumped up and down. "England! England!" All the sweet memories of my public school primer rushed in on me: Puss in Boots, Dick Whittington, Little Boy Blue, Little Miss Moffat, Banbury Cross, Little Bo Peep! "It's the nursery rhymes, Cisco, the fairy tales you hear as a child, that have the most powerful influence. Italy has a strong hold on me, but England is our mother."

"Don't put it that way. Otherwise, if I score with one of her daughters tonight, it'd be incest."

"Oh, you cold Anglo-Saxon bastard! Is that all you can think about? This is England! England! The Sheriff of Nottingham! Alfred the Great! Pease Porridge!"

"I hear a truck." Cisco stuck out his thumb. "Maybe we can get a lift." A giant truck came out of the dark, barely visible. Its dimmed-out lights were shaded toward the ground. Its brakes screeched as it came to a halt.

"Hop in, Yanks!"

"How'd you know we're Americans?"

"You look so well fed, even in the bloody dark!" We could barely understand his accent.

I gave him a pack of cigarettes and began telling him what I felt about England and its beauty, all the while straining to see something of the old motherland through the window that was now streaked with rain. But I saw nothing except darkened warehouses and row after row of wharves discharging cargo from black freighters whose dimly lit winches screeched and clanged across the dark.

"Blimey, do you really like this bloody country that much?" The driver shouted to overcome the noise of a locomotive pulling a train of freight cars through the streets alongside of us.

"Like her? I love her!" And all the way to town, I tried to awaken in that ignorant Liverpudlian a sense of pride for the land of Shakespeare, the repository of ancient ritual and beautiful traditions.

"Come, mate, don't be carried away," the Liverpudlian singsonged. "I can understand about Shakespeare, but as for the beautiful traditions, come the end of this war, an' the bloody king can go fuck himself! And all his capitalist friends to boot!" Before I could react to this unexpected show of sentiment, the driver stopped the truck. "This is it, mates, town center — but if you want to find England, I'd advise you to stick to the back streets. Good luck, Yanks."

He drove off into the blackout, compared to which New York's brownout was like the Great White Way. But slowly our eyes became accustomed to the dark, and we could make out figures twenty feet away. We were in a wide street, patches of which were now and then lit by the shaded headlamps of some passing trucks. There were no people that we could see. Great stone buildings loomed around us, and even in the dark I could sense their massive Victorian presence and the power — banking, insurance, commercial — that emanated from them to the far corners of the Empire.

"Can I help you, gentlemen?" It was a bobby, saluting us and looking exactly as I had imagined him to be.

"Yes, officer, we're American seamen looking for England, and we've got to find her in an hour."

"Turn left at the first crossing — you'll come to the Rose and Crown. Have a look there. Good night, gentlemen."

The pub was blacked out, but we heard a crowd singing through the heavy curtains that covered the doorway. Inside, the brightly lit room was jammed, and on an untuned piano with an open top someone was banging out "Blue Skies" to the accompaniment of everybody in the place. They swayed arm in arm as they sang at top voice.

"Drink up, Yank!" A soldier shoved a large glass of beer into my hands. Another soldier did the same for Cisco, and to show our appreciation we took an extra long swallow of that flat, warm liquid they called beer. Then two singing old ladies shoved their arms under ours and swayed us from side to side in linked rhythm with the rest of the room, heedless of the sloshing beer, looking up into our eyes, grinning and singing, "Never saw the sun shining so bright, never saw things going so right!"

Cisco and I joined in. "Blue skies, all of them blue." It was impossible not to sing, impossible to unlink, and absolutely impossible to pay for a drink. Four pints and ten songs later, Cisco shouted into my ear, "It's ten to eleven."

"Time's up!" I shouted to the old ladies clutching my arms.

"Okay, love. Come again, ducky!" They reluctantly let me go, and the floor was unsteady under my feet.

"It's all that swaying!" I shouted as I leaned on Cisco. "So long everybody, and thanks for the drinks!" I shouted, holding up my fingers in the Churchillian V for victory salute. The piano abruptly changed tunes and pounded out "Give My Regards to Broadway." The entire clientele of the Rose and Crown roared "say hello to Herald Square!" as if they had rehearsed it just that way. We could still hear them halfway down the street.

"We goddamn better find a taxi!" Cisco grabbed my arm and pulled me along with him. "Fine fix you got me into, jumping ship in time of war, and for what — four pints of that stuff. If I didn't know it was beer, I'd swear it was piss!"

■

"Have a good time?" My hungry navy friend shouted as we sped back to the *Sea Pussy*.

"Beautiful!" I shouted back.

"Blonde or brunette?"

"Neither!" shouted Cisco. "I'm the one who got screwed."

My seaman friend looked at Cisco a bit queerly.

"Sex is all he thinks about!" I shouted. "No sense of history! We found a bit of England tonight! Glorious! Glorious!" The speed of the boat and the flying spray combined with the beer to increase my excitement. "For England and Saint George!" I shouted. "Up the British!"

"Up your ass!" shouted Cisco.

I was about to crush him with a smashing comeback when a heavy spray of Mersey water hit me square in the mouth. Then the motor suddenly cut dead and we were alongside the *Sea Pussy*. I led the way up the gangway on tiptoe. "Pat?" I whispered.

"All clear, you lucky bastards!" he whispered back.

Woody was waiting up for us. He made believe he was reading, but he was waiting up for us. Without a word, he turned off his light.

"Don't you want to hear what we did?" I turned his light back on.

"Nope." He turned his light off. "Too sleepy."

Cisco undressed without a word and turned out his light too.

I tried to stave off the waves of guilt. "I don't care what they think!" I thought to myself just before falling asleep. "Nobody got hurt. Tomorrow I could be dead, but at least I saw England, goddamn it!"

■

Bang! Bang! Somebody was pounding on our door. "We're going in! We're going in!" It was our morning caller. "Wake up!" He pushed our door open. "Wake up, you guys! We're goin' in!" The three of us jumped out of bed. I ran up to the boat deck in my shorts. A hundred ships lay between us and the mist-covered harbor.

"Is this Normandy?" I shouted to a seaman climbing down from the bridge.

"No, it's Belfast."

"Belfast?"

"Yeah, Belfast, Ireland."

"Thank you, Saint Michael!" I murmured to myself.

Ireland! Our passengers were ecstatic about going ashore in Ireland instead of Normandy, and the crew was ecstatic because we would get forty-eight hours shore leave and then go straight back to dear old New York.

The ship was electric with anticipation, shouting, laughing, and joking. Grudges were forgotten; chronic grouches stopped grouching; the cooks excelled themselves; we messmen performed like waiters at Maxim's, and bottles of whiskey mysteriously appeared. Such was the mood that prevailed on the *Sea Pussy* for the entire day, and although by nighttime we were still anchored out, the degree of patience was admirable.

"Hell, you gotta wait your turn for dock space."

"One day more or less won't kill us."

"It'll make the cheese more binding."

And so on. The disappointment was considerably lessened by the bum boats that flocked around us, eager to exchange a bottle of their best for a carton of our cigarettes, and instead of finding pubs and women, most of the crew settled down to stud poker and Jamison's whiskey. As for our passengers, things were a lot better — at least there was no more pitching and rolling.

By nine o'clock Woody and I were stoned, each in his own way. Woody threw his head back much more than usual and kept one eyebrow permanently cocked. I grinned a lot. Cisco stayed dead sober, although he drank twice as much as we did. He did his best to dissuade Woody and me from getting into the seven-man poker game. Both of us ignored him and played with warm confidence; Cisco played with cold calculation. By midnight Woody and I had blown our wages to date.

Woody stretched himself. "Oh, well, easy come, easy go."

Cisco won twice as much as he earned in a month.

We didn't pay with the cash we had in our pockets — we saved that for Belfast. Cisco marked our losses in the poker book, which as usual everybody had agreed that Cisco should keep. But when I looked in the book, I saw that he had not debited Woody or me; he had decreased his credit by the amount we had lost. He had done that several times before, but this time he insisted on doing so with much less cursing about the stupidity of our playing, humming under his breath as he undressed for bed. Such was the good mood that was created by the anticipation of shore leave.

The next day the mood slowly changed from eager anticipation to quiet alarm — there was no sign of disembarkation.

"Well, I guess we just have to wait for dock space — right?"

"Sure, of course. Look at all those ships ahead of us."

But by nighttime the ships ahead of us were in the very same place. Not one of them had moved toward any dock that we could see. The afterdinner poker game was played dead sober and strictly cut-throat, and Cisco did not wipe out Woody's loss. I broke even. By the next day it was clear that there would not be any shore leave in Belfast. As ship's chairman, I had the responsibility of going topside for an explanation. The captain just glared at me and walked away, leaving the first mate to explain the situation. A few minutes later I called a meeting in the crew's mess and relayed what I had been told.

"Security my ass!" shouted an oiler who had been dressed spic and span and shaved for the past three days. "How come they let the bum boats swarm all over us if they're so worried about security?"

"Well," I tried to explain, "they might as well let the bum boats operate because it doesn't make any difference. Any spy with a decent pair of binoculars can see what we've got on these ships. The soldiers have to come up for air at least for an hour a day, which means that practically every poop deck in this harbor is crowded with GIs all day long."

"Then why the fuck don't they let us off?"

"Because if they let us ashore and kept our three thousand GIs locked up down below, it would destroy their morale."

"All right then, why the fuck don't they let everybody ashore?" barked a usually mild-mannered ordinary seaman.

"Because right now in this harbor there must be a hundred thousand soldiers waiting, at any moment, for the order" — my voice swelled with the drama of the occasion — "which will send them into the jaws of hell to fight for our freedom! So let's not yap about losing forty-eight hours shore leave!" Thus ended my speech, and very pleased I was with it, until a gravy-soaked roll hit me square in the face. Then my entire audience — except for Woody and Cisco — walked out on me.

A week later we were still anchored out in Belfast harbor. The radio newscasts implied that the German resistance in Normandy was much fiercer than expected and that the Allied forces were stalled only a few miles from the invasion beaches. Everything was behind schedule. It might be many days before we would be ordered to Normandy. Our angry passengers swore that they would rather take their chances against the Nazis immediately than take another day trapped down below in the holds, and with each passing day they became more and more obstreperous. They could no longer be contained within the holds; they demanded and got the run of the ship, and soon the beautiful *Sea Pussy* became a pigsty. The soldiers wandered aimlessly over the decks; or they sat and ate their army food, spilling half of it accidentally or in disgust; or they clustered and drank their bum boat whiskey, of which they seemed to vomit more than they swallowed. And when it rained, which was most of the time, they crowded our alleyways and our messrooms in search of some food that would relieve the boredom of the mush served to them down below. Nor did our music help lift the morale, and after a while, even Woody's guitar was silent.

The morale of the crew was just as foul. There were marked personality changes. Chips, one of the nicest guys on board, handed me a perfectly delicious-looking plate of Irish stew. "Take this plate of shit back to that Spick cook and tell him to shove it up his ass!" That same day there were two arguments between engine-gang and deck-gang hands that were forcibly stopped just short of blows.

Woody was ill-humored too; he sat at his typewriter all day and half the night, glumly banging away without saying a word. O'Brien, a perfectly nice guy who had voted for me, turned sour. "What the hell are you writing now?" he snapped at Woody, who was typing away on the afterdeck.

"Newspaper article."

"What are you, some kind of newspaper man too, for Chrise sake?"

"Am now."

"What paper?"

"If I told you, you'd get mad."

"How the hell do you know I'd get mad?"

"Because our politics are different."

"Well, that don't mean I'm gonna get mad! You got some fucking nerve to accuse me of that! What the hell is the name of the goddamned paper?"

"I call it the *Sabbath Employee*."

"Never heard of it. Anyway, what the fuck is there to get mad about a newspaper called the *Sabbath Employee?*"

"It's official name is the *Sunday Worker*."

"The *Sunday Worker?* That's a no-good fucking Communist newspaper!"

"Told you you'd get mad."

"But that's a no-good Communist news —"

"It's the only paper that printed my stories about the Okie fruit-picking camps." The crew and the soldiers that had gathered around the disputants, in eager anticipation of a fistfight, began to argue angrily among themselves, some for Woody, most of them against him.

The ship's morale degenerated from day to day. I tried to help by giving two lectures, one on the history of the labor movement in the United States and one on Jack London. Both lectures were grudgingly attended by Cisco and Woody, who constituted my entire audience.

"I told you," Cisco grumbled. "The guys want sex, not bullshit." I resented his characterization of my well-prepared lectures, but I kept silent because Cisco was basically right.

The next day there was a near riot on the *Sea Pussy*. For some stupid reason the authorities sent twenty pretty Belfast women on board our ship, ostensibly to cheer us up.

"Godamighty!" Woody burst into our cabin. "A bunch of colleens have just come aboard! Crew's gone crazy! The GIs are out of control, six gunners have fainted in the alleyways, and Bosun's stuck his head in the refrigerator to cool off." Woody raced topside, with me breathing on his back.

The pandemonium was worse than Woody had described, and the women were quickly hustled off the ship. Instead of cheering us, the women's visit made the ship's mood more foul than ever.

Even Cisco, that paragon of kindness, began to show a shocking streak of sadism. The three of us were lying in our bunks after lunch when Cisco suddenly got up with a mean scowl on his face, opened the cabin door, and stood there with his back to us. Then, without the slightest provocation, he loudly broke wind and left, slamming the door behind him. Woody's retaliation was short, sharp, and brutal. That night, as he was getting into his bunk, he broke wind with twice as powerful a blast, less than a foot away from Cisco's face.

Cisco was furious, and when Woody referred to Cisco's earlier unprovoked act of aggression, Cisco became angrier and said that his act, however offensive, did not deserve a response of such magnitude and at such close range. Woody, himself infected by no-shore leave nastiness, refused to show the slightest sign of remorse, and when Cisco furiously insisted on an apology, Woody's answer was an even louder blast. Cisco took Woody's insult as an open declaration of war and immediately launched an amazingly powerful counterattack aimed at bringing about Woody's quick unconditional surrender. But Woody's capacity for waging that kind of war was at least equal to Cisco's, and despite my pleas for an immediate cease-fire, the fighting escalated fiercely.

At lunch Cisco ate nothing but a can of beans; at dinner Woody ate nothing but two cans of beans; and the bombardments lasted through the night, making the cabin practically uninhabitable.

By the next morning, the Fourth of July, both sides began resorting to illegal warfare verging on atrocities. After a particularly vicious salvo, Cisco ran out of the cabin, banged the door behind him, and held it shut, trapping Woody and me — me, an innocent, neutral nonbelligerent. I threatened to call a special session of the union unless both belligerents declared the cabin neutral ground and agreed to confine their war to a no-man's-land such as the poop deck.

Both Woody and Cisco gave me a formal apology, and they agreed to respect the cabin's neutrality, but by lunchtime the escalation reached an insane, mutually destructive level — they added raw onions to the all-bean formula. In the holocaust that followed, both sides ignored the cabin's neutrality, and I was inexorably drawn into the conflict, not on anybody's side, but just blasting away aimlessly, out of sheer despair.

The horror continued into the night until Woody withdrew. When he came back to the cabin, he had a strange smile on his face. The explosion he set off was a quiet one, so quiet that Cisco and I looked at each other, wondering why Woody should be looking so smug — unless he had a secret weapon. And then it hit us!

"Oh, my God!" Cisco waved a white handkerchief in hysterical surrender. "He's stuffed a dead skunk up his ass!"

After the effects of the battle had cleared, we lay in our bunks, silent and totally dejected. Eighteen days without shore leave — what terrible things it can make people do. I jumped down from my bunk. It being much easier to repeat a sin once having committed it, I announced, "I'm going ashore." Woody and Cisco said nothing.

"They've forgotten us! Three thousand troops on board! Eighteen days in this goddamned harbor! They've forgotten us. It must be one of the biggest military goofs of all time!" My mates listened impassively. "God knows how much longer they'll keep us here. I've talked with the bridge — no sign of any orders about moving out, so what the difference would it make if we went ashore for a few hours? I already talked to the Irish guys on the shore launch — a carton of cigarettes each. Pedro and Chico will cover for lunch, and we'd be back in time for dinner. What do you say?"

"We'll talk about it in the morning." Cisco put out his light. "I'm too exhausted to talk about it now."

"Me too." Woody put out his light.

27

Next morning, after breakfast, both of them said, "Let's go."

It was ten o'clock and sunny when we jumped ashore, somewhere in the dock area. We got through the Irish security guards without any trouble, and then it suddenly started to rain, a steady, cold, miserable rain. "It'll clear up soon." I was already beginning to feel guilty about having talked my mates into coming with me. Half an hour later, with the rain still falling and no taxi or bus in sight, we started walking up the long street that led to the crossroads of Belfast. Everything looked dreary in the rain: trolley cars packed with wet passengers; downcast pedestrians, half of them without umbrellas; gray, uninteresting business buildings; a couple of movie houses; and an American-style milk bar.

Cisco dispiritedly suggested that we go to Bangor, which at least was pretty. He had visited Bangor on a previous trip. It was a short train ride along the sea. Bangor was a resort town, but in that rain it had no charm. We had a dreary lunch in a dreary cafe. I tried to liven the meal by telling an old burlesque joke.

First man: I'm taking my girl to the seaside.
Second man: Bangor?
First man: Not yet, but I hope to tonight!

Neither of my mates laughed.

We were back in Belfast by two o'clock. It was still raining. "How about a good movie? That one looks like it could be great. What do you say?" Cisco's glum look wiped the false enthusiasm from my face.

The theater was very large and almost filled. The lights were on and people were lined up, buying ice cream and candy from vendors who hawked their wares in front of the screen. After a while the lights dimmed and the movie started. Fifteen minutes later, when we were just getting interested in the plot, all the lights in the theater were suddenly turned on. On stage were three men. Two of them carried submachine guns. The man in the middle, a mild-looking man with steel-rimmed glasses, shouted in a heavy Irish accent, "Ladies and Gentlemen, we bring you greetings from our comrades who are fighting for the freedom of our beloved Ireland." The audience showed absolutely no sign of panic or even surprise. Many of them around us continued to eat the candy they had just bought. Each aisle had one IRA man with a submachine gun, and at the back of the theater there were three similarly armed men guarding the doors.

"The English say they're fighting for the freedom of mankind," the orator continued, "but the truth is they're only fighting to preserve their empire, which includes the continued separation of Mother Ireland by the force of their tanks, their thugs, and — our traitors!" There was scattered applause. He continued his tirade, quoting facts and figures about the oppression of Catholics in the north and cursing the policy of divide and rule.

"Jesus," said Cisco a little too loudly, "if I know the Irish, he'll go on talking all night."

After another fifteen minutes of the haranguing, I thought of going up to one of the IRA men guarding the doors and explaining to him that we had to get back to our ship, but that seemed inadvisable in view of the fact that the orator kept urging the audience to sabotage the war effort. "Destroy England," he shouted, "and free Ireland!"

After a few minutes we heard sirens outside. The orator brought his speech to a rapid, but dignified, conclusion, and all the gunmen disappeared behind the silver screen. Seconds later squads of police burst into the theater. Eventually the movie continued, but we left.

"Well," I said, "that was fun."

"Hysterical." Cisco looked straight ahead.

Outside it was still raining. I chose a pub, the most cheerful one I could find, but it was dismal compared with the one in Liverpool. We each had three pints of Guinness without conversation. When Cisco got up to get another round, he stopped to talk with a woman in her late twenties. Although she was shabbily dressed, she was attractive. Cisco came back without the drinks. "I'm going up to her place. It's a pound apiece. You guys want to?"

"No thanks — no hard feelings." Woody finished his drink.

"We'll wait here," I added.

"Come on, walk with me. It stopped raining. I won't be long."

Cisco and the woman walked ahead, and we followed them through streets that became poorer and poorer. Smoke-blackened tiny houses all attached, endless row on row, lined both sides of the street. Most of the windows we passed were either bare and dirty or hung with tattered cloths and dirty. And the rain started again.

The woman stopped in front of one of the houses, opened the door, and beckoned us in. The curtained window let in little light, but a candle in front of a statuette of the Madonna helped us to see a man about forty, seated near a fireless grate. He held a diaperless baby in his arms. Two small children were on the floor, fussing over a rag doll. Near the window a boy of about eight was stretched out on a blanket covering two chairs. Even in the poor light I could see his reddened face contorted by a wracking cough.

The man looked at us and at the woman, just for a second, and then looked away. The woman signaled for Cisco to climb the wooden ladder that led to the attic. Cisco froze, and then he turned to the man.

"Your . . . young lady . . . she told us how bad it is for you Catholics. We . . . we're American seamen. We're from the National Maritime Union. Please take this." He pulled some pound notes from his pocket and put them on the table. "Good-bye." Cisco opened the door.

"God bless you." The man did not look at the money.

"Good-bye," Woody and I muttered as we left without looking at the man or the woman.

We walked silently, in the rain, back to our ship.

Our Irish accomplice was waiting to take us back on the launch. Crossing that miserable stretch of gray water was a fitting finish to my ill-conceived adventure, and no longer able to contain my guilt, I blurted out, "You can both go fuck yourselves!"

"That's okay," Cisco said. "You don't have to apologize."

"Of course not." Woody offered me a cigarette.

The *Sea Pussy* loomed ahead of us. What a relief to see her still there. What a joy it would be to get back on board. As we climbed the ship's ladder, we saw the captain waiting for us at the head of the gangway, dressed in immaculate white and flanked by his first mate.

"Welcome aboard, gentlemen." He smiled. "I thought you'd never get here. We'll discuss your adventure after dinner." He continued smiling as he walked away.

"How did the captain find out?" I asked Pedro.

"He called a fuckin' boat drill, an' you was not there."

Word of our adventure had spread to the entire crew. They crowded around us as though we had just returned from visiting a civilization in outer space.

"What was it like?"

"How'd you guys do it?"

"Were the dames great?"

Woody and Cisco deferred to me. I couldn't bear to disappoint the men, and I didn't want to lie. I let out a long sigh. "Boys, there are some things that cannot be described."

Chips cried out, "I don't care what the captain does to you guys, it was worth it!"

As our appointment with the captain drew near, the men began to talk to us with great sympathy. Some said we'd be fined all our wages, and some said we'd have our seamen papers taken away. Others hinted at worse fates, but everybody urged us to be brave and assured us of their moral support.

"All hands on deck!" the loudspeaker blared. "All military personnel on deck!"

"My God!" I jumped up. "What the hell is the captain thinking of doing to us?"

The entire forward deck was jammed with GIs and crew men sitting on the hatch covers, on the deck — everywhere. The captain was on the bridge, looking down on the mass of men. He was flanked by the first mate, the commanding colonel, and an army chaplain. "Men!" our captain called out. "Major Browning, our chaplain."

"Well, boys!" The chaplain's voice rang out. "It is my proud duty, on this Fourth of July, to announce to you that in one hour we shall be on our way to play our part in the liberation of Europe. Some of us will come back and some of us won't, but all of us can be proud that we're fighting for the freedom of our people for generations to come. Our ship leaves in one hour!"

The audience cheered wildly.

The chaplain, deeply moved, his voice choking, said, "I'm mighty proud to see that you can't wait to get your hands on those Nazis."

"Nazis, hell, Chaplain!" someone shouted from the ranks. "It's this lousy ship! We can't wait to get off this lousy ship!"

An even louder cheer greeted that statement.

"Yes, of course. Hah, hah." The chaplain recovered his composure and went on with his memorized speech. "The heroes who fought for the freedom of man, for the freedom of religion, beginning with Abraham, on his great white steed, racing across the white sands of Israel, his white cloak flowing behind him, racing into the setting sun to do battle with the enemy, just as we are ready to do battle with ours . . ."

"Ever hear such a crock of shit?" somebody grumbled a bit too loudly.

The chaplain went on unaware. "The barons who kidnapped the tyrant King John and forced him to sign the Magna Carta — their blood flows in your veins, and . . ."

"Why don't he cut that crap an' let us get back to our crap game?" somebody grumbled even louder.

"Ah still got a hundred dollars to lose," another grumbled, "and if ah get killed with that much in mah pocket, ah'll be damned mad, ah can tell you."

But on and on the impassioned chaplain went, urging us to be unafraid of the horrors that faced us.

"Let the Nazis fire their flamethrowers at us! Let their Stuka bombers pour bombs on our heads . . ."

"Ah wasn't the least bit scared until that sonofabitch started talkin'!" grumbled another soldier.

The *Sea Pussy* 253

"So long as we have faith in the Almighty God, let the Nazis plant their deadly mines that can blow ships to smithereens . . ."

"Plug your ears, Andy," the soldier's voice carried at least ten feet. "You're too young to hear such horrors."

The chaplain went right on, deaf to the fact that all the men were now murmuring to each other and ignoring him totally. Even the captain had left the chaplain's side and disappeared.

"Let the fires of hell burn! Yea and we shall be as ice!" But nobody listened. Then the chaplain came to an abrupt halt.

"What happened?" "What is it?" The men stopped chattering and looked up at the chaplain. Slowly he took off his cap. In the silence we now heard the clanging of the ship's anchors being raised.

"Our Father who art in heaven, . . ."

"Hallowed be thy name," the men answered as they removed their caps, moved, I'm sure, not so much by the chaplain's fervent prayer as by the quiet throb of the engine that now began to turn, carrying us toward the open sea.

28

The ship was eerily quiet that night. The messrooms were deserted and the alleyways empty. The three of us waited for the captain to call us, but I was hopeful that he might have forgotten about us. Cisco said he might postpone, but he would never forget.

I went down to number-three hold to say good-bye to Mando and Boom Boom. The hold was dead quiet and dark — even the crap game had stopped. The only sign of life was the glow of cigarettes from almost every bunk. I worked my way through the narrow aisles to Mando's section.

"Mando," I whispered.

"What do you say, Jimmeh?" he whispered back.

"Take care of yourself."

"You too. Cigarette?"

"No, thanks. I want to say good-bye to Boom Boom too."

"He's in the bunk above me, but don't wake him. He needs his beauty sleep. I'll tell him for you."

"Okay. Thanks — for everything."

"Ah told you, we're in your debt. So long, paisan." We shook hands.

When I got back to the cabin, Cisco and Woody had a bottle of whiskey waiting for me. We talked and drank till just before dawn, and then we went up on the boat deck. Despite the dark we could see a good part of the twenty-five-ship convoy around us. We moved slowly, as slowly as the minesweepers. Soon there was a red glow in the sky ahead of us, and after a while we saw a thin, bright-orange ribbon of fire stretching across part of the horizon. We reckoned the front to be about twenty miles long. As the ribbon widened, we heard the distant rumble of gunfire. When the dawn light began to fill the sky, the ribbon of fire began to fade, but its sound increased.

"Prepare for landing!" our ship's loudspeaker blared. "All military personnel prepare for landing."

Instantly our three thousand GIs poured out of their holds. Each man carried a rifle and a forty-pound pack strapped to his back. Quickly and quietly they lined up on deck. The crew watched them in silence. Sharp mouth-whistle blasts ordered special squads of soldiers to unroll the rope nets over the port side.

Suddenly the roar of planes filled the air — our planes — fighters — right over us — a black umbrella. Straight ahead they roared, protecting us and guiding us straight toward the enemy.

All eyes were on the bay that began to emerge from the mist. It was a green, peaceful-looking bay, seven or eight miles wide and ringed by gray cliffs. It was Omaha Beach. The date was July 5, D day plus twenty-nine. I tried to imagine what it was like beyond those cliffs now. After twenty-nine days and thousands of dead, the front was still only a few miles away. But Omaha Beach itself was secured, so secure that we were not called to our gun stations.

Something went screeching over our ship, low and very fast. Woody looked up open-mouthed as he tried to track another one. "I believe somebody's shooting at us!" he shouted above the roar of the planes.

"They're random German shells," said Cisco without looking up.

I grabbed Woody, who was still staring up open-mouthed, and pulled him back under the covered deck. The rest of the crew sought cover too, except Cisco. He was standing in the middle of the soldiers, who could do nothing but stand where they were, their eyes fixed on the beach.

"Big hero," I grumbled as I pushed my way through the soldiers to Cisco's side. "What the hell are you doing here?"

"Playing post office."

A GI handed Cisco a letter. "I'd sure appreciate that." He shook Cisco's hand.

Another soldier said, "Here's five bucks. Will you call this number collect when you get back, and tell my mother I'm okay?"

"Sure, but keep the money. You'll need it when you get to Paris."

A soldier shoved a letter into my hand. "Will you mail this for me, buddy?"

"Sure, sure." I shoved the letter into my shirt.

In the next few minutes the three of us collected fifty letters and as many phone numbers. We would have gotten a lot more except that we were entering the bay, and a fleet of amphibious landing craft, a couple of hundred of them, were speeding toward us. The convoy's ships were to enter the bay five at a time, get within five hundred yards of the beach, discharge their soldiers from the protected seaward side, and then get out to sea as fast as possible.

The roaring landing craft raced toward their assigned ships, zigzagging and crossing each other like a bunch of crazy ducks. "Landing craft approaching!" the colonel's bullhorn blared.

"Okay, get ready, boys!" shouted a young lieutenant standing near us. "It won't be long now!"

Ten landing craft jostled each other for space alongside us. Each pilot, standing on a small stern deck, struggled to keep his heaving boat close to our still-moving ship, arms and legs grappling with three controls at a time. "Let's go! Let's go!" the pilots shouted up at the soldiers.

"Disembark!" the bullhorn commanded above the roar of the landing craft.

The first line of soldiers rushed to the rail and went over the side as though our ship were on fire. Line after line chased them, scrambling down the nets with their heavy loads, jumping into the bobbing boats, most of the men landing upright. The officers standing at the rail slapped each man on the back as he went over.

The crew members now came out in the open to watch the soldiers. We all went to the rail, as close to the soldiers as we could get. I studied the faces of the soldiers as they climbed over the rail. I tried to spot Mando, but the helmets made the GIs look alike.

Suddenly a gun-crew kid next to me screamed "Johnny!" and threw himself onto a soldier who was climbing over the rail. He pulled the startled soldier back onto the deck. "Johnny! Johnny!"

The stunned soldier held his attacker at arm's length, yelled "Bobby!" and threw his arms around him.

The lieutenant at the rail screamed, "Are you guys crazy?" and tried to break them apart.

"He's my brother!" the soldier and the sailor shouted back.

"Break it up! Break it up!" the lieutenant shouted. "You're holding up the line!"

"I didn't know he was on the ship!" the soldier shouted, clutching his brother.

"He's my brother, he's my brother!" the sailor appealed to the lieutenant.

The lieutenant pushed both of them aside so hard that they stumbled into our arms.

"Thirty days on the same ship!" the brothers kept clutching their heads.

"Jesus, at the very last second!"

"Whattaya hear from Momma an' Poppa . . ."

We turned away from the brothers to give them some privacy. We watched the soldiers scrambling down the nets into the bobbing boat below us.

"Let's go!" the pilot shouted, one hand on the steering wheel, one hand constantly changing gears, one foot on the accelerator, revving and slowing until his deck was full, and away he roared toward the open water. I wondered how many trips he had made since D day.

Boatload after boatload; as fast as one boat pulled away, another took its place, bunches of them, each nudging the others to get to the ship's side for a load of soldiers and then racing away.

Above all the noise we heard the colonel's bullhorn call out, "Thank you *Sea Porpoise!*" Then he climbed down from the bridge and went over the rail, followed by the chaplain.

"All right, soldier! Let's go!" the lieutenant shouted to the navy kid's brother. "You're the last one left!"

The brothers shook hands, and the soldier went over the side with the lieutenant. We watched them jump for the already moving landing craft, and then we ran to the other side of the ship to wave good-bye as the landing craft came around toward the open water.

"Good luck!" we shouted, trying to follow the boat as it zigzagged among the other boats, all racing toward the beach, but our ship was turning now, and our view was cut as we sped away.

Free at last, but our beautiful ship, which had been cramped with three thousand soldiers for thirty days, now seemed a vast empty thing, and as the sounds of Omaha Beach receded, we became increasingly aware of silence. The three of us wandered about aimlessly. The empty alleyways were surreal. The holds were like cemeteries, with graves stacked five high. Where we had been three thousand and eighty-five, now we were eighty-five, and the echoes of singing, shouting, depth charges, and crap games made our loneliness all the more acute.

"You guys want to see Hedy Lamarr?" I asked unenthusiastically. "*White Cargo* starts in ten minutes. Some guys must have seen it five times."

"I think I'd rather lie down and think of Margie." Woody headed for the cabin. Having nothing else to do, Cisco and I followed him. I lay in my bunk enjoying the ship's gentle rolling. Omaha Beach, only twenty minutes behind us, seemed twenty years away. Woody stood at the open porthole, gazing back toward the coast.

"Some things are worth dying for," he said, still gazing out of the porthole.

"Yeah," Cisco said, "like a good piece of ass."

"You are something!" I leaned over the bunk. "The guy's talking serious, and all you can think of is fucking!" I tried to slap Cisco on the head, but he was leaning over, untying his shoes.

"No, he's right." Woody turned to me. "Fucking's worth dying for — fucking and things like — things like Jane Dudley dancing the Harmonica Breakdown."

"What's that?"

"What's what?" Woody looked surprised.

"What's 'Jane Dudley dancing the Harmonica Breakdown'?"

Woody raised his eyebrows. "You mean you've never seen Jane Dudley dance the Harmonica Breakdown?"

"No, Woody." I imitated his amazed voice. "I've never seen Jane Dudley dance the Harmonica Breakdown."

"Well — before — you — die —" Woody's lips were now moving in slow motion and he was slowly rising through the air, strangely floating upward toward the overhead. "Before — you — die — you've — got — to see — Jane — Dud — ley — dance — the — Har — mon — i —ca — Break — down." And he kept rising until his head touched the overhead. I watched in awe as he hung there, and then BOOOOM! I heard the mind-shattering explosion! *We were hit!* An enormous underwater force! Its blast had pierced my brain before I heard it, making me see everything in slow motion, until I was suddenly aware that I was being violently bounced up and down, my brain aware of every detail as our eighteen-thousand-ton ship was lifted out of the sea and bounced up and down, three times, like a rubber ball. On the last bounce the heavy steel girders that ran across our overhead slowly crumbled like cellophane wrapping on a pack of cigarettes. I saw it all very clearly, trapped in my bouncing bunk, until the bunk's moorings broke under my weight, and I was flung headlong toward the steel deck, aware that I was falling, that the jagged edge of the bunk just grazed Cisco's bent-over head. As my head hit the deck, I saw Cisco jump up and stand in front of the door, which had sprung open; his arms outstretched and his legs spread apart, blocking our exit, he shouted, "Take it easy! Take it easy!"

I tried to lift my head, but it was magnetized to the deck, and in that upsidedown position I saw Cisco still blocking our exit, shouting, "Take it easy!" but Woody sneaked under his arms, and Cisco ran after him. I collapsed back onto the deck, thinking that if Cisco hadn't been untying his shoes, the weight of my falling bunk plus my weight would have split open his skull. And then I thought how strange that my last thought before dying should encompass such careful calculations as bunk weight plus body weight plus angle of descent.

Then I blacked out.

29

"Let's go, Jim!"

"Let's go, buddy!" Woody and Cisco were trying to lift me.

The sound of the explosion was still in my ears, and my head was still glued to the deck. "I'm okay. I'm okay." I looked around at the wrecked cabin.

"Let's go! Let's go!" Cisco started pulling me to my feet.

"We didn't realize you weren't with us till we reached topside." Woody helped pull me up.

"You mean you guys came back for me?"

"Hell no, we came back for the guitars." Woody pulled me toward the door.

"And the poker list." Cisco pushed me, and Woody pulled me topside as fast as they could — without the guitars or the poker list.

The boat deck was crowded with men shouting questions and milling about in swirling clouds of black smoke that was escaping from the ship's ruptured innards and pouring out the smokestack. Some of the crew were working furiously on the nearby lifeboat.

"No power!" the bosun shouted to the young third mate standing near him. "We'll have to lower her by hand!"

I looked up at the erupting smokestack. "Let's take one of the rafts!" I gripped Cisco's shoulder. "Ship can blow up any minute!"

"Take it easy." Cisco loosened my grip. "Can't do anything until the captain says abandon ship. Where is he?"

"There he is!" shouted Woody.

The captain was shaking an oil-covered engineer who was shouting, "There's a guy in the engine room!!"

Suddenly Cisco dashed toward the ladder leading below.

"Wait!" I shouted after him. "We can sink any minute!" But he disappeared.

"Woody! Cisco's gone crazy!" I ran for the ladder.

"Wait for me!" Woody shouted.

We caught up with Cisco at the open door leading to the engine-room ladder. Steam came through the doorway.

"Listen." Cisco went out onto the landing. The engine room below was pitch dark, but we heard and felt the steam rushing up at us and smelled the acrid dynamite.

"Help me! Help me! I can't see!" somebody was calling.

Cisco started down the ladder.

"Wait! Goddamnit!" I put my hand on his shoulder. Woody put his hand on mine, and we felt our way to the landing just below us, where we found the injured man.

"Help me! Help me! I can't see! I can't see!"

"It's okay, brother. It's okay." Cisco lifted him, but the man did not respond. We carried him up to the boat deck. He was covered with oil and bleeding from the nose. The purser and somebody else laid him out on the deck and started to work on him. "Where'd you find him?" The purser continued working on the man.

"In the engine room," said Cisco.

"What the hell were you doing in the engine room?" the purser asked without looking up.

"We were just passing by," said Cisco, "when we heard him call for help." The purser looked at us strangely.

"Attention all hands!" the captain's bullhorn blared. "Prepare to abandon ship —"

"Fucking captain must be a poker loser," Cisco grumbled.

"— and stand by for further orders," the bullhorn finished.

"What the hell is he waiting for?" I cried. "What the hell is happening?"

Woody grabbed my arm. "Take it easy. The captain's going down below to find out."

"Cisco," Chips shouted, "all poker debts are canceled."

"Not till the ship sinks," Cisco called back.

"She's gonna sink, all right!" another poker loser shouted, gleefully. Everybody seemed manic or stunned.

"Blown right out of his sandals!" Joe, an able-bodied seaman, had his arms around Adam, the only black man in the crew. "Right out of his fucking sandals! Then he ran and hid in the broom closet. We had to push the door open to get him out." Adam looked dazed.

"A real scared Stepin Fetchit!" Shackleton laughed.

"Stepin Fetchit my ass!" Joe held Adam closer. "We were torpedoed together on the *Dorchester*, and ten minutes later the ship that picked us up was torpedoed. Twice in one day, and he's still shipping out, so don't give me any of that Stepin Fetchit shit!"

"That's right, doan give him any of that shit!" Pedro said as he nursed a bleeding nose.

"How'd you get that?" Woody asked him.

"It's nothin'."

"Go ahead, tell him!" Chico punched the air as he jumped up and down. But Pedro wouldn't tell. "We was watchin' Hedy Lamarr when boom, we was hit! The movie film blow up all over the place! I grab a piece and run up on the deck. Then wise guy Pedro, he try to grab it from me, so I gave him punch in the nose! Let him go and get his own fuckin' Hedy Lamarr!"

"Attention all hands!" the captain called through the bullhorn. He was standing on the bridge, his face and his white uniform smeared with oil. "Stand by your stations. We've been badly hit, but if we can get a tug to tow us across the Channel, we might save the ship. Report all casualties to me and stand by for further orders." He came down from the bridge, followed by the first mate, and moved among the men. When he came to Woody, Cisco, and me, he stopped for a moment, shook his head, and moved on.

"Don't worry about the Belfast thing," the first mate said. "He heard about you guys bringing that man out of the engine room."

We had not been hit by a torpedo; no submarine could have gotten through our defenses. We were hit by an acoustic mine. They lie submerged, beyond the reach of the minesweepers. When they hear a ship, they are drawn up to it and explode with tremendous force. Our engine room was blown apart. We had some wounded, but no dead.

While we waited for a tug, Woody had sneaked away from Cisco and me. He had gone below and was standing there with our three guitars, plus the mandolin and the violin.

"Are you crazy to go down below? And by yourself?" I cried.

"No use the three of us going. It's a one-man job."

When the tug came alongside, there was a lot of bullhorn discussion between the two captains before we finally fixed a heavy hawser from our ship to the powerful tug and started slowly moving toward Southampton.

At sunset we were in Southampton harbor. A British launch came alongside to take us off. "Welcome to Merry England, Yanks!" the pilot shouted as we piled aboard with our salvageable belongings and our instruments.

"She made it!" Cisco shouted as the launch roared away. "All poker debts are payable!"

"Are you kiddin'?" Chips shouted back. "She's gonna sink!"

"She made it. That's all that counts!" shouted a poker winner.

"She's sinking! All debts are canceled!" shouted a poker loser.

Everybody was shouting at each other. "She made it!" "She's sinking!" "She made it!" "She's sinking!"

Woody jumped up onto the stern deck with his guitar strapped to his back and his arms full of instruments. I had to hold him to keep him from falling overboard. He faced our ship and shouted "Goodbye *Sea Pussy!* Sink or swim, you are a gallant lady!" He bowed to her and took his seat again. There was no further talk about her sinking.

As we neared the shore, a terrifying noise came out of the cross-channel sky. A noise from another world, an evil noise. As it roared over us, we saw that it was a plane without a propeller, with fierce orange flames shooting out of its tail.

"It's a buzz bomb!" somebody shouted. The pilotless rocket bomb — the V-1 — was the German secret weapon that was intended to bring about the demoralization and surrender of London.

"Pay it no mind," shouted the pilot as we all ducked, "and watch this!" The pilot pointed to a Spitfire that was speeding to meet the buzz bomb. The Spitfire rose above the V-1, turned sharply, swooped down on it from behind, caught up with it, put its wing under the flying bomb's wing, and flipped it over. The V-1 went hurtling toward the sea, and then we lost sight of it until we saw a flash light up the darkening sky.

"One — two — three —" the pilot shouted, counting like a prizefighter referee, "four — five — six — seven —" Boom! We heard the explosion. "If you count the seconds before you hear it, you can tell how far away the bomb fell!" the pilot shouted. "That one, me lads, landed in the drink."

"There'll always be an England!" I shouted to him.

"Hip, hip, hooray!" he shouted.

"Hip, hip, hooray!" We took up the cheer. "Hip, hip, hooray!"

■

A squad of lovely gray-haired, cheerful Red Cross ladies was waiting for us at the pier with tea trolleys. "There's a nice cuppa for you, me lad." From the pier we were taken by bus to a hostel, where they gave us clean clothes to replace our oil-smeared ones, showering facilities, and a good dinner. After dinner Woody went to sleep, and Cisco and I went out to see Southampton. The blackout didn't matter — the moon lit up the town. Its center was a vast pile of rubble, with nothing left standing except a church and a bank building. We walked through the moonlit ruins, harmonizing song after song.

The next morning the tea ladies, still pushing tea, put us on a train bound for London, where we were to change for a train to Glasgow; from Glasgow we would take a ship to New York. The Southampton-London train looked as romantic as the trains always looked in English movies, with compartments and the long corridor from whose windows you could wave good-bye to your forbidden love.

"Good luck, lads!" The tea ladies waved as the whistle blew and the train began to steam away.

"Good-bye, my darling!" I shouted to them all. "I love you! I'll always love you!" And as we chugged through the beautiful countryside, I re-enacted several English train scenes for my captive audience.

On the outskirts of London we began to see bombed-out houses, and the closer we got to the River Thames, the greater the damage. We looked up at the vast London sky — the battlefield for the Battle of Britain. "Where's St. Paul's? Where's Parliament?" I strained to catch a glimpse of them. In a few minutes the conductor slid our compartment door open, announcing, "Waterloo Station, gentlemen!" In another minute we were pulling into the station's enormous shed.

"Waterloo Station!" I jumped up. "Think of it! Waterloo Station!" I couldn't wait to see the rest of London.

Since the train for Glasgow was leaving from Euston Station at five that evening, we had five hours for sightseeing. The first interesting sight we saw was right there on the station platform. "Fuck the bloody king!" bellowed a monumentally fat man with a huge walrus moustache who was sitting on a six-foot-high pile of mail bags, himself looking like a king on a throne. The coat of his uniform was open, and the heavy silver watch chain across his vest accentuated the vastness of his belly.

"And fuck all of his bloody lords!" he continued bellowing to a co-worker below him.

Woody pointed to the Falstaffian figure. "Now that is more impressive than the dome of Saint Paul's Cathedral."

"What about national unity?" I called out.

"Don't worry," he bellowed down at me. "We'll stick together until we win this bloody war! But after that we'll sweep away the bloody ruling class *and* their bloody empire *and* all of their bloody establishment *and* —"

"Morning, Bill." A majestic-looking bobby strolling by lifted a finger to his helmet.

"Morning, George." The fat man touched his cap and then continued bellowing. "And we'll sweep away all of their bloody lackeys as well!"

I turned to our train conductor, who had caught up with us as we walked toward the gate. "I thought everybody loved Churchill and the king."

"We admire them, and we'll back them all the way — until we win the war and the other one starts."

"You mean the class war?"

"Yes. Old Bill puts it a bit crudely, but he speaks for at least half the nation."

"We'll sweep 'em all out!" the monumental prophet bellowed after us. "Just you bloody well wait and see!"

The crowd in the station gave off a happy hum, and apart from a few army uniforms, you couldn't tell there was a war going on.

In the streets crowds of people walked about calmly. They were all nicely dressed. Some of the men wore caps and sweaters under their jackets; some wore jaunty fedoras and nicely cut suits; and a few wore black derbies, smart black suits, and tightly furled umbrellas. The women were nicely dressed too. Most of the young ones were tall, lean, and fair, and many of them were amazingly beautiful. But the most amazing thing about them was their calm: nobody paid any attention to the approaching buzz bomb.

The three of us ran inside a store as the bomb roared over. "Good morning gentlemen." An elderly lady smiled at us. "What can I do for you?" We were in a ladies' corset shop.

"The bomb! Didn't you hear it?"

"Yes, but you get used to them. As long as you hear them, you're all right." We heard the thud of the bomb's explosion.

"That was at least a half a mile away," she said. "I could tell from its sound that it wouldn't fall near us. Are you American?"

"Yes, ma'am," Woody said. "We're American seamen."

"Oh, my!" She clutched her hands. "I suppose you've been through a great deal."

"A little — but not as much as you."

"Bosh!" She shook his hand. "Do drop in again — anytime."

We walked past Big Ben and the houses of Parliament, we visited Westminister Abbey, and walked toward Buckingham Palace, past many bombed-out houses. At Buckingham Palace Road, just across the street from the palace, we stopped for a traffic light. "Damage around here's pretty bad," Woody said to a bobby standing next to us.

"Not really, sir. The real damage is in the East End, where the docks are — lots of factories — and where our working-class Jewish people live, which is one of the reasons why the Germans concentrated the Blitz there, although the Gerry's have hit the palace a couple of times."

"But of course the king doesn't live there now?" I asked.

"Flag's flying, sir; that means His Majesty's at home. Cheerio, gentlemen, and don't let the Gerrys bother you."

"If you gotta have a king" — Woody looked up at the palace — "that's the kind of king to have."

We took the subway to the East End. We were amazed at the depth of the stations where the people slept side by side during the Blitz, and we saw the inspiring dome of St. Paul, but the most inspiring thing we saw was the people's calm. When next we heard a buzz bomb, we were the only ones to look up at it — but we didn't run for cover.

Woody telephoned the office of the British Broadcasting Corporation to talk to a fan he had there. Cisco and I went to a pub near the BBC to wait for Woody while he went up to see his fan. After too long a time Woody returned with a slightly smug look on his face. "What the hell took you so long?"

"Oh, they asked me to sing three songs on their *Children's Hour*."

We got to Euston Station without a minute to spare. The train was jammed with wounded GIs being sent back to the States with us. Some had no arms; some, no legs. Most of them had been badly wounded and were now strong enough to make the trip. Many of them were air force men; their average life under fire was less than ten minutes. Most of their injuries were to their bottoms, from antiaircraft flak. Many of them had injured or lost their genitals. I was embarrassed by my good luck, losing two out of my three ships and coming out of it unhurt except for a slight loss of hearing. None of the three of us suggested entertaining our fellow passengers; it was too sad a train that raced through the beautiful English countryside.

I spent most of the night tending the more helpless ones, bringing them coffee or sitting with them while they sipped whiskey and water from shaking paper cups, as the Royal Scot sped us toward Glasgow. Riding the Royal Scot, the fastest train in the world, had been one of my ambitions; how bitter that it should be fulfilled this way, surrounded by these suffering, broken men.

Where would our next ship take us? Maybe to the Far East, where I might happily fulfill another ambition: to sit on the verandah of the Repulse Bay Hotel, in Hong Kong, with a long drink in my hand, as Conrad did, or maybe someday in Paris to drink beer on the terrace of the Brasserie Lipp, as Hemingway did.

■

It was seven o'clock in the morning when we pulled into the Glasgow station. We hung out the open windows, waving to the Red Cross ladies, who looked just the same as their English sisters, pushing the same tea trolleys but sounding different.

"Welcome to Scutlond, lods!"

"Glossgoh will take care of you, lods!"

Several priests were jogging along our slow-moving train. "Any RCs in this car?" a red-faced priest called to us.

"Yes, father!" a wounded airman waved to him.

"Church of England?" a minister called. He didn't get anybody from our car, so he dropped back to the car behind us. We came up on another young minister jogging and waving to us.

"Any Presbyterians?" he shouted.

"Hi! Yeah! Right here!" He got two of them.

We were coming up on a jogging, short, heavy man wearing a large round fur hat and a caftan down to his ankles. He struggled to keep up with the train, and as we passed him, I saw the long gray beard and the earlocks of an Orthodox rabbi.

"Rabbi!" I shouted as I opened my compartment door and leaped for the platform. I landed about twenty feet ahead of him. "Rabbi!"

He stopped and spread his arms. "My son!" he shouted in Yiddish. We raced toward each other and embraced. His bear hug almost crushed me. Then he held me at arm's length and breathlessly continued in Yiddish, "From where are you?"

"From America. I'm a merchant seaman from New York," I answered in my poor Yiddish. "And you, Rabbi?"

"From Poland." He released me and stopped smiling. "I was visiting the Jewish community here in Glasgow when the war started. My wife and children are still in Poland. But come, enough of that!" His face lit up again with happy excitement. "Let us find some more Jewish boys, then we'll go to the synagogue and find food and —"

"Rabbi, I'd love to, but —"

"No buts, you must! You must!" He grabbed my shoulders again. "We will —"

"Rabbi!" I put my hands on his shoulders. "Rabbi, I'm sorry — I'm not Jewish. My wife is, but I'm not Jewish!"

The happiness drained from his face. He looked into my eyes for a long moment, and then he hugged me tightly and rocked me. "It's all the same, my son." He said in English, "It's all the same."

I would have gone with the rabbi, but we were immediately hustled onto buses. The rabbi waited until we left. "Shalom!" He waved. "Shalom Aleichum!"

"Aleichum shalom!" I waved back.

"May God bless you!" he called in Hebrew as he threw a kiss to me.

■

The bus took us to Greenock Harbor, where a big liner, the *Erickson*, waited for us. Thousands of us sat on the floor of an enormous dock shed waiting to board her. Suddenly there was a stir in the crowd around us. A company of tough-looking British soldiers, holding submachine guns across their chests, surrounded a couple of hundred prisoners and escorted them to a spot fifty feet from us. Somebody said they were Italians. I got up to find out from what part of Italy they came. I got within ten feet of them when I froze — their uniforms bore the insignia of the Black Flame. They were Mussolini's SS men. When Italy surrendered, they continued to fight under the Germans.

I could not help myself. "Assassins!" I shouted in Italian. The fascists turned toward me, stunned by my outburst. "Shame of the human race!" I continued shouting in Italian. To a man, they rose, growling. The British Tommies glanced back at them but said nothing. "Mad dogs!" I tried to keep my jaw from trembling. I mustn't show weakness. I *must* keep my jaw from trembling. "Murderers of women and children! Butchers of honest men!"

Their growling grew louder, and many of them began to shout back at me, but still the Tommies said nothing. "My brothers died to protect us from you!" I shouted. "You are their murderers!" Christ, I mustn't cry, but the tears rolled down my face. "My brothers were cut to pieces on bloody beaches because of you! Drowned because of you! My brothers burned in flaming oil because of you! So may *you* be burned alive in your masters' death camps!"

All of them were cursing me now, and still the Tommies did nothing. "Men of no honor!" I kept shouting in Italian. "You let your German masters fuck your wives and children!" The fascists began shouting threats of killing me. The Tommies didn't even look back at them.

"Come forward, you cowards!" I shouted. "Come forward, you cuckolds, and make good your threats!" A fascist screamed at me, pulled a knife from under his shirt, and ran toward me. Our bosun was standing near me; I grabbed the knife from his belt and held it low, ready to dig it into the fascists's balls, but the Tommy in front of me turned slightly and without blinking brought the butt of his gun up in a short, sharp jerk that caught the onrushing fascist's forehead and dropped him, unconscious, to the floor.

Cisco took the knife from my hand. I struggled to suck in my breath and realized that I was sobbing. Woody put his arm around my shoulder, and the two of them led me toward the gangway that was already loading the wounded.

The voyage home was uneventful.

THE LAST SHIP

My shore leave passed too quickly. On the last day Cisco and Woody met me at the bar across the street from the union hall. Both of them had long faces. The FBI had taken Woody's seaman papers from him because the *Sunday Worker* had published his article.

"I'm fighting them," Woody said. "By the time you get back from your next trip, Cisco and I'll be ready to ship out with you again."

"Why?" I turned to Cisco. "Aren't you coming with me?"

"No. I'm sorry, buddy. My mother found out about Slim. I'm going west to be with her for a while. We'll wait for you to get back, and then we'll ship out again."

"Sure, sure — of course." I didn't finish my drink.

We said good-bye in front of the bar.

"You'll be all right." Cisco embraced me.

"Take it easy." Woody embraced me. "But take it."

They walked toward 8th Avenue, and I went into the union hall. The dispatcher's voice was squawking over the loudspeaker, ". . . and there's a blonde in every lifeboat."

EPILOGUE

The war ended before we could ship out again. After the war Woody continued writing at a furious pace—songs, poems, essays, and a novel—racing against time, fighting the increasing signs of Huntington's Chorea, the killer disease he had inherited from his mother.

At the age of forty-two my wonderful Woody was no longer able to control his muscles and had to be hospitalized. But his mind remained crystal clear, and although he couldn't write anymore, he saw a new generation grow up on his songs. Singers and composers, not only in his own country, but all over the world, looked to Woody for inspiration, as did his own son, Arlo Guthrie, and Bob Dylan. And there were other satisfactions: President Johnson suggested that Woody's song "This Land Is Your Land" be made the national anthem, the U.S. government awarded Woody a special honor, and a station of the Bonneville Power Authority was named for him.

When the end came, after ten years, I went to see Woody for the last time. I asked him if he loved me. He blinked his eyes once. It was the only way he could say "Yes."

Cisco had said his good-bye to Woody and me a few years earlier. At the age of forty-two my beautiful Cisco was killed by cancer. At the time of his death Cisco too had begun to achieve success in concerts and recordings, and the State Department had sent him on a tour of India.

Some of Cisco's friends and I accompanied him to the plane that was to take him to California, where he wanted to die. At the plane's gangway we embraced. "Good-bye, my brother," was all he said.

In California, just before he died, Cisco said, "What happened to Woody and me are just mistakes of nature, things that will someday be overcome, but that's not nearly as great a tragedy as millions of people

blown to hell in a war which could be avoided. Those are the real trag-
edies of life."

Cisco and Woody died young—by the law of averages I should live a
long time. Woody wrote a song about us called "Seamen Three"; my
favorite line is "Cisco, Jimmy, and me—if you ever see one, you'd see all
three."

INDEX OF NAMES & SONG TITLES

VINCENT J. "JIM" LONGHI shipped out in the Merchant Marine with his buddies Woody Guthrie and Cisco Houston in the spring of 1943. After the war, he joined the rank-and-file longshoremen on the New York waterfront in their struggles against corruption, serving as their lawyer and spokesman. To bring attention to their cause, he began to write. His first play, *Two Fingers of Pride*, gave the actor Steve McQueen his first job. *Climb the Greased Pole* was staged at the Mermaid Theatre in London, *The Lincoln Mask* played on Broadway, and *Canto XI* is bound for a Russian production. Longhi lives in New York City with his wife, Gabrielle.